WARS AND BATTLES OF
ANCIENT GREECE

WARS AND BATTLES OF ANCIENT GREECE

PAUL CHRYSTAL

FONTHILL

'ὁ πόλεμος βίαιος διδάσκαλος' (war is a violent teacher).
Thucydides' assessment of the atrocities committed during the civil conflict on
Corcyra (Corfu).

History of the Peloponnesian War 3, 82

Fonthill Media Language Policy

Fonthill Media publishes in the international English language market. One language edition is published worldwide. As there are minor differences in spelling and presentation, especially with regard to American English and British English, a policy is necessary to define which form of English to use. The Fonthill Policy is to use the form of English native to the author. Paul Chrystal was born and educated in Scotland; therefore, British English has been adopted in this publication.

Fonthill Media Limited
Fonthill Media LLC
www.fonthillmedia.com
office@fonthillmedia.com

First published in the United Kingdom and the United States of America 2018

British Library Cataloguing in Publication Data:
A catalogue record for this book is available from the British Library

ISBN 978-1-78155-681-8

Typeset in 10.5pt on 13pt MinonPro
Printed and bound in England

Acknowledgements

Thanks to Professor Amy Smith at the Ure Museum of Greek Archaeology, University of Reading for permission to use a number of photographs of their exhibits (www.reading.ac.uk/Ure/index.php).

By the Same Author

Roman Republic into Roman Empire: the 1st Century BCE Civil Wars in Ancient Rome (2018)

Roman Record Keeping & Communication (2018)

Women in Ancient Greece: Seclusion, Exclusion, or Illusion? (2017)

When in Rome: A Social History of Rome (2017)

Women and War in the Ancient World (2017)

Roman Military Disasters (2016)

Wars and Battles of the Roman Republic (2015)

Roman Women: The Women Who Influenced Roman History (2015)

Contents

Timeline of Ancient Greek Wars

c. 1250 BCE: End of Trojan War

c. 1200 BCE: Fall of Mycenaean civilisation

1100–800 BCE: Dark Ages in Greece

800–500 BCE: Greek colonisation of the Mediterranean and Black Sea.

800–700 BCE: Homer's *Iliad* composed.

750–650 BCE: Rise of the *polis*, the Greek city-state.

c. 750–*c.* 350 BCE: Hoplites are the major players in Greek land warfare.

730–660 BCE: Sparta defeats Messenia.

c. 700 BCE: Corinthians adopt the trireme from the Phoenicians; Lelantine War between Chalcis and Eretrea.

669 BCE: Sparta defeated by Argos at Hysiae.

660 BCE: Corcyra wins a naval battle against their founding city of Corinth.

c. 650 BCE: Sparta crushes Messenian revolt.

580–376 BCE: Carthage and Greece fight for control of Sicily.

560 BCE: Tegea defeats Sparta at the Battle of Fetters.

c. 550–*c.* 366 BCE: Peloponnesian League alliance between Sparta, Corinth, Elis, and Tegea, which establishes Spartan hegemony over the Peloponnese.

550 BCE: Sparta defeats Argos at Battle of the Champions.

539 BCE: Etruscan and Carthaginian alliance expels the Greeks from Corsica.

525 BCE: Sparta and Corinth unsuccessfully attack Polycrates of Samos.

499–494 BCE: Ionian cities rebel against Persian rule.

494–493 BCE: Spartan forces under Cleomenes I attack Argos; crush Argives at Sepeia.

493 BCE: The first fortifications built at Athens's port of Piraeus.

492 BCE: Darius I of Persia invades Greece.

490 BCE: A combined force of Greek hoplites defeat the Persians at Marathon.

c. 483 BCE: Themistocles persuades the Athenians to expand their fleet, which saves them at Salamis and becomes the basis of their power.

480 BCE: The indecisive battle of Artemision between the Greek and Persian fleets of Xerxes I. The Greeks withdraw to Salamis; Battle of Thermopylae. 300 Spartans

under King Leonidas and other Greek allies hold back the Persians led by Xerxes I for three days but are ultimately defeated; Battle of Salamis where the Greek naval fleet led by Themistocles defeats the invading armada of Xerxes I of Persia; Gelon, tyrant of Syracuse, defeats the Carthaginians at the battle of Himera; Agrigento defeats Carthage at the battle of Himera; Thebes allies with Persia during Xerxes invasion of Greece.

479 BCE: Xerxes's Persian forces are defeated by Greek forces at Plataea and Mycale effectively ending Persia's expansionist ambitions in Greece.

478 BCE: Spartan general Pausanias takes both Cyprus and Byzantium.

476–463 BCE: Delian League operations are led by Athenian commander Cimon.

c. 475 BCE: Athenian general Cimon defeats Spartan general Pausanias and takes Byzantium.

471 BCE: Sparta defeats Arcadians at Dipaea.

c. 466 BCE: Cimon twice defeats the Persians at Eurymedon on the southern coast of Asia Minor.

465–463 BCE: Cimon conquers Chersonesus in Thrace and the north-Aegean island of Thasos.

460–445 BCE: First Peloponnesian War.

457 BCE: Sparta wins the battle of Tanagra. Athens defeats the Boeotians at Oenophyta.

453 BCE: Pericles erects trophy at Nemea after Athenian victory over the Sikyonians.

450 BCE: Cimon dies on Cyprus fighting the Persians.

448 BCE: Pericles leads the Athenian forces in the Battle of Delphi.

447 BCE: Boeotians defeat Athenians at first Battle of Coronea.

440 BCE: Hoplites increasingly more lightly armoured, as new battle tactics require more mobility. Athenians successfully besiege island of Samos.

433 BCE: A naval battle between the victorious combined forces of Corcyra and Athens against Corinth.

431–404 BCE: The Cycladic city-states side with Athens in the Peloponnesian War against Sparta and her allies.

431–404 BCE: Thebes sides with Sparta against Athens in the Peloponnesian War.

431 BCE: Athens invades Megara.

431–404 BCE: The 2nd Peloponnesian War between Athens and Sparta (the Delian League and the Peloponnesian League) which took in all of Greece. Thucydides begins his *History of the Peloponnesian War*.

430 BCE: Athens struck by plague.

429 BCE: Peloponnesian forces led by Sparta lay siege to Plataea. Death of Pericles; Athens successfully campaigns in the Corinthian Gulf regions during the Peloponnesian War.

427 BCE: Plataea finally falls to the Spartans after two years.

425 BCE: Athenians capture Pylos. Spartan general Brasidas injured in attempting to re-take the city; Athens defeats Sparta at Pylos under command of Cleon and Demosthenes; Athenian and Corinthian hoplites fight a street battle in the suburbs of Solygeia.

424 BCE: A force of Athenian peltasts defeat Spartan hoplites on Sphaktria in the Peloponnese; the Athenian expeditions against Megara and Boeotia fail with a particularly heavy defeat near Delium; Brasidas's campaign in Thrace; Brasidas takes Amphipolis, Thucydides failed to prevent this and is exiled.

422 BCE: The Athenians, led by Cleon, try to re-take Amphipolis but are defeated by Brasidas; Brasidas employs Myrkinian and Chalkidian peltasts to defeat a force of Athenian hoplites at Amphipolis.

418 BCE: Sparta, led by Agis II, defeats Argos and her allies at the Battle of Mantinaea.

c. 415 BCE: Alcibiades persuades the Athenian assembly to send a military expedition to Sicily. Mutilation of the herms in Athens; Herodotus's *Histories* published.

415–413 BCE: Athenian expedition to attack Syracuse. Spartan garrison at Decelea.

414 BCE: Athens builds fortifications at Sounion.

413 BCE: The Athenian expedition in Sicily ends in a calamitous defeat; the Athenian generals Nicias and Demosthenes are executed.

412 BCE: The Spartan general Astyochus sacks Kos; Sparta allies with Persia.

410 BCE: Alcibiades leads the Athenian fleet to victory over Sparta at Cyzicus.

407 BCE: Athenian general Alcibiades makes his naval base on Samos.

c. 407 BCE: The Athenian fleet is defeated by Lysander of Sparta at Notium.

406 BCE: Agrigento is attacked and destroyed by Carthage.

405 BCE: Athenian naval defeat at Aegospotami.

404 BCE: End of the Peloponnesian War.

Maps

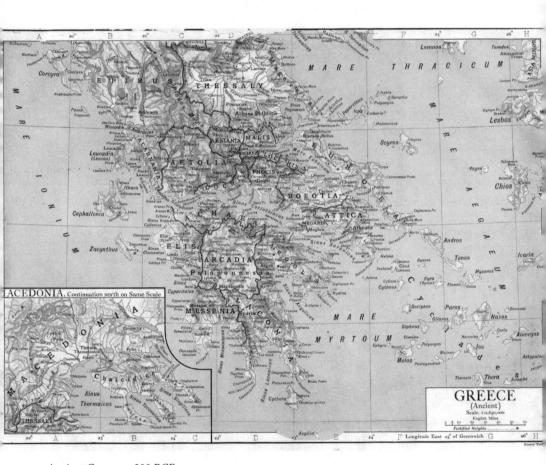

Ancient Greece, *c.* 300 BCE.

The Greek World during the Persian Wars (500–479 BC)

★ Ionian revolt
✕ *Main battle*
▬ Greek opponents of Persia
▬ Greek neutral states
▬ Persian empire
▬ Persian vassal states
— Ionian rebels (498 BC)
— Mardonius (492 BC)
— Artaphernes/Datis (490 BC)
— Xerxes/Mardonius (480 BC)

0   50   100 km

Above: Greece during the Persian Wars.

Below: Greek and Phoenician colonies, *c.* 500 BCE.

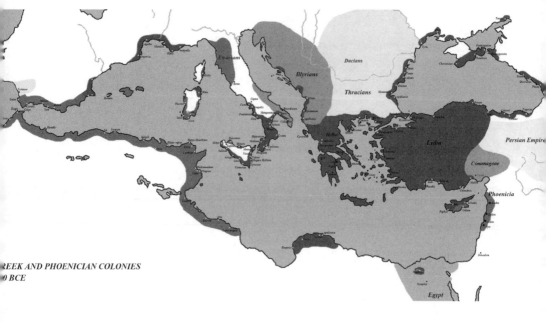

REEK AND PHOENICIAN COLONIES
0 BCE

The Ionian Revolt.

BATTLE OF MARATHON
Greek Double Envelopment,
490 B.C.

SCALE OF MILES
0   1/4   1/2   3/4   1

Above: Battle of Marathon. (*Department of History, United States Military Academy*)

Below: Battle of Salamis. (*Department of History, United States Military Academy*)

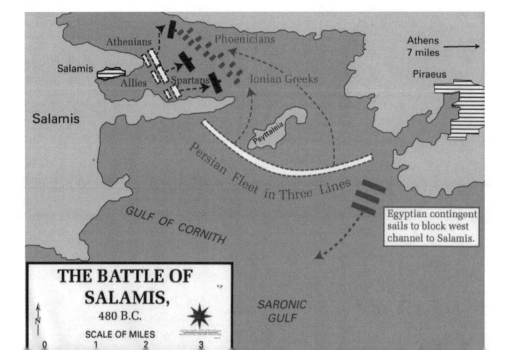

THE BATTLE OF SALAMIS,
480 B.C.
SCALE OF MILES
0   1   2   3

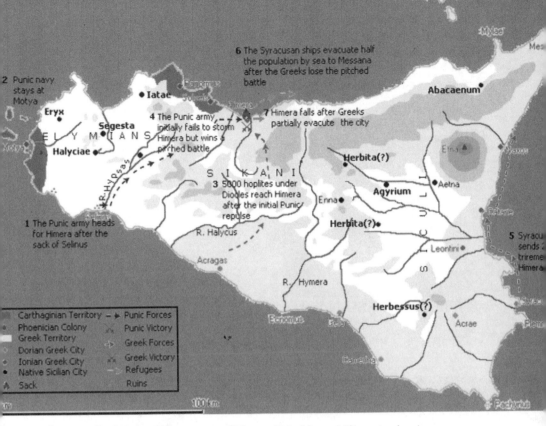

Above: Battle of Himera. (*Department of History, United States Military Academy*)

Below: Battle of Thermopylae. (*Department of History, United States Military Academy*)

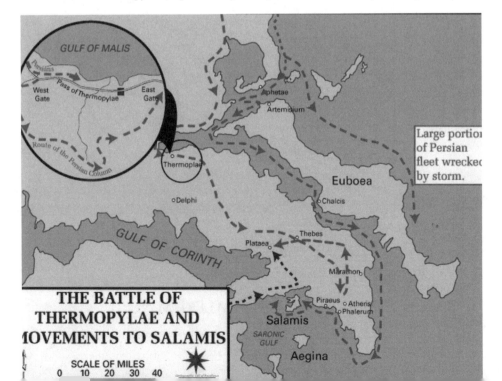

Left: The Peloponnesian War.

Below: The Long Walls of Athens.

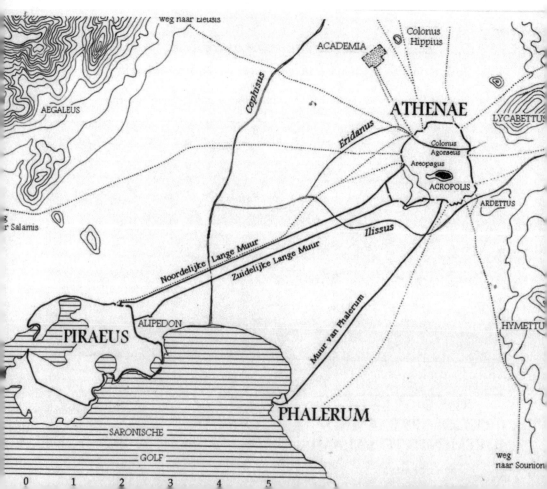

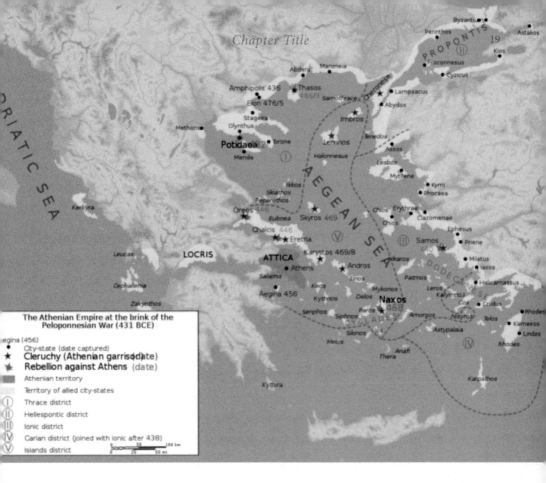

The Athenian Empire at the brink of the
Peloponnesian War (431 BCE)

egina (456)
- City-state (date captured)
★ Cleruchy (Athenian garrison) (date)
✦ Rebellion against Athens (date)
- Athenian territory
- Territory of allied city-states
Ⓘ Thrace district
Ⓘ Hellespontic district
Ⓘ Ionic district
Ⓘ Carian district (joined with Ionic after 438)
Ⓥ Islands district

Above: The eve of the Peloponnesian War.

Right: The siege of Syracuse.

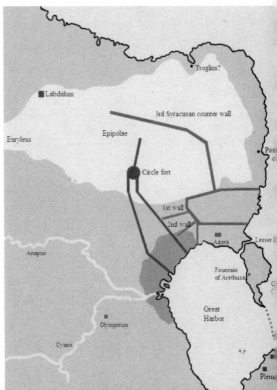

Introduction

One of the most popular and published areas of ancient history is war in the Greek and Roman worlds. The number of books, magazine and journal articles, web pages, and blogs on every conceivable aspect of war in the ancient world is endless, and continues to grow. So why add to the plethora of literature already available? What makes this book worthy of publication in an already crowded market? *Wars and Battles of Ancient Greece* is not just another arid account of wars and battles, with endless, often exaggerated, casualty figures and repetitive tactics. It is different from most other books in the field because it has context as its focus—each of the battles covered is, where sources permit, placed in its historical, political, and social context: why was the battle fought, how was it fought, what was the outcome, and what happened next? No war or battle was ever fought in isolation—there is always a prelude, a *casus belli*, and a series of consequences. These are revealed wherever possible for each of the wars and battles.

In order to reinforce our focus on context, the book includes chapters covering topics fundamental to the study of war in classical antiquity—warfare in civilisations and cultures before Greece; the Greek war machine; and Greek women and conflict, which is rarely, if ever, covered in books on Greek war or Greek women.

Throughout the book, I have strived to tease out unique points of military interest where they exist for the battles, highlighting the first or last appearance of major figures and weapons, describing the significance of a certain action, and its consequences. So, we highlight psychological warfare; 'friendly fire'; the rise of the Greek navy; ethnic cleansing; war rape; siege machinery; armour and weaponry; women on the front line and in support; and strategies and tactics.

Wars and Battles of Ancient Greece is the thrilling story of Greece's endless battling and warring, be it focused on Athens, Sparta, or Sicily. For much of the time covered by the book, somewhere, an army of Greeks was doing battle with a foreign army or, much more likely, with another Greek army. Generally speaking, Athens, from the start of the Persian Wars in 490 BCE to the Battle of Chaeronea in 338 BCE was, on average, fighting more than two years out of every three and never saw peace for a period as long as ten years. This book tells the fascinating and gripping story of Greece's wars and battles from Mycenaean conflicts to the end of the Peloponnesian War in 404 BCE. Wars and battles defined these years; war was the norm. Indeed, as Yvon Garlan has said, 'peace was understood … simply as the absence of war'.[1]

War Before the Greeks

Warfare and conflict, of course, were well-established in ancient societies before the Greeks. Territorial defence or expansion, mineral deposits, naked aggression, trade protectionism, the need to eat, drink, and procreate in safety, and despotism all played their part, long before the Greeks, in fuelling wars, conflict, and confrontation. War has been a constant for as long as man has had lands, a food and water supply, and women and children to protect.

It seems probable that regular unrest started to manifest around 6500 BCE, about the same time as the nomadic hunter-gatherer started to settle down, graduating from a nomadic life in his search for food to living in a settlement from which he emerged each day to hunt and returned home each evening to eat, procreate, and protect. Later, population growth and the quest for living space on fertile land would have caused additional conflict as mountain people, for example, came down to occupy lands already settled and cultivated by other tribes, themselves either indigenous or immigrant.

In Mesopotamia around 3500 BCE, great change came about when defensive ditches around farmsteads and homesteads developed into walled defences and citadels to defend the new cities and to assert conspicuous power and control over neighbouring, weaker settlements.

Early descriptions of war date from around 3200 BCE with the Sumerians of Mesopotamia—the city-states of Ur, Lagash, Uruk, and Kish squabbled internally with each other while they struggled externally with the nearby Elamite kingdom. Early depictions of war include the Standard of Ur (2500 BCE) wall panel, and the Stele of the Vultures of Lagash (2330 BCE), which show kings leading orderly ranks and disciplined formations of men into battle. The Standard depicts two-man war chariots drawn by four mules, and close formation spearmen; the Stele commemorates the long-running conflict between Umma and Lagash over a tract of agricultural land on their borders and shows soldiers in even closer formation—a sight not seen again for some 1,800 years when they re-emerged in the shape of the Greek hoplite phalanx. The British Museum describes the Standard as follows, illustrating as it does the importance of war in Sumerian society:

The main panels are known as 'War' and 'Peace'. 'War' shows one of the earliest representations of a Sumerian army. Chariots, each pulled by four donkeys, trample enemies; infantry with cloaks carry spears; enemy soldiers are killed with axes, others are paraded naked and presented to the king who holds a spear.

The 'Peace' panel depicts animals, fish and other goods brought in procession to a banquet. Seated figures, wearing woollen fleeces or fringed skirts, drink to the accompaniment of a musician playing a lyre. Banquet scenes such as this are common on cylinder seals of the period, such as on the seal of the 'Queen' Pu-abi, also in the British Museum.[1]

The limestone stele is typical of victory stele of the time and displays a mythological and an historical side. The historical side is divided into four; the upper register shows Eannatum, the king of Lagash, leading troops into battle, with their enemies trampled underfoot. The vultures, after which the stele gets its name, circle above, gruesomely carrying the decapitated heads of the enemy in their beaks. The next register depicts soldiers marching with spears behind the king, who is in a chariot also bearing a spear. In the third register a cow is shown tethered to a pole while a naked priest standing on a pile of animal carcasses performs a libation; to the left is a heap of naked bodies surrounded by skirted workers carrying baskets on their heads. The damaged fourth register shows a hand holding a spear touching the head of an enemy. The land dispute ends in a battle after which the leader of Umma swears that he will not trespass into the territory of the Lagash again; if he does, he will have the gods to answer to.

More evidence of early conflict comes with a famous slate palette from 3000 BCE Egypt graphically depicting King Narmer slaying his foes.[2] In Mesopotamia around 2500 BCE, Naram-Sim desecrated the temple of Enlil and devastated Nippur, Enlil's city. In mindless retaliation Enlil unleashed the ferocious Gutians—an uncontrollable people with the mentality of dogs and the faces of apes. They swarmed all over the land like locusts, destroying everything, including Nippur. Later, the Sumerian king, Shulgi (2029–1982 BCE), not only destroyed the Gutians in battle but laid waste to their lands, reducing it, and their economy and society, to a virtual desert; the Gutians were scattered far and wide.[3]

The gradual emergence of the bow and its archers had a significant impact on warfare. The first serious exponent of belligerent archery came with the Akkadian army of Sargon. Sargon had moved south in search of fertile land after the salinisation of his own country. The victory steles of Sargon's son, Rimus (r. 2278–2270 BCE), and of the Akkadian king Naram-Sin (r. *c.* 2254–2218 BCE) both depict bows being deployed; their range was 250–300 yards.

The first recorded engagement was the Battle of Megiddo (biblical Armageddon) in northern Palestine, which was fought in 1469 BCE between Egypt and an alliance of Canaanite kingdoms; they were deployed by the Egyptian pharaoh Tuthmosis III. Megiddo is also the world's first dateable battle for which we can trace location, outcome, and combatants. It also marks another early example of the use of the bow, and the first recorded body count.

At the same time, treaties and coalitions proliferated: Naram-Sin allied with Elam in south-west Iran. The Hittites were particularly accommodating: see, for example, King Shuppiluliuma's concord with Niqmaddu, king of Ugarit in northern Syria in the middle of the fourteenth century. Dynastic marriages and the forging of alliances between families were widespread: one notable instance was the marriage of the daughter of Ashur-uballit of Assyria to the king of Babylonia around 1500 BCE.[4]

As noted, the protection of state boundaries, living space, and economic and mineral resources were, as now, common causes of war and battles. Around the same time as the Ashur-uballit marriage, Assyrians were attacked by the Mittannians, who were anxious to annex the rich agricultural lands along the Tigris; the Assyrians repulsed them and from then on made punitive raids on Mittannian tribesmen to prevent further incursions, thereby expanding their own territory. The Israelites theologised their reprisals when Yahweh decreed that the raiding Amalekites would be expunged from memory for all time—an early *damnatio memoriae*—for their attacks on and appropriation of Israelite settlements. The hateful curse endured into the time of Samuel and Saul (*c.* 1100 BCE) when the former ordered the latter to exterminate the Amalekites down to the last woman, child, and baby and to erase their agrarian economy.[4] So we get one of our earliest record of instances of the extermination of women and children, and of ethnic cleansing; no doubt, the slaughter of the women was preceded by wholesale rape and other atrocities.

The Assyrians were the champions of logistics: they laid down the rules for lines of supply, supply depots (*ekal masharti*), arsenals, barracks, and transport columns—rules and protocols which are still followed to this day. Their expertise in maintaining an armed, watered, fuelled, and fed army allowed them a hitherto unheard-of reach and penetration (up to 300 miles) at an awesome speed of up to 30 miles a day on horses on ancient highways.

Assyrian naval warfare was launched with Sennacherib in the early seventh century; he brought in Syrian shipbuilders to build a fleet at Nineveh to oppose the Elamites. Crewed by Phoenicians, the Assyrians sailed as far down the Tigris as the great river would permit and then followed a canal linked to the Euphrates, through which they entered the Persian Gulf; from there, they advanced into Elamite territory with their horses and soldiers. The Assyrians were notorious for ransacking and torching enemy lands once their armies had replenished and eaten their fill of local grain, oil, wine, and dates. Sargon II and Sennacherib, his son, were seasoned devastators with enemy irrigation systems, granaries, and fruit orchards all falling victim.

Another way in which the belligerent Assyrians were pioneers was in their understanding of the value and importance of loyalty and subservience. Any suspicious people they encountered were uprooted and resettled far from home; those trusted to be loyal were integrated into the army, regardless of ethnicity. The bonds between victor and vanquished were further strengthened by a policy of linguistic and religious tolerance and receptiveness; Assyrian armies were further reinforced by allowing the defeated to form ancillary units, using their own armour and weapons.

The Assyrians were devotees both of siege warfare and, like the Egyptians, the use of chariots. They could boast an impressive arsenal of siege craft—metal-tipped battering rams, mobile assault towers crammed with archers, miners expert in tunnelling under walls, engineers adept at chipping away at foundations and gates, and shock spearmen scaling walls. Chariots were to become largely obsolete over time and survived only in remote societies, such as the Celts in Britannia.

Under Sargon II (r. 721–705 BCE), the charioteers moved forward onto the back of their horses, marking the evolution from charioteer to mounted archer and the introduction of cavalry. Generally speaking, the key to Assyria's success probably lies in their willingness to learn from their enemies and to blend progressive new ideas and strategies into their military thinking. The use of propaganda to promote Assyria both as a terror to be avoided and as an attractive ally was equally successful.

Yahweh's sanction of the Amalekite genocide noted above indicates that a warring state's actions was thought to be justified and mitigated by the will of god. Divine approval has been necessary before the opening of hostilities in many theatres of war down the ages. Omens in the ancient world were interpreted and had to be favourable; failure to observe them could be costly. An imprudent and impious Naram-Sin lost 250,000 men when he chose to ignore his ill omens before one battle.

Divine sanction was also useful in justifying and mitigating atrocities. The Assyrians had a shocking reputation—as did some Egyptians, not least Amenophis II (1439–1413 BCE), who massacred all surviving opposition at Ugarit. The Egyptians too were notorious for mutilating the defeated; for example, the battle of Megiddo yielded eighty-three severed hands. The walls of the temple at Medinet Habu show piles of phalluses and hands hacked from Libyan invaders and their allies by Rameses III (1193–1162 BCE). Ashurbanipal, the Assyrian king who reigned from 668 to 627 BCE, rejoiced in the fact that 'I will hack up the flesh [of the defeated] and then carry it with me, to show off in other countries'. His ostentatious brutality is widely depicted; one picture shows him implanting a dog chain through the cheek and jaw of a vanquished Bedouin king, Yatha, and then reducing him to a humiliating life in a dog kennel guarding the gate of Ninevah or pulling the royal chariot.[5]

Babylon was a particular threat. When Ashurbanipal destroyed the city, he tore out the Babylonians' tongues, smashed the Babylonians to death with the statuary, and fed their corpses, cut into little pieces, to the dogs, pigs, zibu birds, vultures, and fish. Ashur-etil-ilani (r. 627–623 BCE), Ashurbanipal's heir, had a predilection for cutting open the bellies of his opponents 'as though they were young rams'. In the Bible, we read of the children of the defeated being dashed to death, and pregnant women ripped open.[6] War rape was a constant: again in the Bible, the prophet Zechariah announces 'I will gather all the nations against Jerusalem to battle, and the city shall be taken and the houses plundered and the women raped ...' Isaiah's vision was equally apocalyptic: 'Their little children will be dashed to death before their eyes. Their homes will be sacked, and their wives will be raped'. In Lamentations, 'Women have been violated in Zion, and virgins in the towns of Judah'.[7]

Throughout its long history, Egypt consistently justified its many military conflicts as valid defence against the violation of its borders by, for example, the Hittites or the Hyksos (Rulers of Desert Uplands), or as necessary when Egyptian trade was threatened. The Middle Kingdom Egyptians of around 1900 BCE were among the first exponents of the battering ram, depicted on the Beni Hasan wall painting with its metal tip and protective hut. Scorched earth and the erasing of whole nations as well as mass deportation and displacement of conquered peoples were routine. The horse-drawn chariot, the bow, bronze weapons, scale armour, and state-of-the-art daggers and swords had come into play; they formed part of the Egyptian military armamentarium by 1600 BCE.

The Papyrus Lansing was composed in the reign of the Pharaoh Senusret III, the fifth ruler of the twelfth dynasty of Egypt from 1878–1839 BCE. It provides us with a fascinating, if biased, account of Egyptian society at the time and, indirectly, the important role played by the military in that society. It is written by the scribe Nebmare-nakht to his younger apprentice Wenemdiamun, persuading him that the profession of a scribe is the best while decrying other occupations such as farmer, merchant, or soldier. What a wretched life soldiering was—dirty, salty water every three days; relentless uphill marching, with no rest, clothes, or sandals; a body racked with disease; desertion punished by the extermination of the whole family and an anonymous, unremembered death at the end of an unremembered life.

Given the river Nile, the Nile delta, and the Mediterranean, it is not surprising that naval warfare played a major role in Egyptian conflict. The Theban Kamose saw action in the revolt against the Hyksos, delighting in his victory and the resulting booty: having sailed upstream from Thebes he, 'happy in heart', encountered the fortress of a collaborator; 'I was on him [like] a hawk ... I razed his wall, I slew his people, I caused his wife to go down to the river bank—[presumably a euphemism for rape]. My soldiers were like lions with their prey, with serfs, cattle milk, fat and honey, dividing up their possessions'. The Hyksos capital of Avaris was eventually taken after a naval victory by Amosis (r. 1552–1524 BCE).

Mycenaean Military
(*c.* 1600–1100 BCE)

It seems likely that waves of immigration to the Aegean area took place during the 3,000 years that cover the Neolithic Age (6000–3000 BCE) by agricultural peoples in search of fertile, workable plains, ample fresh water, a good climate, and plenty of deer, goats, boar, and bears. These immigrants probably came from what was later Anatolia, Cilicia, Syria, and Palestine. Pots, axes, and adzes have been found in abundance throughout the region, notably in Thessaly and Crete. Early evidence of weapons include finds of slings, clay sling bolts, flint, and obsidian arrowheads on the islands. On the mainland, copper knife blades and a copper axe (from Knossos) have been excavated.

The real picture regarding the existence of warfare in Minoan Crete, which flourished from about 2700 BCE and 1420 BCE, continues to elude. Archaeology has revealed weaponry, grand fortifications, and warlike long boats but many scholars explain these away as flamboyant expressions of status. There is no firm evidence for a Minoan army, or for Minoan expansionism outside Crete. Minoan art is decidely short on military subject matter with, for example, depictions of armed warriors being stabbed in the throat with swords put down to ritual or blood sport. Others, however, contend that war was familiar to the Minoans using evidence gleaned from, for example, skeletal remains in graves which exhibit military traumas and injuries.[1] The remains from the Hagios Charalambos cave in Crete, dated to the Middle Minoan period, provide us with a large and well-preserved collection of cranial traumas, giving some of the most crucial evidence for a military prescence in Minoan society. At least sixteen cases of cranial trauma have been found, the majority on male skulls, mostly 'on the frontal or on the left parietal, consistent with an instinctive rightward turn of the head to avoid probably a missile or to avoid a blow from a right-handed assailant'.[2]

Most battlefield traumas from the Minoan burials implicate the skull, but there is also evidence of skull traumas from the Mycenaean burials. This ties in with what we learn from Homer in which the cranium was the target of choice for most violent blows. From the total fifty-four injuries described in the *Iliad* and the *Odyssey*, twenty-nine injuries involved the head, twenty-two the neck, and three both areas, while there were thirty-nine fatal injuries to the head, face, and cervical spine.

Indeed, Mycenaean Greece also reveals its military side with the numerous weapons excavated, the prolific depictions of warriors and combat in contemporary art, and by Linear B records, which give us details about the organisation of the military personnel. The tablets relating to military issues were named '*orchha*' (in Linear B script: o-ka, oρχα)—a word related to '*orchos*' (όρχος, military group)—which probably means the military unit.

It was, however, the palace centres that administered and coordinated the development of its sophisticated military infrastructure with materiel production and logistics. This militarism was to inspire and influence later Greek culture and societies, not least Homer's epics and the works of the epic cycle, which exposed the heroic nature of the Mycenaean warrior elite. The three most important palaces were at Knossos, Phaistos, and Mallia, but numerous smaller palaces have been discovered at, for example, Arkhanes, Gournia, and Monasteraki, each guarding a small plain or valley.

Power and might in late Bronze Age Greece was shared between warrior kingdoms; Mycenae was the dominant force but there was rivalry from Tiryns, Pylos, and Thebes. Records from Pylos reveal that every rural community, the *damos*, had to supply a quota of men for service in the army; the aristocracy was similarly obliged. The (*W*) *anax* (the king) was, of course, at the top of the palace hierarchy but the second in command was the *laphagetas*—the leader of the army, the military commander. The *laphagetas* was the palace's military leader in time of war, the official who made the war plans and strategy. The high status of the military official illustrates very clearly the importance of the military in Mycenaean politics and society.

The shaft graves found at Mycenae provide evidence of a militaristic society. Grave circle 'B' from the seventeenth–sixteenth century BCE has twenty-six graves: fourteen are shaft graves and twelve cists containing twenty-four skeletons; six of the shaft graves were family tombs in which several occupants were found. The males have with them drinking vessels and various weapons—swords, daggers, and arrowheads—indicating the existence of an elite warrior class in Mycenaean society. Grave Nu has revealed traces of a boar's tusk helmet, typical of Mycenaean warfare. Many of the males show signs of trauma: healed skull and spinal injuries most likely incurred on the battlefield, while some of them probably died in battle of their injuries.

The sixteenth-century-BCE grave circle 'A' is a royal cemetery near the Lion Gate, the main entrance of the citadel of Mycenae. It started off outside the walls but was later enclosed in the acropolis when the fortifications were extended in the thirteenth century BCE.

The circle, 27.5 m in diameter, comprises six shaft graves, accomodating nineteen bodies (eight men, nine women, and two children) along with gold death masks, full sets of weapons (spearheads, swords, bows, and daggers) ornate staffs, and gold and silver cups. In addition, golden belts may have been used as baldrics to hold the rectangular or figure of eight shields. Depictions on the objects show fighting and hunting scenes and it is likely that some of the weaponry at least was ceremonial rather than military: some swords are decorated on the blades while the hilts are often covered with richly decorated gold sheet and the pommels consist of handsomely carved lumps of ivory, alabaster, or marble. The site was famously excavated by Heinrich Schliemann in 1876.

From about the fifteenth century BCE, the Mycenaeans were spreading towards the Aegean, the Anatolian coast, and over to Cyprus. The Mycenaean military is characterised by heavy infantry carrying spears (the main weapon), large shields, and occasionally armour. A significant change came in the thirteenth century BCE when tactics and weaponry became more uniform and flexible and weapons became smaller and lighter. Most of the features we see in the later hoplite panoply of classical Greece were in evidence by this time.

The role of war chariots is disputed but it seems that during the sixteenth–fourteenth centuries they had a combat role, but later in the thirteenth century BCE, they were lighter (rail chariots) used more for battlefield transport. There were also cavalrymen in their military mix. Archery was common; other weapons included maces, axes, slings, and javelins. Shields covered most of the body; 'figure-of-eight' shields were the most common type made of layers of bull-hide sometimes reinforced with bronze plates. The boar's tusk helmet was the most popular and became the most identifiable piece of Mycenaean armour. Boar's tusk helmets consisted of a felt-lined leather cap, with several rows of cut boar's tusk sewn onto it.

The palaces obviously had to be defended; they made good use of awesome symbolism with walls built in what became known as Cyclopean style: huge, unworked boulders more than 8-m (26-feet) thick and weighing several metric tonnes.

The shallow draughts of Mycenaean ships allowed them to be beached in sandy bays. The largest ships may have had a crew of around forty-five oarsmen, with one rudder, a captain, two officers, and a squad of warriors.

As noted, around 1450 BCE, Greece was divided into a series of militaristic kingdoms, the most important in Mycenae, Tiryns, Pylos, and Thebes. Before the end of the century, this martial civilisation replaced the former priestess-dominated civilisation of Minoan Cretans in the Aegean expanding towards the Aegean Islands and Anatolian coast. Mycenaean soldiers also found work as mercenaries in foreign armies, like Egypt.

It is the Hittites who provide us with evidence of some of the first Mycenaean military actiivity in the region. Contemporary Hittite texts mention Ahhiyawa, a Hittite translation of Mycenaean Greece, or Achaeans in Homeric Greek. Ahhiyawa bolstered its position in western Anatolia from *c.* 1400 to *c.* 1220 BCE when the kings of Ahhiyawa dealt with the Hittite kings militarily and diplomatically. Ahhiyawa meddled in Anatolian affairs, supported by anti-Hittite uprisings or through local vassal rulers. An example from 1400 BCE, shows Attarsiya (possibly Atreus) launching a campaign with war chariots to attack Hittite regions before an invasion of Cyprus, eventually overthrowing the local Hittites. Attarsiya's campaigns are the earliest recorded Mycenaean Greek military activity against the Hittites. The Trojan War may have its origins in the Hittite-Ahhiyawan conflict in Wilusa, the Hittite name for Troy, in the thirteenth century BCE. Around 1250 BCE, population movement and internal strife may be among the causes of the final destruction of the Mycenaean palaces in the twelfth century BCE, all despite a programme of huge strengthening and expansion of the fortifications at various sites.

In 2006, archaeologists working at the Mycenaean palace on the island of Salamis unearthed a bronze scale that was part of a larger quilted piece of armour, a cuirass. What is remarkable is that this scale was stamped with the royal cartouche of Ramesses II (r. *c.* 1279–1213 BCE) and shines new light on the military activities of the Greeks during the Late Bronze Age outside of the Aegean. Also, this was not typical of the armour worn by the Mycenaeans during the Late Bronze Age: Mycenaean warriors wore a full suit of body armour or panoply. It consisted of a body cuirass, shoulder guards, breast plates, lower body protection plates, greaves, and lower arm-guards, all weighing around 18 kg. The best-known example was discovered at the village of Dendra in the Argolid dated to the end of the fifteenth century BCE. It is part of the Late Helladic (LHIIIa) Dendra Panoply, comprising fifteen separate pieces of bronze sheet, held together with leather thongs, that encased the wearer from neck to knees. This panoply includes both greaves and lower arm-guards.

The cartouche reinforces the belief that the Greeks of the Late Bronze Age served as mercenaries overseas as documented in an inscription of Ramesses II's at Abu Simbel, which describes how, in the second year of his reign, Ramesses defeated raiders invading the Egyptian coast at the Nile delta; they were known as the Sherden or the Shardana and are believed to have come from the Aegean region. Ramesses II takes them prisoner and gives them an opportunity to join his personal bodyguard. The Sherden also served the Pharaoh in his battle against the Hittites at Qadesh in 1274 BCE.

A more recent find in 2009 involved a Mycenaean palace near Xirokampi, in Laconia. Apart from clay vessels, figurines, and frescoes, there are three Linear 'B' tablets, one of which features an inventory of about 500 daggers; another is an inventory for textiles.

The other power players in the region at the time were the so-called Sea Peoples—an obscure race of piratical marauders who wreaked irrevocable destruction and havoc on the Mediterranean civilisations they came into contact with. They are conjectured to have originated from western Asia Minor, the Aegean, the Mediterrannean islands, or Southern Europe and are believed to have attacked Anatolia, Syria, Canaan, Phoenicia, Cyprus, and, most emphatically, Egypt before and during the collapse of the Late Bronze Age (1200–900 BCE). They disappeared from the scene as quickly as they had arrived, taking with them the civilisations of the Hittites, Canaanites, Mycenaeans, and Minoans. They attacked Egypt twice: in 1207 BCE during the reign of Merneptah and in 1177 BCE in the reign of Ramesses II.

When Merneptah heard news of the attack on Egypt, 'His majesty was enraged at their report, like a lion'. Merneptah states that he quelled the invasion, killing 6,000 troops and taking 9,000 prisoners cutting off the penises of all of the uncircumcised enemy dead and the hands of all those who were circumcised.

In the second year of Rameses's reign, he repulsed an attack from the Sea Peoples on the Shardana, on the Nile Delta, and took some of the raiders prisoner, as recorded on Tanis Stele II: 'the unruly Sherden whom no one had ever known how to defeat, they came boldly sailing in their warships from the middle of the sea, none being able to withstand them'. The Shardana prisoners were subsequently incorporated into the Egyptian army for service on the Hittite frontier, and fought as Egyptian soldiers in the Battle of Kadesh.

Some scholars believe, though, that there was more to the Sea Peoples than just random bands of piratical raiding parties and that they were, in fact, part of a huge migration of peoples displaced by earthquake or drought.[3]

The Ancient Greek War Machine

Ancient Greece, of course, was never one single identifiable civilisation or nation state in the way that, say, Rome was; rather, Ancient Greece comprised a number of independent city-states and societies that existed more or less independently at different times. So we have, for example, the Minoan civilisation on Crete, and, on the mainland or on islands nearby Sparta, Mycenae, Athens, Crete, and Macedonia, all exerting power and influence, and often only really coming together to do battle, trade, or forge alliances. Add to this the various Greek colonies scattered around the Mediterranean and the Black Sea and there is a very complex picture geographically, militarily, politically, economically, and socially; ancient Greece was anything but homogenous—the ancient Greeks were never one people.

The Athenians, Spartans and other city-states, and the Macedonians all engaged in warfare at one time or another. The city-state (*polis*) has its origin in the Mycenaean Greeks who, based around Athens, established twelve fortified cities in the tenth century along the Aegean coast, looking to Athens as their centre. These were supplanted by barbaric invaders from the north, the Dorians, who captured the cities, grabbed the lands and enslaved the inhabitants.

In Crete, political rights in the period 850–750 BCE were granted only to those rich enough to bear arms, thus forging a society in which allegiance to the state far outweighed any domestic obligations. Military service began at seventeen with strict discipline, athletics, military exercises, hunting and mock battles. By nineteen, cadets were assigned to a mess for which the fees were paid for out of public funds. Marriage was permitted but wives lived separately and family life was kept to a minimum. Later migrations to the Greek mainland saw the exportation of this way of life, notably to Sparta where we can recognise many aspects of the Cretan military lifestyle and where the distinction between the franchised warrior and the serf devoid of rights was at its most pronounced.

The Romans have a reputation for being serial warmongers. It is less well-known that many Greeks were equally belligerent. As Finley points out: 'Athens ... was at war on average more than two years out of every three between the Persian wars and the defeat ... at Chaeronea in 338 BCE, and ... it never enjoyed ten consecutive years of peace in all that period'. Thucydides tells us that early Greek wars were largely squabbles over territory; one of the first, he says, was the Lelantine War between Chalkis and Eretrea in Euboea, which took place between *c.* 710 and 650 BCE.[1] The war was triggered by a dispute over the much coveted fertile Lelantine Plain; the conflict spread and sucked in a number of other city-states. According to Thucydides, it was the only war to take place in Greece between the time of the Trojan War (around 1300 BCE) and the Persian Wars (499–449 BCE), in which multiple cities united in alliances rather than single *poleis* were involved. The Persian Wars themselves, in which the cities of Greece eventually repulsed the Persians, is famous for its battles of Marathon, Thermopylae, Salamis, and Plataea. The thirty-year war was pivotal in Greek history, leading to the Athens-led Delian League, a huge expansion of Athenian influence, and the establishment of Athenian democracy.

Conflict between Athens and Sparta was inevitable and consumed much of the latter part of the fifth century; the Peloponnesian War from 431–404 BCE was the most significant, fought against the Peloponnesian League under Sparta. Historians have traditionally divided the war into three phases. The first part, the Archidamian War, saw Sparta attacking Attica and Athens deploying its superior navy in raids on the Peloponnesian coast. The 421 BCE Peace of Nicias brought this phase to an end, but the peace was short-lived. In 415 BCE, Athens sent a huge expeditionary force to attack Syracuse; it turned into a huge disaster that anticipated the destruction of the entire force in 413 BCE. The Decelean War, or the Ionian War, followed in which Sparta was allied to Persia; ultimately, Athens lost her naval supremacy at the catastrophic battle of Aegospotami, leading to Athens's surrender in the following year.

Before this time, there was little in the way of strategy or tactics with land armies on either side content to confront each other, literally, head-on. The Greek model of combat was based on the hoplite phalanx supported by missile-hurling troops. The hoplites were infantry recruited from the middle classes (the *zeugites*), who could afford the expensive heavy armour; this comprised a breastplate (*linothorax*), greaves, a helmet, and a large, round, concave shield (the *aspis* or *hoplon*, made from wood and iron, 3 feet in diameter). Close combat was the order of the day with troops standing shoulder to shoulder eight rows deep. Hoplites also carried long spears (the *dory*) and a sword (*xiphos*). There was little or no room for individual combat: every hoplite depended on the men on either side holding their ground and not exposing him. Lightly armed skirmishers, the *psiloi*, were another element of Greek armies at this time.

When large-scale naval warfare and the maintenance of a standing fleet came, it had a significant impact on Athenian politics, society, and economics. A large number of rowers were obviously required to crew the ships and skilled craftsmen were needed to build, maintain, and repair the fleets. This caused a demographic shift from country village to urban *polis*, raising hitherto less significant social issues and, to some extent, the politicisation of the workers as *thetes*. All of this contributed one way or another to the establishment of democracy in Athens.

The trireme was the standard warship, comprising three banks of oars operated by a crew of 200 or so men, 170 of whom were oarsmen. A battering ram was provided by a metal beak on the prow. Bigger models—quadriremes and quinqueremes—simply had additional decks of oars. Demetrius in the Hellenistic age went further still with his *hexeres* (sixes) and *hepteres* (sevens). At the other extreme, the *penteconter* sported a single bank of fifty oars.

Initially, the ship was used to carry platoons of troops or marines whose objective was to board enemy vessels and either sink or commandeer them. Soon, this tactic gave way to employing the ship itself as a weapon, unceremoniously ramming the enemy with its beak, ideally amidships. A refinement of this crude but effective tactic was to attack the enemy vessel head on, diverting at the last minute and running down the side, shearing off all the enemy oars.

Greek naval warfare dawned with the Peloponnesian War. Sparta, commanded by Lysander, eventually defeated the Athenian navy by cutting off the seaborne supplies going into Piraeus, and defeating the Athenian fleet at Aegospotami where Lysander sank 168 ships and captured up to 4,000 Athenian sailors. In the meantime, Alcibiades had defected to Sparta (and later back to Athens again); the Athenian army (5,000 infantry and light-armoured troops) and navy (100 or so ships) had been virtually exterminated at Syracuse where a bad omen—a lunar eclipse—had delayed their retreat and they were run down and killed or enslaved by the Spartan cavalry. The Spartans were later joined by Persia and by disaffected Athenian allies. Athens was brought to its knees politically and economically, as well as militarily. Sparta, however, was on the rise.[2]

Sparta was very much a militaristic society but perhaps not to the extent that we are often led to believe. Caution needs to be exercised with the sources as much of what we know about Sparta is given to us by Athenian writers whose work is freighted with bias against and hostility towards an arch-enemy. Nevertheless, Lycurgus in the eighth century BCE famously said that Sparta's walls were made of men, not bricks; Sparta was a well-oiled war machine which required a ready and constant supply of warriors.[3] The men were pre-occupied with their military careers and, though marrying from their mid-twenties, saw very little of domestic or family life before the age of thirty. Even then they still dined in their mess with their brothers in arms and devoted most of their time to the military (*syssitia*). Spartan women, consequently, had a crucial economic role in bringing up their children and running the household. They were responsible for raising sons until they were seven when they left to join the junior army (*agoge*) to begin military training. For that reason, it was considered important that women of the citizen class be physically and mentally equipped for conception and motherhood. The Spartan mother remained at home like other Greek women to a large extent but she was educated in the arts and received training in athletics, dancing and chariot racing: a strong, fit, and educated mother delivered strong babies for a strong army.

Training for boys included endurance exercises and competitive sports; combat training began at eighteen. At twenty, the trainees moved into barracks. At thirty, they were eligible for full citizenship and, if selected, became an 'equal'; this entailed suppressing the helots and remaining on standby for war.

By about 473 BCE, Sparta was the pre-eminent power on the Peloponnesian peninsula and was leader of the Peloponnesian League. She achieved this status in three protracted but successful wars in which she defeated Messenia to the west (940–920 BCE and 750–650 BCE), Arcadia to the north (570–470 BCE), and Argolis to the north-east (670–494 BCE). In the Greek wars against Persia, the Spartan forces were crucial in the battles of Plataea and Thermopylae; the end of the hostilities, however, saw Sparta withdraw into relative isolation, deepened by the machinations of Pausanius, by a destructive earthquake and by revolts by their allies. This allowed Athens to flourish and, eventually, led to confrontation in the Peloponnesian wars.[4]

Land ownership was vital to the Greek citizen soldier, and it defined Greek military activity at this time. The part-time Greek soldier depended on his 15 acres or less to grow his grain, olives, and wine; this livelihood permitted him to live and sell off his surplus to turn a profit and pay for weapons and armour, among other things. This in turn gave him the franchise and an indirect role in politics and government. Any threat to this routine was obviously a serious affair and goes some way to account for the episodic rather than protracted nature of Greek belligerence: incursions needed a speedy outcome because the undefended smallholding back home was vulnerable to attack, not to mention neglect and productivity issues if left untended for too long. As a result, victors rarely pressed home their successes because they were keen to get home, as were the defeated for the very same reason. If an enemy remained intractable then they would simply be attacked later, usually the following year.

A phalanx might lose up to 15 per cent of its strength in an unsuccessful engagement, be it through death in the fray or in flight, or by post battle wound infections such as peritonitis. This obviously had important economic and social ramifications.

The Greeks did little without the sanction of the gods—joining battle was no exception. Armies on the move were always accompanied by a flock of sheep ready for sacrifice (the rites of bloodletting, or *sphagia*); sacrifices were evident at every critical juncture, such as crossing a river, invading a border, striking camp, and starting the battle. Often, the sacrifices were preceded by a meal washed down by generous amounts of alcohol; this meal might be their last, and the alcohol delivered courage and abandon.

Mythical and Semi-Mythical Wars

The Trojan War (Twelfth–Eleventh Century BCE)

It is Homer's *Iliad* that provides us with our most detailed account of a very short episode in the tenth year of the Trojan War; this is extended by the Greek tragedians, Apollodorus, fragments of the epic cycle of poems and the Roman poets Ovid and Virgil who tell us about the aftermath and the experiences of some of the protagonists of the war and their relatives. The question is: how much of this is mythology and how much is based on real historical events?

Despite accepting some poetic license and hyperbole on the part of Homer, many classical authors, including Herodotus, Thucydides and Dio Chrysostom, believed the Trojan War to be historical and a crucial conflict in the region, and that it took place around the Dardanelles in the the thirteenth or twelfth century BCE.[1] Scepticism had set in by the mid-nineteenth century CE when the war and the Troy itself were relegated to mythology. However, in 1868, German archaeologist Heinrich Schliemann was persuaded by Frank Calvert that Troy was a real city located near modern day Hissarlik in Turkey. This is now widely accepted on the basis of excavations conducted by Schliemann, among others. Schliemann's famous 1873 haul apparently included thirteen spearheads, fourteen battle axes, daggers, and a sword.

Somewhere between 1194 and 1184 BCE is the favoured date for the legendary fall of Troy at the hands of the Mycenaean Greek armies, under the command of Agamemnon, and with the tragic deployment of the duplicitous Trojan horse. This calamity for the Trojans took place ten years after the start of the war on Troy. Scholars who advocate the historicity of the Trojan War prefer that date in the twelfth century BCE, as given by Eratosthenes; this corresponds with archaeological evidence for a destructive conflagration at Troy VIIa, Hissarlik, and with the end of the Bronze Age. Excavations have revealed Troy VIIa to be a walled city with fortified towers up to 30 feet high with foundations 59 feet deep. Troy VIIa covered 50 acres or so with a population between 5,000–10,000 inhabitants; it was, by the standards of the day, a major city. Michael Wood notes that scholarly scepticism about Schliemann's identification has been dispelled by the more recent archaeological discoveries, linguistic research, and translations of clay-tablet records of contemporaneous diplomacy: 'Now, more than ever, in the 125 years since Schliemann put his spade into Hisarlik, there appears to be a historical basis to the tale of Troy'.[2] Further excavations have revealed that at the time of the siege Troy was full of bins and pits dug for the emergency storage of grain and other staples, dragged in by country folk seeking refuge and making preparations for a long blockade. The numerous shanties discovered were just as indicative of a city preparing to sit out a protracted siege.

So, while it is very likely that a war and a siege of some kind did take place, it is equally likely that all the descriptions given by Homer and other literary sources bear little relation to actual events in that war.[3] The power in the region was held by the Hittites in Anatolia who held sway in the region from 1700 to 1200 BCE from Troy to today's Turkish–Syrian border, and the Mycenaeans on the mainland, with Troy languishing in the middle. Indeed, Homer by no means provides our only literary evidence: Hittite texts also shine light on the Trojan War or Wars. Joachim Latacz has identified the 'Achaioi' of the *Iliad* with the inhabitants of Ahhiyawa, believing that 'the *Iliad* preserved through oral hexameters the memory of one or more acts of aggression perpetrated by the Ahhiyawans (Hittite for Achaeans) against Wilusa (Hittite for Troy is (W)Ilios) in the thirteenth century BCE'.[4] Hittite archives reveal descriptions of four wars fought at Wilios in the late Bronze Age, any one of which, or all of which, could have been Homer's Trojan War. The records also give the name of one of the kings involved as *Alaxandsu*, Hittite for Greek Alexander, who is most likely the same person as Alexander or Paris of Ilios.

This is Manfred Korfmann's illuminating article on the subject; at the time he wrote this, he was director of excavations at Hissarlik:

Troy appears to have been destroyed around 1180 B.C. (this date corresponds to the end of our excavation of levels Troy VI or VIIa), probably by a war the city lost. There is evidence of a conflagration, some skeletons, and heaps of sling bullets. People who have successfully defended their city would have gathered their sling bullets and put them away for another event, but a victorious conqueror would have done nothing with them. But this does not mean that the conflict was the war—even though ancient tradition usually places it around this time. After a transitional period of a few decades, a new population from the eastern Balkans or the northwestern Black Sea region evidently settled in the ruins of what was probably a much weakened city …

The main argument against associating these ruins with the great city described in the Iliad has been that Troy in the Late Bronze Age was a wholly insignificant town and not a place worth fighting over. Our new excavations and the progress of research in southeastern Europe has changed such views regarding Troy considerably. It appears that this city was, by the standards of this region at that time, very large indeed …

According to the archaeological and historical findings of the past decade especially, it is now more likely than not that there were several armed conflicts in and around Troy at the end of the Late Bronze Age. At present we do not know whether all or some of these conflicts were distilled in later memory into the 'Trojan War' or whether among them there was an especially memorable, single 'Trojan War.' However, everything currently suggests that Homer should be taken seriously, that his story of a military conflict between Greeks and the inhabitants of Troy is based on a memory of historical events—whatever these may have been. If someone came up to me at the excavation one day and expressed his or her belief that the Trojan War did indeed happen here, my response as an archaeologist working at Troy would be: Why not?[5]

In a letter to *The Times*, M. L. West said:

> Hisarlik is the major prehistoric site in northwest Anatolia … There is no doubt that it is Homer's Troy at least in the sense that the poet of the Iliad knew the place and assumed its topography in his narrative. There is archaeological evidence that it had been destroyed by an enemy force in the 12th century BCE. Nearly all scholars accept that the Greek tradition about the Trojan War is based on some memory of this.
>
> On the other hand, we know that an epic tradition is liable grossly to distort the facts, and to be all but worthless as a historical source. We must therefore remain sceptical on such questions as who exactly destroyed Troy, in what circumstances, and from what motive … Troy probably fell to a much smaller group of attackers in a much shorter time.[6]

The catalogue of 1,186 ships in Book 2 of the *Iliad* (lines 494–759) gives a reasonably accurate picture of Bronze Age naval might as supported by archaeological evidence, even though some cities are missing and others are there but should not be—the inevitable result of facts being handed down generation by generation until Homer's day. The cremations of Patroclus and Hector (*Iliad* 18, 138–257 and 24, 784–804) are likewise supported by archaeology even though cremation was much more popular in Homer's Iron Age days than it was in the Bronze Age. The evidence is a fourteenth-century cremation with remains buried in urns in level VIh at Hissarlik. Boar's tusk helmets, as detailed by Homer (*Iliad* 10, 260–265), were long gone by the time Homer was writing, but Bronze Age examples have been dug up at Tiryns on the mainland, at Knossos on Crete and on the island of Delos. The Tower shield of Ajax described by Homer is Bronze Age, even earlier than the Trojan War (*Iliad* 7, 219–223). These huge shields and the helmets are depicted on the Miniature Fresco painted on a wall in a house in Akrotiri on Santorini from the seventeenth century BCE, long before the putative date of the Trojan War. The full suit of armour (the panoply) from 1450 BCE found at Dendra near Mycenae lends credence to Homer's decriptions of Hector wearing full armour at *Iliad* 6, 117–118 and 11, 65. As the years went by, these and other Bronze Age details quite naturally became 'polluted' by the introduction of Iron Age elements relating to armour, tactics, fortifications, and other military details, the more so as the process of oral transmission continued apace and the bards came closer to Homer's own times. However, we have shown that the archaeological evidence gives credible support to Homer's picture of a Bronze Age culture at the time of the Trojan War.

What is unlikely, though, is that Helen was the *casus belli* for the Trojan War. It is more probably that her abduction was used as a pretext for a war in which trade was the primary catalyst for conflict between the Greeks and the Trojans.

Amazonomachy

Equally controversial, if not more so, are the Amazons and questions surrounding their historicity. Amazonomachy is a battle involving Amazon warriors. The only sure thing that can be said about the Amazons is that nothing much about them can be said for sure. A lot of information relating to the Amazons remains mired in controversy or shrouded in speculation. Herodotus believed them to be related to the Scythians and located them vaguely between Scythia and Sarmatia, roughly modern Ukraine.[7] Others would put them in Pontus, Anatolia, on the river Don, or in Libya. The Greeks called the river Don '*Tanais*', but the Scythians called it the 'Amazon', a nod to the fact that the woman fighters inhabited the area—Pliny the Elder suggests the valley of the Terme River in central northern Turkey between the cities of Ordu and Samsun.

In Greek mythology, the legendary capital of the Amazons, Themiscyra, as found on the river Thermodon, may have been their home; it also mentions a mountain named after them (the modern Mason Dagi), as well as a settlement called Amazonium; Herodotus first mentions their capital Themiscyra.[8] Philostratus places the Amazons in the Taurus Mountains; Ammianus locates them east of Tanais, as neighbours of the Alans. They were, therefore, distant and liminal people.

Herodotus further tells that the Sarmatians were descendants of Amazons and Scythians, and that their wives observed their ancient maternal customs, 'frequently hunting on horseback with their husbands; in war taking the field; and wearing the very same dress as the men'. He goes on to say how a group of Amazons was blown across the Maeotian Lake (the Sea of Azov) into Scythia (today's southeastern Crimea). They mastered the Scythian language and agreed to marry Scythian men, on the condition that they would not be required to follow the customs of Scythian women.[9] Domesticity springs to mind. They then moved north-east, settling beyond the Tanais (Don) river, and became the ancestors of the Sarmatians. Herodotus adds that the Sarmatians fought with the Scythians against Darius the Great in the fifth century BCE.

In Roman times, Julius Caesar reminded the Senate of the conquest of large parts of Asia by Semiramis and the Amazons. Strabo compares successful Amazon raids against Lycia and Cilicia with resistance by Lydian cavalry against the invaders.[10] Gnaeus Pompeius Trogus reports how the Amazons originated from a Cappadocian colony of two Scythian princes, Ylinos and Scolopetos.

Their name has become a byword for female warriors in general. Obvious battlefield skills apart, Amazons were great colonists and civilisers: they are said to have founded many cities including Smyrna, Paphos, Ephesus, and Magnesia; as natural horse-borne fighters, they are also credited with inventing the cavalry.

Hippolyta was an Amazon queen.[11] One of the many Hippolyta myths involves Theseus; some versions say he abducted her, and others that she fell in love with Theseus and betrayed the Amazons by absconding with him. In any event, she ended up in Athens where she was to marry Theseus, making her the only Amazon to marry and causing the other angry Amazons to attack Athens in what became known as the Attic War; this was a conflict that they lost to Athenian forces under Theseus or Heracles. Plutarch assures us, though, that 'the invasion of Attica would seem to have been no slight or womanish enterprise'.[12] The Attic War is commemorated as an amazonomachy, in marble bas-reliefs as on the Parthenon, in the sculptures of the Mausoleum of Halicarnassus, in reliefs from the frieze of the Temple of Apollo at Bassae (now in the British Museum), on the shield of the statue of Athena Parthenos, and on wall paintings in the Theseum and in the Stoa Poikile. Pliny the Elder records five bronze statues of Amazons in the Artemision of Ephesus.[13]

Another queen of the Amazons, Myrina not only epitomises the military capabilities of the Amazons but demonstates for us what great builders, town planners, and civilisers the Amazons reputedly were. Her tomb in Troad is mentioned in the *Iliad* and according to Diodorus Siculus, she led a military expedition in Libya and was victorious over the Atlantians, laying waste their city, Cerne.[14] She struck a peace treaty with Horus of Egypt, and conquered the Syrians, the Arabians, and the Cilicians. She subdued Greater Phrygia, from the Taurus Mountains to the Caicus River, and several Aegean islands, including Lesbos. Myrina died when her army was eventually defeated by Mopsus the Thracian and Sipylus the Scythian.

Jordanes's *Getica* (written *c.* 560 CE) tells how the ancestors of the Goths, descendants of Magog, originally inhabited Scythia, on the Sea of Azov between the Dnieper and Don rivers and how, having repulsed a raid by a neighbouring tribe, while the menfolk were away fighting Pharaoh Vesosis, the women formed their own army under Marpesia and crossed the Don to invade Asia. The invading women were in fact descended from the Amazons: they procreated with men once a year, conquered Armenia, Syria, and all of Asia Minor as far as Ionia and Aeolia. Jordanes also relates how they fought with Hercules, and in the Trojan War, how a contingent of them lived in the Caucasus Mountains until the time of Alexander. He mentions by name the Queens Menalippe, Hippolyta, and Penthesilea.

Thalestris was another Amazon queen and mistress of Alexander the Great. They went lion hunting together but, more interestingly, spent thirteen nights in lovemaking; thirteen is significant—it is a sacred fertility number for moon worshippers, and relates to the number of moons in a year. Despite such torrid sex, Thalestris died without issue, dashing her hopes of a child by Alexander.

Gigantomachy

Gigantes (giants) presented a major problem for the Olympian gods. They were a race of prodigious strength and violent aggression, though not always of great size. They are best known for their *Gigantomachia*, their battles with the Olympians to win control of the world and the cosmos. According to Hesiod (*Theogony* 176ff), the Giants were born of Gaia (Earth), from the blood spilt when Uranus (Sky) was castrated by his Titan son, Cronus.

Gigantes are often depicted as humanoid, man-sized hoplites. The subjugated Giants were buried under volcanoes and are said to be what causes volcanic eruptions and earthquakes. Hesiod describes their martial characteristics, as born 'with gleaming armour, holding long spears in their hands'. The importance of their role in Greek culture is reflected in the ubiquity of Gigantomachy in Greek art. There are more than 600 representations cataloged in the *Lexicon Iconographicum Mythologiae Classicae* (*LIMC*).

The cause of the war between Gigantes and Olympians is somewhat obscure. The most detailed account comes from Apollodorus in the first or second century CE (1, 6, 1–2). The scholia to the *Iliad* refer to the rape of Hera by the giant Eurymedon, and according to scholia to Pindar's *Isthmian* 6, it was the Giant Alcyoneus's stealing of the cattle of Helios that started the Gigantomachy. Apollodorus mentions this but also suggests a mother's revenge as the motive for the war, saying that Gaia bore the Giants because of her anger over the Titans who had been subdued and imprisoned by the Olympians. As soon as the Giants are born, they start hurling 'rocks and burning oaks at the sky' (1, 3, 6).

The sheer gall of the Gigantes in trying to overthrow the Olympians was seen as the last word in hubris, with the gods themselves meting out punishment for the Giants for their arrogant challenge to the authority of the gods. The Gigantomachy is also a continuation of the struggle between Gaia and Uranus, earth and sky, and the primal opposition between female and male. Over seventy Gigantes have been identified.

The Messenian Wars (724–682 BCE)

With the battles of the Messenian Wars, we stay in the shadowy double-world in which the mythological and historical are blurred. Pausanias is our main source for a series of conflicts engendered by an expansionist Sparta, covetous of the fertile lands of Messenia around Macaria, and assimilating other Laconians as *perioeci* ('people who live around us'). The Messenian Wars were the culmination of years of mutual enmity between the intransigent Messenians and the Spartans, which saw Messenians raping Spartan virgins on sacred ground during a festival at the temple of Artemis Limnatis around 768 BCE, or, alternatively, beardless Spartan soldiers masquerading as virgins in a bid to assassinate the Messenian aristocracy.[15]

Spartans were murdered by Messenians so the Spartans led a surpise attack on their enemy by assaulting Ampheia, where Messenians were slayed in their beds. The Spartans sacked the city then turned it into a garrison as a base for further operations against Messenia.[16] The Messenian women and children were taken prisoner; the men who had survived the massacre were enslaved.[17] The Messenians were outraged: the king, Euphaes, exhorted the Messenian menfolk and mobilised the entire citizenry and organised a training programme.[18]

Euphaes fortified and garrisoned his towns but avoided direct forays against the Spartan army for two campaigning seasons while the Spartans stole anything moveable, especially grain and money. The Messenians could only attack undefended Spartan border communities when the opportunity arose, beginning a war of cat and mouse. By the summer of 739 BCE, Euphaes had had enough—his agricultural lands were now under Spartan control—and resolved to take the war to the Spartans at Ampheia, to 'unleash the full blast of Messenian anger'.[19] Euphaes set off, his baggage train laden with timbers intended for a marching fort from which to attack the Spartans. Meanwhile, the Spartans had called up reinforcements and sent a force upstream to outflank the Messenians, preventing them from building any fort; Euphaes saw this coming. The Spartans faced the Messenians between Ithome and Taygetus. Their approach was no surprise to Euphaes who selected a site with one side bordering an impassable ravine between the Messenians and the Spartans. He followed the Spartans on his side of the ravine with 500 cavalry and light infantry under Pytharatos and Antandros where they prevented the Spartans from crossing. They completed work on the fort the next day.

With nowhere to go, the Spartan army withdrew from Messenia; the Messenians could count this inconclusive engagement as a victory. The next year, the armies met at Taygetus somewhere in Messenia, near Ampheia. The battle is described as mainly a heavy infantry engagement with the addition of some light infantry in the shape of Dryopians, an ethnic group of Pelasgians, and a unit of Cretan archers. The Messenians were somewhat reckless and disorganised while the more professional Spartans held firm in what can be described as a phalanx formation.[20]

The Messenians withdrew to their hilltop fortress at Mount Ithome, north of Messene from where they consulted the oracle at Delphi. The sacrifice of a royal virgin was the solution; the daughter of Aristodemus, a Messenian hero, was chosen. The Spartans' reaction was to desist from attacking Ithome for six years, before then advancing and killing the Messenian king. Aristodemus was crowned the new Messenian king. After five years, both armies were worn down so they agreed to settle matters in a pitched battle. Aristodemus drove the Spartans back into Sparta. An attempt at intelligence gathering (spying) by the Spartans failed when Aristodemus sent 100 Spartans who had been 'exiled' to Mt Ithone back to Sparta.

Sparta then consulted Delphi again and destroyed the Messenian army as a result of the advice they received. Aristodemus took some unfavourable omens and then, depressed as a result, his own life; a besieged Ithome fell and was destroyed. The surviving Messenians either fled abroad or were captured and enslaved as helots.[21]

After thirty-five years or so of Spartan rule, in 685 BCE, a helot uprising among the Messenians sparked a Second Messenian War in which the Messenians invaded Sparta. A skirmish at Derae proved inconclusive but a Messenian called Aristomenes was invited to take the crown after excelling in the battle. Aristomenes had no interest in kingship but did agree to be general of the Messenian forces when again he distinguished himself.[22] The following year, the Spartans and Messenians faced each other in pitched battle at Boar's Barrow in Stenyclerus on the northern plain; Aristomenes broke the Spartan line and routed them as they fled.[23]

Yet the Spartans were by no means finished: in 682 BCE, they confronted the Messenians at Great Foss, deploying subterfuge when they bribed Aristocrates, king of the Arcadians and supposed allies of Messenia. Aristocrates withdrew his army at the last minute from the Messenian line, leaving them exposed and at the mercy of the Spartans. Aristomenes was captured but escaped; he gathered the survivors and retreated to the stronghold of Mount Eira; here they remained for eleven years until it was captured and destroyed. The Spartans released the women and children along with Aristomenes; the rest were again reduced to helots. The Spartans had been buoyed up by the leadership and war songs of the lame poet Tyrtaeus whose verses give us some insight into the Messenian Wars.[24] Tyrtaeus's poetry advises Spartans how to handle their weapons and wear their armour; the *Suda* tells us:

Tyrtaeus, son of Archembrotus, [was] a Laconian or Milesian elegiac poet and pipe-player. It is said that by means of his songs he urged on the Lacedaemonians in their war with the Messenians and in this way enabled them to get the upper hand.

The Lelantine War (*c.* 710–650 BCE)

The Lelantine War, or the war between Chalcidians and Eretrians (πόλεμος Χαλκιδέων καὶ Ἐρετριῶν), was a conflict between the two *poleis* Chalcis and Eretria in Euboea. As recently as 750 BCE, the two cities had jointly founded Cumae in Italy. The *casus belli* was apparently the possession of the fertile Lelantine Plain between the two cities on Euboea, noted especially for its vines, perhaps exacerbated by a lengthy drought.[25] The conflict spread rapidly, involving many more *poleis* joining either side; in the end, much of Greece was at war. Thucydides marks out the war as being exceptional because it was the only war between the semi-mythical Trojan War and the Persian Wars of the early fifth century BCE in which cities in alliances rather than single *poleis* were implicated.[26]

The war took place before there was any historiography, so there are no contempory written sources for the events. Some scholars even argue that the Lelantine War is mythical or a pure fiction.[27]

Hostilities opened in 710 BCE and although both cities probably had large fleets, the war was fought on land. Just as there was no historical writing, so there were no hoplites. The war predated the introduction of hoplite warfare and was presumably fought between lightly armed swordsmen, or indeed mainly cavalry engagements. This was the time when Eritrea was at its height and could field something in the region of 3,000 hoplites, 600 cavalrymen, and sixty chariots.

The war was never just about claims on the Lelantine plain. Trade was at the heart of the conflict, specifically, the right to trade between the islands of the Cyclades and the mainland. Chalcis controlled the 'Euripus Strait', the narrowest point between the island of Euboea and the mainland; Eretria controlled the islands of Andros, Tenos, and Ceos. Other cities knew all too well that backing the winning side would also allow them access to trade routeds through the strait and the islands. An indication to the importance of trade can be seen by the proliferation of new colonies both cities founded around this time.

It seems likely that Miletus was involved on the side of Eretria and Samos; Thessaly sided with Chalcis, Aegina, Corinth, and Megara; Chios and Erythrai possibly took part as well. Aegina was active in trade with Egypt, where its main competitor was Samos. Samos was allied with Chalcis, which suggests that Aegina supported Eretria. Corinth and Megara were at war for nearly all of the Archaic period, due mainly to the Corinthian conquest of the Perachora peninsula which had originally belonged to Megara.

The decisive action was around 700 BCE when Calchas destroyed the Eretrian mother town of Lefkandi. This severed Eretria's link with the Lelantine Plain; Eretria's ally Miletus devastated the southern Euboean town of Karystos. At the same time, Miletus rose to become the dominant power in the eastern Aegean. It was probably Calchis who eventually came out on top and the end of the war came about, probably, with the intervention of a Thessalian cavalry army, led by Kleomachos of Pharsalos.

Defeat reduced Euboea, not so long before the leading light of Greece, to something of a backwater and an economic nonentity; both victors Chalcis and Eretria lost their former commercial and political importance. Corinthian vase painting had taken over the preeminence formerly enjoyed by Euboean pottery in the Mediterranean markets. Colonisation was now dominated by the *poleis* of Asia Minor, such as Miletus and Phokaia. If Theognis is believed, the two cities fought again over the Lelantine plain in the sixth century.

Other Battles of the Seventh and Sixth Centuries BCE

The Argive-Spartan Feud (669–494 BCE)

The Argolid city of Hysiae was a stronghold south-west of Argos and east of Tegea, near the border with Sparta. The battle here probably occurred during the reign of Pheidon II, the Argive tyrant.[1] This Argive victory enabled her to assume dominance among the Peloponnesian states. Hoplite warfare was becoming the norm around this time with the development of the *aspis*, especially in Argos. Phaidon II was probably the inventor of the hoplite phalanx. An *aspis* (ἀσπίς, plural ἀσπίδες), also known as a *hoplon*, was the heavy wooden shield wielded by the hoplite.[2]

The Battle of the Fetters was a conflict between Sparta and Arcadia in around 550 BCE, in which the Arcadians defeated the Spartans who were intent on a land grab from the Arcadians. Herodotus tells us that the Spartans consulted the oracle at Delphi before making a decision on military action. The response that came back told them that, while they would not conquer all of Arcadia, it remained possible for Tegea to fall, as the oracle would 'give you Tegea to dance in with stamping feet and her fair plain to measure out the line'. The Spartans, however, misinterpreted the oracle, believing that it referred to them measuring out the line to divide Tegea into *kleroi* (the land allocated to each Spartan citizen on coming of age). Accordingly, they marched into battle fully prepared, carrying rods with which to parcel out their new land and fetters with which to shackle the Arcadian helots. Ironically, they became prisoners of war shackled in their own chains. The fetters were displayed for centuries in the temple of Athene Alea, in Tegea.

The Battle of Thyreatis (or the Battle of the 300 Champions) in 545 BCE can claim to be one of the oddest of all ancient Greek battles. It was fought over the territory of Thyrea, owned by Argos but occupied by Sparta. The Argives marched on Thyrea, intent on taking it back; Argive military pride was at stake, as was the abundant local olive economy. The sides agreed that a duel be fought between 300 of the best men on each side. At the end of a grueling and bloody day, only three men were still alive: two Argives and a Spartan. The Argives left, confident they had won while the Spartan remained on the field of battle and collected the discarded arms. The next day, both sides claimed victory: the Argives on the numerical strength of their two survivors, the Spartans because they still had a man on the battlefield. A full-scale battle ensued which the Spartans won.[3]

The battle of Sepeia in 494 BCE finally clinched for Sparta the dominance over the Argives for supremacy in the Peloponnese. Based on information revealed to him by the oracle at Delphi, Cleomenes I of Sparta was inspired to lead an army to take Argos at Sepeia near Tiryns. A different oracle had warned the Argives of impending doom and to beware Spartan duplicity. So, in obedience to this, they instructed their herald to listen to what the Spartan herald said and repeat it verbatim to his Argive troops. Cleomenes soon caught on and told his men to charge and attack when given the order to take breakfast. The Argives were massacred as they ate and when the thousand or so survivors took refuge in a sacred grove nearby, Cleomenes simply set fire to it, ruthlessly killing all within.[4]

Pallene (546 BCE)

The popular tyrant Peisistratus rose to fame after capturing the port of Nisaea in Megara in a coup in 564 BCE. After this, three factions vied for power in Athens: Lycurgus led the Pedieis, the people who lived on the plains producing grain, giving them power during the food shortage. The Paralioi lived along the coast; led by Megakles, the Paralioi controlled the sea and much of Athens's trade. The Hyperakrioi were hill people and easily the poorest of the Athenians, bartering in honey and wool. Peisistratos organised this faction; they easily outnumbered the other two parties put together.

With the support of Megakles, Peisistratus declared himself tyrant. It was never plain sailing, though: Peisistratos was removed from office and exiled twice during his reign. The first time was around 555 BCE, but when the Pedieis and the Paralioi fell out, Peisistratos returned to Athens, entering the city in spectacular fashion sharing a golden chariot with a statuesque woman Athena look-alike. Many came back to him in the belief that he had the favour of the goddess. During his second exile, he acquired resources from the Laurion silver mines near Athens and won the support of the Eritreans and the Thebans; in 546 BCE, he landed at Marathon to successfully attack his enemies at Pallene, 11 miles east of Athens. He remained tyrant of Athens until his death in 527 BCE.[5]

River Helorus (492 BCE)

Hippocrates, the tyrant of Gela in Sicily, was busy building an empire for himself on the island. He had his eye on Syracuse and to that end attacked the Syracusans on the banks of the river Helorus. Although he was victorious, Hippocrates was deterred from attacking Syracuse by Corinth and Corcyra.[6]

Battles with the Etruscans (*c.* 540–505 BCE)

More than thirty Greek city-states established colonies around the Mediterranean by this time. The age of expansion between 734 and 500 BCE was spearheaded by individual city-states (*poleis*) acting with political and commercial autonomy. The *poleis* were keen to acquire more land, to foster trade and to stamp their influence at a distance from the mother city, the metropolis. Phocaea was one of these ambitious *poleis* with a portfolio that included Massalia (around 600 BCE); this was a key colony in southern France (modern Marseille) and, later, Elea, in Magna Graecia (*c.* 540 BCE).

Another was Alalia on the east coast of Corsica. When Phocaea itself fell to Cyrus the Great of Persia in 546 BCE, many Phocaeans emigrated to Alalia, facilitated by the good terms they enjoyed with the Greek colonies along the Strait of Messina and the toll-free passage they enjoyed in the region.

The problem was that the Greek city-states were not the only powers trawling the region hungry for new settlements and trade opportunities. The Phoenician Carthaginians and the Etruscans were in similarly acquisitive mode. Phocaea's Alalia was only established five years when the Carthaginians decided to do something about what they considered an invasion of their territory. The Greeks were also seen to be encroaching on Carthaginian and Etruscan trade from Corsica and were suspected of eyeing up their colonies in northern Italy and Sardinia. So, the Etruscans and Carthaginians joined forces to oppose the Greeks and around 540 BCE, they launched a fleet of 120 pentekonters to face the sixty Phocaean pentekonters. Herodotus reports on the battle, also known as the Battle of Sardinia Sea, with a healthy dose of false facts, describing the outcome as a Cadmean victory for the Phocaeans despite his own report that forty Phocaean vessels were sunk while the other twenty were rendered unseaworthy, their beaks damaged beyond repair.[7] The Phocaeans picked up their families and departed ignominiously for Rhegion on the Italian mainland. Greek prisoners were stoned to death at Caere by the Etruscans; the Carthaginians sold their prisoners into slavery.[8]

The rivalry continued, with two significant naval battles between Carthage and Massalia; Carthage lost both but still succeeded in closing the Straits of Gibraltar to Greek shipping, thus stalling the Greek expansion in Spain by 480 BCE. One of the earliest Greek colonies was Cumae near Naples, established by 750 BCE and one of the gems of Magna Graecia. The Capuan Etruscans coveted thriving Cumae and in 524 BCE prepared to take it by recruiting a horde of allies comprising the Dauni and Aurunci from southern Italy to make an (exaggerated) army of 500,000 infantry and 18,000 cavalry as opposed to the 4,500 Cumaean foot and 800 horse. Whatever the numbers, the sheer size of the Etruscan force was to be its undoing; squeezed into a narrow defile, only the cavalry was able to manoeuvre effectively. The Etruscan alliance fled.[9]

It was here that Aristodemus first rose to fame when, as *strategos* (general), he led the Cumaean victory. Aristodemus (*c.* 550–*c.* 490 BCE) was nicknamed Malakos ('soft' or 'malleable' or even 'effeminate') and became a tyrant of Cumae winning popularity due to his opposition to the city's aristocracy. He was himself eventually assassinated by the aristocrats around 490 BCE but not before he had banished the male descendants of the exiled nobles from the town, making them perform servile labour in the fields. Slaves were freed and granted citizenship, the citizens were disarmed and de-politicised.[10]

Antipathy and enmity festered among the rich over all this anti-aristocracy liberal democracy. In 506 BCE, when Aricia, a Latin town some 15 miles south east of Rome, was besieged by the Etruscans, the Aricians appealed to Cumae for military assistance. The aristocrats saw in this as an opportunity get rid of Aristodemus so they sent him north with a small army of mercenaries on some battered old boats. Aristodemus persuaded the Aricians to come out and fight and then challenged the Etruscans to do battle, which they did. The Aricians immediately ran back into their city but the Cumaean force stood firm. Aristodemus covered himself in glory when he personally slew the Etruscan commander. On returning to Cumae, he did likewise to the aristocrat leaders.[11]

The War of Sybaris (511 BCE)

Sybaris was a flourishing colony in the Gulf of Tarentum; life there was so relaxed and prosperous: the word sybarite in English has come to mean a person steeped in luxury and self-indulgence. One of the decisive acts of a tyrant there, Telys, was to expel some of the wealthiest libertines in town. These found refuge in nearby Croton, much to the displeasure of Telys who gave the people of Croton an unequivocal ultimatum: get rid of the Sybarites or expect war. One of the leading citizens of Croton at the time was Pythagoras—more noted for his theorems than for diplomacy, it seems. He advised granting asylum to the Sybarites, whatever the consequences.

Telys responded by drawing up a force allegedly of 300,000 men, all led by an Olympic champion by the name of Milo. This was the battle of the River Traeis. Yet Telys had not bargained for the mollifying effect on his men of years of unremitting hedonism. When the Crotoniate fifers struck up, the Sybarite cavalry horses broke into dance, thus throwing the army into confusion. The rather more disciplined soldiers from Croton slaughtered the invaders, taking no prisoners. As a *coup de grâce*, they diverted the river Crathis through Sybaris, thus expunging all evidence of the city.[12]

The Ionian Revolt (499–493 BCE)

Cyrus the Great was the founder of the Achaemenid Empire, otherwise known as the First Persian Empire. He built this by conquering the Median Empire, then the Lydian Empire, and eventually the Neo-Babylonian Empire. He led an expedition into central Asia, which resulted in major campaigns that were described by Herodotus as having brought 'into subjection every nation without exception'.

Cyrus the Great, however, is remembered not just for his military prowess but also for his good works in human rights, politics, and for a general influence on both Eastern and Western civilisations, leaving, for example, his stamp on the national identity of modern Iran. Achaemenid influence also extended as far as Athens, where many Athenians adopted Achaemenid Persian culture as their own, in a form of reciprocal cultural exchange.

We have to go back as far as 700 BCE to see how Miletus emerged as the most important of the Ionian cities.[1] Culturally, it spawned the first philosophers and was one of the first Greek cities to adopt writing and coinage. It founded colonies (Pliny the Elder says over ninety) from the Propontis and on the coasts of the Black Sea: these became major hubs for Ionian trade. Miletus occupied and fortified Mount Mycale and took control of the sanctuary of Apollo at Didyma, the one and only Greek oracle in Asia, with the huge prestige that brought. It was at its zenith around 500 BCE under the rule of Aristagoras.

It was the Persians who posed the first real external threat to the city-states of ancient Greece. The Ionian Revolt was a series of conflicts between the Achaemenid Empire of Persia and Greek city-states; it started in 499 BCE, eliding into the Persian Wars at Marathon in 490 BCE and continuing until 449 BCE.

The trouble had started as far back as 547 BCE when the Greek cities of Ionia and Aeolia on the coast of Asia Minor fell to Persia. The Persians first crossed into Europe in around 513 BCE when Darius attacked Scythian nomads north of the Danube, followed by the conquest of parts of Thrace in 512 BCE. This gave the Persians a foothold in Europe and allowed them to threaten the Greek grain trade routes in and around the Black Sea. The cities of mainland Greece were the next objective but the

Persian expansionist policy was interrupted by the Ionian Revolt. Either Croesus of Lydia or the Persians had installed tyrants to rule each of the Ionian city-states. Over time, this became an increasing cause of resentment, not least because conscription by the Persians into their armies was ever-increasing. In addition, Persian expansion into Egypt, the Black Sea regions, and Thrace started to restrict and delimit Greek markets and sources of mercenaries, as well as increasing taxation.

In 499 BCE, Aristagoras was deputy governor of Miletus, a *polis* on the western coast of Anatolia. Aristagoras was one of two key players in the run up to the Ionian Revolt. The other was Histiaeus, Aristagoras's uncle and father-in-law and tyrant at Miletus by 513 BCE, installed there and dependant on Darius. Histiaeus reciprocated by supporting Darius militarily in the region for which Darius rewarded him with the gift of a fertile and strategically important part of Thrace, Myrcinus, with permission to build a city there.[2] However, Darius was tipped off by a relative, Megabazus, son of Megabates the Persian commander in Xerxes's fleet regarding the likelihood of rebellion; Darius called Histiaeus to Susa and detained him there long-term under virtual house arrest.

Just before 500 BCE, the populace in Naxos had seized control of the island, expelling the aristocrats and establishing a democracy. Disaffected exiles from Naxos approached Aristagoras, the satrap, to help restore them to power and control the island.[3] Aristagoras saw the capture of Naxos as a chance to bolster his position in Miletus and so proposed to Artaphernes that if he provided an army, Aristagoras would take the island in Darius's name, and would then give Artaphernes a share of the booty to cover the cost of raising the army. Aristagoras argued that once Naxos fell, the other Cyclades would quickly follow, including Euboea—all expediting Persian expansion in the region. Artaphernes agreed in principle and obtained from Darius approval to launch the expedition: a fleet of 200 triremes was assembled to attack Naxos the following year under the command of Megabates.[4] In a bid to fox the Naxians, the fleet first sailed north, towards the Hellespont, then doubled back at Chios and headed south for Naxos.[5]

Chaos soon reigned. Aristagoras and Megabates apparently squabbled after one of Megabates's routine inspections when Megabates found one ship from Myndus which had failed to post sentries. Megabates had the captain of the ship, Scylax, stuck into one of the ship's oar holes with his head protruding outside and his body inside the vessel. Aristagoras was outraged by this and confronted an obdurate Megabates. Aristagoras let Scylax loose himself; an angry Megabates then allegegly (and treasonously) disclosed the imminent attack to the Naxians who were able to equip themselves amply with food and water for the impending siege. Herodotus reports that the 'Naxians have 8,000 men that bear shields', that is 8,000 men were able to equip themselves as hoplites.[6]

Four months later, the expeditionary force ran out of money and had no choice but to lift the siege. The only consolation was that before leaving, they built a stronghold for the exiled Naxian aristocrats on the island so that they had a base from which to quickly return, as events permitted.[7] Aristagoras read the writing on the wall and saw that his position as tyrant was compromised as he had alienated the Persians and was unable to repay Artaphernes. In desperation, and encouraged by proxy by a Histiaeus ever on the lookout for an escape from Susa, he then set about inciting the whole of Ionia to rebel against Darius, fanning the fires of Ionian discontent.[8] This was, in reality, an attempt to replace Persian rule with Milesian. As we have seen, the Ionian cities had good reason to rebel, to dismantle the barbarian tyrannies and establish democracies.

To sustain the uprising more allies were desperately needed. Aristagoras began by summoning a council at Miletus, which voted in favour of war. He asked each of the rebel cities to provide a general for their own forces. In the winter of 499 BCE, Aristagoras sailed to mainland Greece to try to recruit allies. The Spartans under king Cleomenes I were not interested; they were still smarting from the recent failure of an expedition against Polycrates of Samos.[9] Yet Athens and Eretria came on board. Athens at this time was a fledgling democracy, having overthrown the tyrant Hippias. Later, Hippias made an unsuccessful attempt to regain power in Athens, helped by the Spartans. Hippias fled to Artaphernes, and tried to persuade him to take Athens. Athenian ambassadors tried to dissuade Artaphernes from this action, but Artaphernes simply told the Athenians to restore Hippias as tyrant if they wanted to avoid punishment. The Athenians' reaction was to declare themselves at war with Persia.[10] It was therefore no wonder then that Athens was happy to support the Ionian cities.

Eretria, an old ally, signed up, probably because they saw Persia as a threat to their trade or to repay the support the Milesians had given them in the Lelantine War many years previously between *c*. 710 and 650 BCE.[11] The next spring, 498 BCE, the Athenians dispatched a fleet of twenty triremes, joined by five from Eretria, and set sail for Ionia, meeting the main Ionian force near Ephesus. The Ephesians then escorted this force through mountains to Sardis, Artaphernes's regional capital.

The Greeks took the Persians by surprise: they captured the lower part of the city and sacked the rest while Artaphernes retreated to the citadel. The rebels' indiscipline, however, was to be their undoing: they embarked on an orgy of pillage during which one soldier torched a house, starting a conflagration, which consumed the whole city, including the famous sanctuary of Cybele. The Lydians, an alliance with whom was coveted by the rebel forces, joined the Persians; a reinforcing Persian army approached Sardis, giving the Ionians no option but to retreat. Their only common expedition thus ended in disaster. The Persian troops were probably mainly cavalry adept at wearing an enemy down with continuous salvoes of missiles delivered from horseback. In the event, the Persians routed the Greeks in the battle which ensued at Ephesus.[12] The Eretrian general, Eualcides, was killed; the surviving Ionians returned to their own cities, while the Athenians and Eretrians sailed back to Greece.[13] They had seen an Ionian army in action and were not impressed; moreover, they had their own interests to safeguard in the shape of constant Aeginetan raids on the coast of Attica. The Athenians withdrew their support and ignored all further calls for help.

Despite this reverse the revolt continued to spread: the Ionians sailed to the Hellespont and Propontis, taking Byzantium and the other cities close by. The Carians and Cypriots also joined the Ionian cause, preoccupying the Persians until 495 BCE and giving the Ionians some respite.[14] Aristagoras must have seen how untenable his position was and renounced leadership of both Miletus and of the revolt and settled in Thrace where he took control of the city that Histiaeus had founded, Myrcinus (site of the later Amphipolis), and started agitating against the local Thracian population. For his troubles, however, he was killed by the Edonians in 497 or 496 BCE.[15]

In Cyprus, revolt was total, except for Amathus in the south. The Cypriot leader was Onesilus, brother of the king of Salamis, Gorgus, who was against revolt. Onesilus locked his brother out of Salamis and seized his crown. Gorgus defected to the Persians while Onesilus began to besiege Amathus.[16] This revolt was potentially disastrous for Darius: a hostile Cyprus could sever the sea lanes to Egypt and threaten Phoenicia. In the spring of 497 BCE, the Persians under Artybius and reinforced by Phoenicians set sail for Cyprus. When Onesilus heard that a Persian force was on its way, he sent to Ionia, asking them to send reinforcements, which they did, 'in great force'. The Ionians initiated a sea battle and defeated the Phoenicians at Cape Cleides.[17] In the simultaneous land battle at Salamis, the Cypriots at first had the upper hand and killed Artybius. However, the wholesale defection of two contingents of Greeks to the Persians was a fatal blow: they were routed and Onesilus was killed and his brother restored to power.

Herodotus passes over the Persian assault on Paphos, but archaeology reveals Persian siege works from which we can deduce that the attackers built a siege ramp between two towers. The defenders dug four tunnels under the walls, some to undermine the mound and some against the siege towers. Persian arrow heads have been found while the defender's missile weapons are scattered across the ramp area.

Soli was the most stubborn; the siege there lasted for four months before the city eventually fell after the Persians tunnelled under the city walls. The fall of Soli ended resistance to the Persians on Cyprus. The revolt in Cyprus was over.

That same year (497 BCE), three of Darius's sons-in-law—Daurises, Hymaees, and Otanes—were given commands of three armies so as to enable them to exterminate three more strands of the Ionian revolt. At first, Daurises invaded the Hellespont, where one by one he besieged and took Dardanus, Abydos, Percote, Lampsacus, and Paesus, each in a single day according to Herodotus.

Hymaees advanced on the Propontis and took the city of Cius; he then marched on the Hellespont to capture many Aeolian cities as well as some of the cities in the Troad. However, he then fell ill and died. Otanes, with Artaphernes, took his campaign to Ionia where they captured Ionian Clazomenae and Aeolian Cyme.[18]

Daurises headed south into Caria to confront the Carians at the 'White Pillars', on the Marsyas river (modern Çine), a tributary of the Meander. Pixodorus, a relative of the king of Cilicia, recommended that the Carians should cross the river and fight with it at their backs, thereby precluding retreat, but the Carians had other thoughts and made the Persians cross the river to fight them. In the end, the dogged Carians eventually folded under the weight of Persian numbers; Herodotus reports casualties at 10,000 Carians and 2,000 Persians.[19]

The demoralised survivors of Marsyas retreated to the sanctuary of a sacred grove of Zeus at Labraunda where they discussed their next course of action: surrender to the Persians or leave Asia for good. The day was saved by reinforcements in the form of a Milesian army. The Persians, however, attacked and inflicted another heavy defeat.[20]

In 496 BCE, the Carians continued the fight when they set an ambush for Daurises on the road through Pedasus. The Persians, as predicted, arrived at Pedasus after nightfall: the ambush was most successful: the Persian army was exterminated and Daurises and two other Persian commanders, Amorges and Sisimaces, as well as a Lydian named Myrsus, son of Gyges, were killed. Stalemate then set in for a year or so.[21]

Soon after, Histiaeus was released from the virtual house arrest in Susa imposed on him by Darius. This was on the promise that he would bring an end to the Ionian revolt. On arrival in Sardis, he was met by Artaphernes who bluntly accused him of fomenting the rebellion with Aristagoras: 'I will tell you, Histiaeus, the truth of this business: it was you who stitched this shoe, and Aristagoras who put it on.' Wisely, Histiaeus fled that night to Chios and made his way back to Miletus where he was made equally unwelcome and expelled. He went next to Mytilene in Lesbos and persuaded the Lesbians to give him eight triremes in which he sailed for Byzantium with anyone who would follow him. There he established himself as a pirate, seizing any ship that attempted to sail through the Bosporus, unless the crew agreed to serve with him.[22]

By the sixth year of the revolt, 494 BCE, the Persian forces had taken stock and reorganised themselves into one army, supported by a fleet supplied by the Cypriots, Egyptians, Cilicians, and Phoenicians. The Persians had resolved to attack the very heart of this seemingly intractable revolt and so headed straight for Miletus. The Ionians, for their part, had decided at a council in Panonium to defend Miletus by sea, leaving the Milesians responsible for the defence of Miletus itself. Defeating the Persian fleet would guarantee the safety of Miletus. The Persians tried diplomacy, promising immunity in exchange for surrender, but promising severe punishment in case of continued resistance. Herodotus reports that none of the cities took up the offer.[23]

The Ionian fleet, made up of 353 triremes, came together for the decisive battle at Lade Island, off the coast of Miletus. The Milesians formed the eastern wing of the fleet, and provided eighty ships; the Prieneans provided twelve, Myous three, Teos eighteen, and Chios 100. The Erythraeans sent eight and the Phocaeans sent three. Non-Ionian Lesbos in Aeolia contributed seventy ships. Finally, the Samians formed the western end of the fleet with sixty ships. Substantial as this was, the Persian fleet numbered 600 ships many of which came from Phoenicia.

Morale was low among the Ionians; this was partly due to Dionysius, commander of the minute Phocaean contingent, who was given command of the fleet. He introduced a boot camp programme of intense training for one week, which led some Ionians then to mutinously refuse to continue with the training. Moreover, when the Persians tried to get some of the Ionians to defect, they did so at the first sign of a Persian attack; forty-nine of the sixty Samian ships and the Lesbians deserted the battle (one third of the fleet), causing the collapse of the Ionian battle line. The names of the crews of the eleven ships were later inscribed on a column in the town square. The Chians and some others remained to fight valiantly but the battle was lost.[24] The survivors sailed north across the bay and reached the southern shores of Mt Mycale. When they tried to escape north across the peninsula, they were massacred as soon as they entered Ephesian territory.

Meanwhile, Miletus was besieged by the Persians 'mining the walls and using every device against it, until they captured it in its entirety'. Most of the men were butchered, and the women and children were sold into slavery. Archaeological evidence reveals extensive signs of destruction from around this time. Miletus was 'left devoid of Milesians'; the Persians took the city and coastal land for themselves, and gave the rest to Carians from Pedasus.

The sanctuary at Didyma was sacked and razed, revenge for the Milesian destruction of the sanctuary of Cybele at Sardis. The captive Milesians were settled on the coast of the Persian Gulf, near the mouth of the Tigris. Many of the Samians were invited by the people of Zancle to settle on the coast of Sicily, which they did along with the Milesians who had escaped from the Persians. Samos itself was spared from destruction by the Persians because of their defection at Lade. Most of Caria now surrendered to the Persians.[25]

Histiaeus then set himself up as leader of the revolt and left Byzantium with his forces for Chios. When the Chians rebuffed him, he destroyed the remnants of the Chian fleet. The Chians then had a change of mind and agreed to Histiaeus's leadership.[26]

Histiaeus then assembled a large force of Ionians and Aeolians with a view to besiege Thasos but, when news reached him that the Persian fleet was sailing from Miletus to attack the rest of Ionia, he immediately returned to Lesbos. His army had to be fed so he organised foraging expeditions near Atarneus and Myus. However, his intelligence was not all it might have been and a large Persian force under Harpagus which was in the area (Bakir Çayi) intercepted one foraging party near Malene. The resulting battle was equally fought until a Persian cavalry charge tipped the balance and the Greek line was routed. Histiaeus gave himself up to the Persians, in the arrogant belief no doubt that he could win a pardon from Darius. However, he had to wait a while before he could get to Darius, and when he did, it was not in his preferred way; he was taken to Artaphernes instead, who, only too familiar with Histiaeus's record of treachery, impaled him on a stake and sent his embalmed head to Darius.[27] Darius, however, was not impressed—he ordered Histiaeus's head to be cleaned up and buried with honours as that of a benefactor of the King.

The year 493 BCE saw the end of the Ionian Revolt. The Persians wintered at Miletus, before taking the islands of Chios, Lesbos, and Tenedos. In each case, they formed a 'human-net' of troops, sweeping across the whole island to ensnare any of the enemy that remained. They then captured each of the remaining cities of Ionia. Miletus suffered most. Herodotus tells us that the Persians chose the best-looking boys from each city and castrated them, thereby making sure that no more Miletian citizens would ever be born again; the most beautiful girls were sent to the king's harem; the Persians then burnt the temples of the cities.[28] A year later, Phrynicus produced the tragedy *The Capture of Miletus* in Athens. The Athenians fined him for reminding them of their loss. That Herodotus may be exaggerating is suggested by the fact that just thirteen years later, the cities were able to equip a large fleet for the second Persian invasion of Greece.[29]

The Persians finished the job when they re-took the settlements on the Asian side of the Propontis, while the Persian fleet sailed up the European coast of the Hellespont, taking out each settlement in turn.[30] One of these was the Chersonese where Miltiades, who would later command the Athenian army at Marathon, was tyrant: he was compelled to flee into exile to Athens.

Darius had not forgotten Sardis; how could he? Herodotus tells us that after Sardis Darius took his bow, shot an arrow into the sky, and exclaimed: 'Zeus, allow me to take vengeance on the Athenians!'. At the same time, he ordered one of his servants to say to him every day before dinner, three times: 'Master, remember the Athenians'.[31]

Nevertheless, the Persians initiated a more conciliatory policy. In 493 BCE, Artaphernes called to Sardis representatives from each of the Ionian states and ordered them to set up a system of arbitration. He also measured each state's land area and set new levels of tribute that more accurately reflected their size.

In 492 BCE, Darius appointed his son-in-law Mardonius as the commander in Asia Minor. Herodotus says that he had been sent to punish Athens and Eretria for supporting the rebels, but he also set about replacing the tyrants, who had been restored after the failure of the revolt, with new democratic regimes.

Our knowledge and the veracity of the Ionian Revolt are, of course, subject to the bias and vagaries of Herodotus's account, his being the only one that has survived; caution is obviously needed. He consistently exaggerates the shortcomings of the Ionians, their disorganisation and the actions of the tyrants; on the other hand, the Ionian achievements are minimised while the rivalry between *poleis* is emphasised. To Herodotus, the revolt was doomed from the start.[32]

That said, there were positives: the Ionians did prove that it might well be possible to throw off the Persian yoke, and the integrity of the Persian empire had been threatened; the Ionian states remained a thorn in the side in respect of Persia's future stability; Mardonius lightened the oppression of thee Ionians by replacing the tyrants; Artaphernes lightened their tax burden; and Persian expansionism was hindered.[33]

The Persian Wars
(492–448 BCE)

The First Persian Invasion of Greece

Revenge and expansionism remained the order of the day, and so it was in 492 BCE that the first Persian invasion of Greece was launched: Mardonius took Thrace and Macedon; the fleet then crossed to Thasos, taking that, and then sailed as far as Acanthus in Chalcidice. Here the campaign came to an abrupt end when Mardonius's fleet was destroyed in a storm off Mt Athos. According to Herodotus, 300 ships were wrecked, with the loss of 20,000 men.[1] Things got even worse when the survivors camped in Macedon and the Brygians, a local Thracian tribe, night raided the Persian camp, killing many of the Persians, and wounding Mardonius. Despite this, Mardonius subjugated the Brygians, before leading his army back to the Hellespont; the now ramshackle navy also fell back.[2]

In 490 BCE, a second force poured across the Aegean under the command of Datis and Artaphernes; the Persian force sailed from Cilicia to Rhodes. We know from Lindian Chronicle records that Datis unsuccessfully besieged Lindos, and then headed for Naxos, which he devastated.[3] He then subjugated the Cyclades island by island taking hostages and troops from each island. At Delos, the inhabitants fled but, having exerted Persian power at Naxos, Datis now showed clemency where the individual islands submitted to him. To demonstrate this, he burned 300 talents of frankincense on the altar of Apollo on Delos. At Karystos on Euboea, however, the inhabitants were defiant: the citizens refused to give hostages so the Persians laid siege and devastated their land until they submitted.[4] The Persians' first major objective lay ahead at Eritrea.

The Eritreans had three simple choices—they could flee the city; they could endure a siege, or they could submit to the Persians; the decision was to remain in the city and face a siege. The Eretrians successfully appealed to the Athenians to send reinforcements: the Athenians ordered the 4,000 Athenian colonists at the nearby Euboean city of Chalcis to go to help the Eretrians. However, they were told by a prominent citizen, Aeschines, of the schism among the Eretrians; he advised them to go home and save themselves so they sailed away to Oropus, forsaking Eritrea.

The Eretrians failed to reach a clear plan of action; in Herodotus's words, 'it seems that all the plans of the Eretrians were unsound; they sent to the Athenians for aid, but their counsels were divided'. On the seventh day, two prominent Eretrians—Euphorbus and Philagrus—betrayed the city to the Persians, which was consequently razed, the temples and shrines looted and burned. The Persians enslaved all the remaining townsfolk, no doubt subjecting the women to rape.[5]

Herodotus reports a fleet of 600 triremes, probably a combined force of triremes and transport ships.[6] He does not hazard a guess on the size of the Persian army, but there are a number of other estimates—Simonides, a near-contemporary, numbers it at 200,000; Cornelius Nepos suggests 200,000 infantrymen and 10,000 cavalry; Plutarch and Pausanias independently give 300,000, as does the *Suda*; Plato and Lysias estimate 500,000; and Justin 600,000.[7]

Athens, via Marathon, was next. One of the outcomes of the decisive battle of Marathon enabled Athens to believe in its ability to defend itself and to see a long term political and military future in the region. The Athenians proved that the mighty Persians could be defeated and that organised resistance was a worthwhile policy. For that reason, the battle has commonly been called 'a defining moment in the development of European culture'. It was a huge victory for Athens, not least in term of morale and confidence.

Once again, our main source is Herodotus, although we are now helped by the *Bibliotheca Historica* of Diodorus Siculus, written in the first century BCE and partially based on the work of the earlier Greek historian Ephorus. Plutarch, Ctesias of Cnidus, and the playwright Aeschylus also add to the mix.

In 491 BCE, Darius resorted to diplomacy by sending ambassadors to all the Greek city-states, asking for 'earth and water', a token of submission. Sensibly, most cities complied, fearing Persian reprisals. In Athens, however, the ambassadors were tried and then executed; in Sparta, they were just thrown down a well. The effect of the summary treatment of Athenians and Spartans was to bring the two states together against Persia. However, the concord was short-lived when domestic turmoil erupted in Sparta. Aegina had complied with the Persian ambassadors, causing the Athenians anxiety over the possibility that Persia would use Aegina as a naval base. When Athens asked Sparta to intervene, Cleomenes went to Aegina to confront the Aeginetans only to have them appeal to Cleomenes's fellow king Demaratus, who inconveniently supported their stance. Cleomenes declared Demaratus illegitimate, with the backing of the (amply bribed) priests at Delphi. Demaratus was replaced by his cousin Leotychides. The Aeginetans capitulated in the face of the two Spartan kings. In Sparta, news emerged of the bribes Cleomenes had paid and he was expelled from the city. He was eventually invited back but, as most people considered him a lunatic, he was imprisoned only to be found dead in his cell next day. Leonidas I then succeeded his half-brother.

In September 490 BCE, the Persians arrived in numbers, having taken Eretria; an invasion force of about 20,000 infantry and cavalry poured from a Persian armada of

600 triremes north of Athens. This was the embodiment of the revenge that Darius has promised. Valuable intelligence was gained from the exiled and disaffected Athenian tyrant Hippias.

In response, Athens mobilised 10,000 hoplites: the two armies clashed on the plain of Marathon 26 miles north of Athens—a site favourable to the Persian cavalry, surrounded as it was by hills and sea. The Athenians were bolstered by 1,000 troops from Plataea; the Persian force was again commanded by Datis and Artaphernes. Surveying the scene, the Greeks had pause for thought. They sought help from the Spartans, dispatching a runner to cover the 140 miles; the famous Pheidippides, who arrived at his destination the very next day, was the man sent. The Spartans, however, were unavoidably detained by a religious festival that they could not abandon until after the next full moon, six days hence. This was the Carneia, one of Sparta's important national festivals, held in honour of Apollo Carneus. When the Spartans eventually showed up, it was all over, despite the urgent speed with which they covered the ground.

There was indecision in the Greek camp as to whether to wait for the Spartans or do battle immediately; Callimachus had the casting vote. Miltiades passionately and effectively urged him not to hesitate and to join battle, possibly in the knowledge that the decisive Persian cavalry had not turned up and that the Persians were moving on Athens.[8] 'For if you agree with me that we should fight, you make your country free and your city the best in all of Greece. But if you choose not to fight, we will lose it all'.

He commanded the Greek hoplites to form a line equal in length to that of the Persians. Then, in an act of apparent tactical madness because he lacked supporting cavalry and archers, Miltiades ordered his men to attack the Persian line, breaking into a run when within range of the Persian bows. Predictably, the centre of the Greek line collapsed in the chaos, but the flanks swung round, engulfed and slaughtered the Persians.[9] About 6,400 Persians died that day compared with Greek losses of 192 and eleven Plataeans.[10] The mound under which the Greek dead were buried is still visible today. Simonides wrote the eulogy:

Ἑλλήνων προμαχοῦντες Ἀθηναῖοι Μαραθῶνι
χρυσοφόρων Μήδων ἐστόρεσαν δύναμιν
　　(Fighting at the forefront of the Greeks, the Athenians at Marathon
　　laid low the army of the gilded Medes.)

This is how Herodotus described the carnage:

The Athenians ... charged the barbarians at a run. Now the distance between the two armies was little short of eight furlongs [approximately a mile]. The Persians, therefore, when they saw the Greeks coming on at speed, made ready to receive them, although it seemed to them that the Athenians were bereft of their senses, and bent upon their own destruction; for they saw a mere handful of men coming on at a run without either horsemen or archers. They were the first Greeks we know of to charge their enemy at a run and the first to face the sight of the Median dress and the men who wore it. For till then the Greeks were terrified even to hear the names of the Medes.[11]

Defeat at Marathon would have meant total defeat and annihilation for Athens, since the Athenian army mustered at Marathon was the only Athenian army there was. It was imperative, therefore, that they keep the Persian army pinned down, blocking both exits from the plain, and preventing the Persians from going on to attack Athens. The Athenians chased the Persians back to their ships, capturing seven vessels. Herodotus tells the story how Cynaegirus, brother of the dramatist Aeschylus, took part in the battle; he grabbed hold of one Persian trireme and started pulling it towards the shore (no doubt with some assistance unacknowledged by Herodotus). A Persian sailor saw him and cut off his hand; Cynaegirus died of his wound.[12]

The surviving Persians sailed round Cape Sounion to try an assault on what they thought was an undefended Athens. The Greeks, however, made a forced march back to Athens and repelled the Persians, who then headed home.[13]

Given that the battle of Marathon was so pivotal in the future of Athens and of ancient Greece in general, it is hardly surprising that a number of legends grew up around the battle. The most famous concerns the runner Pheidippides who took news to Athens regarding the outcome of the battle. We have already met him running the 280-mile round trip from Marathon to Sparta, disappointed, no doubt, to discover that the Spartans had other priorities. After the battle, he may have had to join the rapid, armour-encumbered march back to Athens to head off the Persians.

Herodotus adds that Pheidippides was paid a visit by the god Pan *en route* to Sparta; Pan asked why the Athenians did not ever honour him. An awe-struck Pheidippides spluttered in reply that that would all change and that the Athenians would honour him from then on. The god was happy with this promise and appeared in the battle of Marathon to inflict on the Persians the irrational fear that was to bear his name: 'panic'. After the battle, a sacred precinct was established for Pan on the north slope of the Acropolis, and a sacrifice was offered every year.[14]

The victory won similar favour for Artemis Agrotera (Artemis the Huntress) after a vow made by Athens before the conflict to sacrifice a number of goats equal to the number of Persians slain. So great was the number (6,400) that the decision had to be modified to offer 500 goats a year until the number was fulfilled. Xenophon records that in his day, some ninety years after the battle, goats were still being slaughtered in sacrifice.[15]

Plutarch tells us that the Athenians saw the ghost of King Theseus, mythical hero of Athens, leading the army in full battle regalia in the charge against the Persians.[16] Pausanias adds:

They say too that there chanced to be present in the battle a man of rustic appearance and dress. Having slaughtered many of the foreigners with a plough he was seen no more after the engagement. When the Athenians made enquiries at the oracle, the god merely ordered them to honor Echetlaeus ('he of the Plough-tail') as a hero.[17]

The most famous legend has Pheidippides running all the way from Marathon to Athens after the battle, to announce the jubilant Greek victory with 'joy to you' νενικήκαμεν 'we've won!' With his job done, he dropped down dead from exhaustion. The story is first published in Plutarch's *On the Glory of Athens*, who quotes from Heracleides of Pontus, naming the runner as Thersipus of Erchius or Eucles.[18] It was Lucian who gives us Philippides (and not Pheidippides).[19]

The feat—real or otherwise—was adopted in 1896 by the creators of the modern Olympic Games as the marathon event, based on the legendary version of events, with the competitors running from Marathon to Athens. The distance eventually became fixed at 26 miles and 385 yards, the approximate distance from Marathon to Athens.

We have already noted how huge a victory this was for Athens militarily, politically and psychologically; moreover, Marathon is considered to be the starting point for the golden age of Athens, which ushered in, no less, the birth of western culture as we know it. Marathon bolstered the nascent democracy at Athens; it also demonstrated that Athens was the force in Greece. From a military point of view, the battle proved the efficacy of the hoplite phalanx. Although always vulnerable to cavalry, the phalanx was nevertheless a powerful and deadly fighting formation.

Darius, however, was not finished by any means. He set about raising a massive new army and navy but his plans were temporarily delayed when, in 486 BCE, his Egyptian subjects revolted. Darius died while preparing an attack on Egypt, and his throne passed to his son Xerxes I. Xerxes wasted no time in crushing the Egyptians and revived the preparations for the invasion of Greece. The second Persian invasion of Greece began in 480 BCE.

Meanwhile, in Athens in 482 BCE, Themistocles had used the revenues acquired from a recently discovered silver mine in Laurion to finance a 200-trireme fleet. Xerxes had sent ambassadors around Greece asking for 'earth and water' (submission), but pointedly omitted Athens and Sparta. The effect of this was to drive Athens and Sparta into alliance and support began to gravitate to these two *poleis*.[20] A congress of states was convened at Corinth in late autumn of 481 BCE from which the Athenians and Spartans emerged as the leaders of the Greek resistance; seventy of the 700 or so Greek *poleis* joined the alliance, which is quite remarkable given the fractured and fractious nature of the Greek political world, and since many of the *poleis* in attendance were still at war with each other. The others stayed neutral or yielded to Xerxes. Notable for their absence from the rebel faction was Thebes, which was long suspected of complicity with the Persians. That said, 400 Theban hoplites did join the allies. Herodotus loosely calls this confederation 'οἱ Έλληνες' (the Greeks); they had the power to send envoys requesting assistance and to dispatch troops from the member states for defence, after joint consultation.[21]

Sparta first emerged as a political force and entity around the tenth century BCE when invading Dorians subjugated the local population. By 650 BCE, it had become a significant military landpower in ancient Greece. Many aspects of Spartan society and its political system set it apart from other *poleis*; uniquely, life there was focused on military training and excellence. Spartans were classified as Spartiates (Spartan citizens, who enjoyed full rights), *mothakes* (non-Spartan free men raised as Spartans), *perioikoi* (freedmen), and helots (state-owned serfs, enslaved non-Spartan local population). It was the Spartiates who underwent the rigorous *agoge* training and education regimen; Spartan military phalanges were among the best.

Spartan women enjoyed considerably more rights, freedom, and equality than women elsewhere in the ancient world. Plutarch's *Moralia* includes a collection of 'Sayings of Spartan Women', including one attributed to Gorgo, the wife of Leonidas I: when asked by an Attica woman why Spartan women were the only women in the world who could dominate men, she replied 'Because we are the only women who are mothers of men'.

We have noted how Sparta was an out and out military society. Lycurgus in the eighth century BCE summed it up when he said that Sparta's walls were built of men, not bricks. Sparta was a well-oiled war machine that always needed a ready and constant replenishment of soldiers.

Training for boys included testing endurance exercises and competitive sports, and combat training started at eighteen; all of it was designed to turn out troops of the highest fitness and caliber to fill the ranks of their crack units. Interestingly, exercises included special operations intelligence gathering against the helots. Those helots under surveillance who were deemed 'unsuitable' or 'inconvenient' in any way by the intelligence officers were winnowed out in an annual bout of social cleansing.

The Second Persian Invasion of Greece (480–479 BCE)

After four years of preparation, spring 480 BCE saw the beginning of the invasion when the Persians crossed the Hellespont (the Dardanelles) and advanced through Thrace and Macedon to Thessaly. Before that, there was much necessary planning, equipment, supplies and ordnance manufacture and acquisition, and conscription. The campaign, however, was delayed for one year due to another revolt in Egypt and one in Babylonia.[22] Herodotus records forty-six states from which troops were mustered in Cappadocia and then led by Xerxes to Sardis where they wintered. They then moved to Abydos.[23]

Xerxes's groundbreaking pontoon bridges were used to convey his army across the Hellespont to Europe, along with a canal dug across the isthmus of Mount Athos—two extraordinary feats of civil and military engineering. At Abydos, two bridges were built to link with the opposite side near Sestos spanning some 1,300 m; however, these were destroyed by a storm before the army arrived. Xerxes was furious and beheaded those responsible for building the bridges before throwing fetters into the straits, administering 300 lashes and branding the river with red-hot irons while the soldiers stood by remonstrating at the water. For the replacements, 360 penteconters and triremes were used to construct the north-easterly bridge and 314 ships were used

for the south-westerly bridge. Screens were erected on either side of the bridges to stop the horses and other animals from panicking when they saw the sea below.[24] The actual crossing took seven days and nights; the army used the north-easterly bridge while the baggage train took the southwesterly bridge.[25]

The size of Xerxes's army has been hotly disputed since classical times. Herodotus records that there were 2.5 million military personnel, along with the same number of ancillary staff. The contemporary poet Simonides says four million; Ctesias, in the *Persica*, with the benefit of Persian records, gives 800,000 (without support personnel). Modern estimates are between 300,000–500,000.[26] Herodotus writes that the Persian fleet comprised 1,207 triremes plus 3,000 transport and supply ships, including fifty-oared galleys (penteconters).[27]

Five capacious food depots were established along the route; animals were bought and fattened up, while locals were ordered to grind their grains into flour. It took three months or so to travel the 360 miles from the Hellespont to Therma (Thessaloniki), pausing at Doriskos to rendezvous with the fleet. Here, Xerxes dispensed with the national units and reorganised the troops into tactical units.[28]

In the the spring of 480 BCE, a Thessalian plan to convene in the narrow Vale of Tempe, on the borders of Thessaly, to block Xerxes's advance was rejected on the advice of Alexander I of Macedon; he argued that the vale could be bypassed by at least two other passes.[29] 'Plan B' was proposed by Themistocles, who pointed out that the route south to Boeotia, Attica, and the Peloponnese would require Xerxes to travel through the very narrow pass at Thermopylae—easily blockable by the allies. The gap between the Trachinian cliffs and the Malian Gulf was only wide enough to take a single carriage.[30] To prevent the Persians bypassing Thermopylae by sea, the allied navy would block the straits of Artemisium. This joint army-navy operation was adopted by the congress. Meanwhile, the cities of the Peloponnese set about making defences for the Isthmus of Corinth, while the women and children of Athens were evacuated to the Peloponnesian city of Troezen.

The Persians timed their advance well: not only was it the period of the general truce observed during the Olympic games, but the Spartan festival of Carneia was in full swing—the very same festival that precluded any Spartan involvement in the battle of Marathon. However, the Spartans, realising the enormity of the crisis, suspended their religious obligations and dispatched Leonidas I with the Hippeis, his personal bodyguard of 300 men. The squad was carefully selected in the interests of maintaining the male Spartan population: young soldiers without offspring were replaced by veterans who already had fathered sons. Leonidas had support from the Peloponnesian cities allied to Sparta, and other forces joining *en route* to Thermopylae. The allies with their modest force of 6,000–7,000 Spartans, Thespians, and Thebans, waited for Xerxes to arrive.

Having arrived at Themopylae, the Persians were in no great rush to join battle; expecting the Greeks to retire, they waited for three days for the Greek retreat. Yet the Greeks knew only too well that their positions were perfectly suited to hoplite warfare: the Persians would have to attack the phalanx head on with likely devastating consequences.[31]

The allies held out bravely for two days, before they were outflanked by the Persians using a mountain path betrayed to the Persians by Ephialtes of Trachis, a local Greek, and deserted by the Phocians who were tasked with defending this route.[32] Xerxes had dispatched his elite guards under Hydarnes, the crack Immortals, on a night march to outflank the allies. Leonidas saw what was happening and dismissed most of his army, remaining with 300 Spartans, 700 Thespians, 400 Thebans, and a few hundred others. The rest of the Thebans deserted, insisting that they had been coerced into joining the alliance; the Persians were not impressed, though, and branded them as traitors. On the third day of the battle, those that were left attacked the Persians. In the end, though, the allies were inevitably wiped out and the pass at Thermopylae was open to the Persians.[33]

Persia lost 20,000 troops in the battle, something of a Pyrrhic victory for them. In an attempt to hide the facts, Xerxes had all but 1,000 of the casualties buried in concealed mass graves. Diodorus, uniquely, reports a different finale in which Leonidas and the Spartans launched a night raid on the Persian camp, hunting for Xerxes. This too ended in doom for the Spartans.[34]

While all this was going on, the Greek fleet of 271 triremes was off Artemisium on the north coast of Euboea; the swifter Persian fleet was tracking down the coast shadowing their army, finally ending up off the Magnesian coast north of Cape Sepias. Things did not go well for the Persians: a destructive storm ripped into their fleet and, over two days, wrecked about 400 of their 1,200 ships. A flotilla of 200 vessels was similarly destroyed while on a mission to block the escape route of the Greek fleet.[35]

Battle was joined. The Greeks manoeuvred themselves into a crescent formation, with the wings drawn back to prevent the Persians sailing around the Greek line.[36] The Persians lost thirty ships, either captured or sunk by the Greeks.[37] They spent the following day repairing their fleet while fifty-three ships from Athens arrived to reinforce the Greek navy.[38] Day three saw a full-scale battle—the allies tried to block the Straits of Artemisium; the Persians formed their ships into a semicircle in a bid to encircle the allied fleet, which responded by attacking head on. In the end, both sides had suffered roughly equal losses—losses that the Greeks could ill afford; in reality, half the Athenian ships (the largest contingent in the fleet) were damaged or lost.[39] The Greeks could not sustain further losses on that scale so deliberated whether they should withdraw from Artemisium. Themistocles ordered his men to slaughter and barbecue the flocks of the Euboeans, to prevent the Persians getting them. Abronichus arrived with the dreadful news from Thermopylae: the Straits of Artemisium were now devoid of any strategic importance so the allies sailed away.[40] Artemisium was, then, inconclusive, but it did pave the way for a rather more decisive naval battle and a land battle of some significance. It boosted morale no end and proved to the Greeks that they could take on the Persian fleet. It gave the Greek crews much-needed battle experience, which they would put to invaluable use at the battle of Salamis; one way or another, the engagement and the losses caused by the storms reduced the opposition numbers considerably, making the Persian fleet potentially a much more assailable foe at Salamis.[41] Pindar puts it well: Artemisium was 'where the sons of the Athenians laid the shining foundation-stone of freedom'.[42]

Herodotus reports that when the Persians heard of the Greeks' departure, they were incredulous that they had thus been given the gift of conquering Boeotia and Attica; they proceeded to sack the region around Histiaea.[43] The allied fleet, meanwhile, headed for Salamis, an island in the northern part of the Saronic Gulf, to help evacuate the remaining Athenians from the city. The gulf is barely a mile wide at its narrowest point between Attica and Salamis while the wider southern end is restricted by the Cynosura promontory and the isle of Psyttalea. On the way, Themistocles attempted to persuade Ionian Greek crews in the Persian fleet to defect to him by leaving notices at all the springs of water.[44] The Persians razed and sacked the Boeotian cities that had not come over to them—Plataea and Thespiae—and then marched on a largely deserted Athens while the allies (mainly Peloponnesians) set about defending the Isthmus of Corinth, demolishing the single road that led through it, and building a wall across it.[45]

The Greek navy set up a blockade to prevent the Persian navy accessing the Saronic Gulf and thereby landing ground forces on the Peloponnese. Themistocles went one stage further when he persuaded his allies (perhaps relying on a veiled threat to pull his forces out) to go for a decisive victory. The Phoenicians were lying off Psyttalea with the Greeks on the other side of the islet; the Egyptians were probably between the west coast of Salamis and Megaris. Themistocles enticed the Persian fleet into the Straits of Salamis where the narrow confines allowed the allied fleet to destroy the best part of the Persian navy in a night battle, thus extinguishing the Persian threat to the Peloponnese as Xerxes made his way back to Asia.[46]

How did this happen? False facts and subterfuge both played a part. Themistocles sent a servant, Sicinnus, to Xerxes, with news that Themistocles was 'on Xerxes' side and would rather that your affairs prevail, not the Hellenes'. Themistocles spread the rumour that the allied command was in disarray, that the Peloponnesians' plan was to evacuate that night, and so, to be victorious, all the Persians had to do was to block the straits.[47] Themistocles, of course, was slyly making the exact opposite happen; he was luring the Persian fleet into the Straits. News of a Greek schism and an easy victory were all music to Xerxes's ears: the Persian fleet set sail to block the Straits and an arrogant Xerxes had a throne set up on the slopes of Mount Aigaleo overlooking the straits, so as to get a clear view of the proceedings as they unfolded, noting the commanders who excelled, and those who did not.

Despite some controversy over whether to fight, the Greeks spent the evening preparing to do battle while the Persians floundered around looking for evacuating Greeks. The next day, battle was joined. Herodotus tells us that there were 378 triremes in the Greek fleet with 600–800 in the Persian.[48]

If there was one hero in the battle of Salamis, it was undoubtedly Artemisia I of Caria, all the more remarkable for being a remarkable woman in a man's world.[49] Artemisia (fl. 480 BCE) was born in Halicarnassus (modern Bodrum in Turkey and birthplace of Herodotus). She was queen of Halicarnassus and commander of the Carian navy. Herodotus reports that she acquitted herself in exemplary fashion; to him, her deeds were a *thaûma* (miracle, marvel). Herodotus marvels at her because she is actually a woman fighting against the Greeks: ἐπὶ τὴν Ἑλλάδα στρατευσαμένης γυναικός; she gives the best advice to Xerxes (γνώμας ἀρίστας βασιλέϊ ἀπεδέξατο). He admires her manliness (ἀνδρηίης) and her eagerness to step up and lead the Halicarnassians after her husband's death. The use of the epithet *andreia* is significant: it, of course, means 'bravery' but its etymology is from *andros*, meaning a man; bravery for the Greeks was inextricably bound up with manhood and was the preserve of men so its use to describe a woman as such is exceptional. Herodotus uses *andreia* only this once to qualify a woman's actions and it is to describe Artemisia's bravery. Indeed, Artemisia had already won a prestigious seat on Xerxes's councils of war, dispensing the best of advice and winning the epithet *androboulos* (advising like a man).[50] It is hard to envisage a woman sitting on a Greek council of war. This is how Greek Herodotus introduces Persian Artemisia:

> I must speak of a certain leader named Artemisia, whose participation in the attack on Greece, notwithstanding that she was a woman, moves me to special wonder. She had obtained the sovereign power after the death of her husband ... She ruled over the Halicarnassians [despite having a grown-up son], the men of Cos, of Nisyrus, and of Calydna; and the five triremes which she furnished to the Persians were, next to the Sidonian, the most famous ships in the fleet. She likewise gave to Xerxes sounder counsel than any of his other allies.

Before the battle of Salamis, Xerxes called all his naval commanders together at Phalerum and sent Mardonius, his second-in-command, to ask whether or not they thought he should fight the battle. All advised him to fight, except Artemisia. Herodotus reports her wise counsel and in so doing demonstrates that she can clearly see 'the bigger picture':

> Tell the King to spare his ships and not to engage in a naval battle because our enemies are much stronger than us by sea, as indeed men are to women. And why does he need to risk a naval battle anyway? Athens, the reason for undertaking this expedition is already his and the rest of Greece too ... If Xerxes chooses not to rush into a naval encounter, but instead keeps his ships close to the shore and either keeps them there or moves them towards the Peloponnese, victory would be his. The Greeks can't hold out against him for very long. They will leave for their cities, because they don't have food stored up on this island ... But if he hurries to engage I am afraid that his Persian navy will be defeated and the land-forces will be weakened as well. In addition, he should also consider that he has certain untrustworthy allies, like the Egyptians, the Cyprians, the Kilikians and the Pamphylians, who are completely useless.

Herodotus 8, 68

Xerxes, though impressed, fought the battle anyway. He watched Artemisia demonstrating tactical brilliance when she was pursued by the ship of Ameinias of

Pallene.[51] To shake him off, she attacked and rammed an allied Persian vessel fighting on her own side and so hoodwinked Ameinias into assuming that she was an ally of his; quite reasonably, Ameinias then gave up the chase. Yet her ingenuity came at a price: the friendly victim, sadly, was manned by people of Persian ally Calyndos and went down with all hands in what is one of the earliest recorded instances of tactical, intentional 'friendly fire'. A confused Xerxes, looking on, assumed that she had successfully attacked an enemy Greek ship, and seeing the indifferent performance of his other commanders, famously commented 'My men have become women, and my women men'.[52] The baffled Xerxes summed it all up with: 'O Zeus, surely you have formed women out of man's materials, and men out of woman's.' Xerxes was oviously not the only man that day who was impressed by the military actions of a woman. Herodotus continues:

> Now if [Ameinias] had known that Artemisia was sailing in this ship, he would not have given up until either he had captured her or had been taken himself; for orders had been given to the Athenian captains, and moreover a reward was offered of 10,000 drachmas for the man who took her alive; since they thought it intolerable that a woman should fight Athens.[53]

Artemisia made inspired use of the Persian and Greek flags she had cleverly stowed on board:

> Artemisia always … carried on board with her Greek, as well as barbarian, colours. When she chased a Greek ship, she hoisted the barbarian colours; but when she was chased by a Greek ship, she hoisted the Greek colours so that the enemy might mistake her for a Greek, and give up the pursuit.
>
> Polyaenus, *Strategems* 8, 53

More tactical wizardry, and that friendly fire, followed, as explained in the words of tactical expert Polyaenus:

> Artemisia … found that the Persians were defeated, and she herself was near to falling into the hands of the Greeks. She ordered the Persian colours to be taken down, and the master of the ship to bear down upon, and attack a Persian vessel, that was passing by her. The Greeks, seeing this, supposed her to be one of their allies; they drew off and left her alone, directing their forces against other parts of the Persian fleet. Artemisia in the meantime sheered off, and escaped safely to Caria.[54]

After the battle, Xerxes rewarded her sterling performance as the best of all his commanders with a complete suit of Greek armour; rubbing salt into male wounds and exemplifying hurt pride, he simultaneousely awarded the captain of her ship a distaff and spindle—unmistakable motifs of womanliness.

More sound Artemisian advice followed when Xerxes asked her whether he should now lead his troops to the Peloponnese himself, or whether he would withdraw from Greece and leave his general Mardonius to do it. Artemisia replied that he should retreat back to Asia Minor and advocated the plan suggested by Mardonius, who requested 300,000 Persian soldiers with which he would defeat the Greeks.

According to Herodotus, her considered response was as follows:

> I think that you should retire and leave Mardonius behind with those whom he wishes to have. If he succeeds, the honour will be yours because your subordinate carrid it out. If on the other hand, he fails, it would be no great matter as you would be safe … In addition, if Mardonius were to suffer a disaster who would care? He is just your servant and the Greeks will have but a poor triumph. As for yourself, you will be going home with the object for your campaign accomplished, for you have razed Athens.

> Herodotus 8, 102

Xerxes took her advice this time, leaving Mardonius to prosecute the war in Greece.

Herodotus repeatedly shows Artemisia stepping outside the traditional boundaries ordained for women and intruding into a male world where, in Greece, she would have no place.[55] She does this because the Persians at the time were, he implies, lacking *andreia* and a leader fit for purpose. Herodotus was quite content to swallow what would surely have been his personal innate suspicion of obtrusive women, and particularly obtrusive barbarian women, if it allowed him to denigrate, by implication, Xerxes and show him to be a weak leader. Artemisia is mentioned by the Old Men in Aristophanes's *Lysistrata* with awe, as something of an Amazon.[56]

Diodorus tells us that the Persians lost at least 200 ships, the Greeks a mere forty.[57] Xerxes's real fear, of course, was that the Persian army would be trapped in Greece if the Greeks should destroy his bridges, his only way home.

Mardonius left Attica and wintered in Boeotia and Thessaly; he tried to tempt the Athenian army with generous terms while the Athenian civilians were thus able to return to their burnt-out city for the time being.[58]

Salamis was pivotal in the wars between Greece and Persia. The ensuing battles on both land and sea at Plataea and Mycale formed the climax of the wars with Persia. The victories ground out by the Greek allies here finally extinguished the Persian threat to Greek control of its own homeland.

When the Athenians demanded in early 479 BCE that the allies march north, the allies declined; the Athenian fleet refused to join the allied navy now under the command of the Spartan king Leotychides and positioned off Delos. What was left of the Persian fleet was off Samos: both sides were reluctant to do battle. Mardonius stayed in Thessaly, resulting in stalemate. Mardonius tried to win a breakthrough when he enlisted Alexander I of Macedon as mediator, empowering him to offer peace, self-determination, and territory. The defiant Athenians, however, vowed never to surrender.

The snubbed Persians headed south; Athens was evacuated again and left to the mercy of the Persians. Mardonius reiterated his offer of peace to the Athenian refugees on Salamis. Athens, Megara, and Plataea sent envoys to Sparta demanding aid and threatening to accept the Persian terms if it was not forthcoming. The Spartans procrastinated; they were celebrating the festival of Hyacinthus at the time. One Chileos of Tegea who happened to be there as a guest highlighted to the Spartans the peril that awaited Greece should the Athenians surrender.[59] Mardonius recaptured Athens, destroying what was left of it with the Greek army still absent guarding the Isthmus of Corinth.[60] He then retreated to Thebes in the hope of luring the Greeks into territory eminently suitable for the Persian cavalry and to confront the Greeks near Plataea, a city still recovering having been razed to the ground in 480 BCE. It seems probable, though, that Mardonius was avoiding a fight, still preferring diplomacy.

The Athenians sent 8,000 hoplites, led by Aristides, along with 600 Plataean exiles to join the allied army. The Persians, meanwhile, built a camp on the plain at Plataea on the banks of the Asopus River.[61] The Greeks, under the command of Pausanias, were not going to be drawn onto the plain, it being highly favourable terrain for the Persian cavalry; eleven days of stalemate ensued. Consequently, the Greek army entered Boeotia over the passes of Mount Cithaeron, arriving near Plataea but, significantly, in positions above the Persian camp. Mardonius was well aware that a successful attack was out of the question so he employed subterfuge to tempt the Greeks on to the plain. This may well be the conspiracy Plutarch tells us about among some prominent Athenians who were plotting to betray the Allied cause. He also deployed sporadic cavalry raids against the Greeks, but this petered out when the Persian cavalry commander Masistius was killed.

Buoyed up by this, the Greeks advanced, maintaining their higher ground advantage when they camped in a new and better position that was also better watered. Mardonius drew up his forces, ready for battle. However, stalemate ensued once again; this was explained by Herodotus by the bad omens received on both sides. Eight days of inactivity followed, notable only for the arrival of Athenian reinforcements.[62] It was Mardonius who finally broke the stalemate when he dispatched his cavalry to attack the passes of Mount Cithaeron; a consignment of Greek provisions was captured, and more skirmishing raids followed over the next two days. Mardonius's cavalry then succeeded in blocking the Gargaphian Spring, the only source of water for the Greek army: the Asopus was off limits because it was covered by Persian archers.[63] Lack of food and fresh water forced the Greeks to retreat under cover of darkness to a position before Plataea, from where they could guard the passes and have access to fresh water.[64]

Mardonius sensed victory and ordered his forces to pursue the Greeks, but the Spartans, Tegeans, and Athenians halted and gave battle, routing the Persian forces and killing Mardonius. Thebes surrendered after a short siege and the Thebans were executed. Plataea has been called 'the greatest land battle in classical Greek history'.

On the same day in 479 BCE, under the command of Leotychides, the Greek fleet of 110 ships under Xanthippos of Athens attacked what remained of the Persian fleet at Mycale in response to a plea by the islanders of Samos. The Greeks sailed to Samos while the Persians, oddly, dismissed the fleet of their Phoenician allies. The Persians, in a bid to avoid battle, then sailed for Mycale directly opposite Samos where they joined a huge army of 60,000 men under Tigranes. The Persians built a defensive rampart and disarmed the Samians; they also neutralised the Milesians, another ally with potential for desertion by having them guard the mountain passes around Mycale. Undeterred, the Greek marines swarmed ashore, defeated the Persians, looted the camp and torched all the Persian boats. The Ionians, with some encouragement from the allies, defected to the Greeks and joined in the assault on the Persians.[65]

The allies set sail for the Hellespont with a view to destroying the pontoon bridges, only to find that the bridges had already been decommissioned.[66] The Athenians then attacked the Persian-held Chersonesos, a Greek colony in what is today the Gallipoli peninsula, expelling the Persians who retreated to the fortress of Sestos where the Athenians laid siege to them. Among their number was Oeobazus of Cardia, who was in possession of the cables and other equipment from the pontoon bridges. After some months, Sestos eventually fell to the Athenians.[67]

Oeobazus was captured by some Thracians. The Athenians eventually caught Artayctes, the Persian governor, whom they took prisoner; he was then crucified by the people of Elaeus, a town on the Thracian Chersonese that Artayctes had sacked while governor of the Chersonesos. The Athenians then sailed back to Athens, taking their pontoon bridge cables with them as war trophies.[68]

However, there was still unfinished business. In 478 BCE, the allies invaded Cyprus deploying a fleet comprising twenty Peloponnesian and thirty Athenian ships and others under the command of Pausanias. Thucydides says that they 'subdued most of the island' but we do not know more than that.

From Cyprus, the Greek fleet sailed to Byzantium, which they besieged and took. With Sestos and Byzantium under their control, the allies now commanded the Bosporus between Europe and Asia, with access to the commercial spoils of the Black Sea.[69]

Yet all did not go well: an arrogant and 'violent' Pausanias alienated many of the allies; the Athenians were asked to take command, which they agreed to do. The Spartans recalled Pausanias and arrested him on charges of collaborating with the Persians. He was acquitted but never saw his command again. The Spartans sent Dorkis to Byzantium to replace Pausanias (who starved himself to death after being arraigned a second time for colluding with the enemy). However, the Allies refused to be led by the Spartans; Dorkis returned to Sparta.[70]

So the Persian threat and appetite for revenge for Sardis all those years ago evaporated. Militarily, Athens came out of Plataea as the supreme naval power in Greece. Mycale and Plataea both left no one in any doubt of the superiority of the hoplite over the lightly armed Persian infantry, as first shown at Marathon.

Wars and Battles of the Delian League (478–431 BCE)

With Sparta's enthusiasm for any further involvement in a pan-Greek alliance growing increasingly tepid, the Athenians went on to form the Delian League in 478 BCE; the objective was to create a cohesive Greek network among city-states and defend against further Persian assaults—in the words of Thucydides, to 'avenge the wrongs they suffered by ravaging the territory of the [Persian] king'.[1] This, of course, all cost money so signatories had to provide military support, ships and materiel, or pay a war tax to the joint treasury; most chose the tax. Athens was the arbiter and also provided the military commander of the allied armed forces. The treasurers too were Athenian, the ten *hellenotamiae*. League members swore to have the same friends and enemies, permanently binding oaths of loyalty. Each member, Athens included, regardless of size, had one vote. It was the Athenian Aristides who devoted himself to running the alliance.[2]

The Delian League was divided into five fiscal districts:

Thrace (the northern Aegean): sixty-two towns, of which Ainos, Argilos, Mende, Potideia, Samothrace, Scione, Sermylia, Strepsa, Thasos, and Torone paid more than five talents.

Hellespont: forty-five towns, Abydus, Byzantium, Chalkedon, the Chersonese, Cyzicus, Lampsacus, Perinthus, and Selymbria paying more than five talents.

Ionia (the eastern Aegean): thirty-five towns, including Cyme, Ephesus, Erythrae, Miletus, and Teos.

Caria: eighty-one towns, including Camirus, Cnidus, Cos, Ialysus, Lindus, Phaselis, and Telmessus.

The islands: twenty-nine towns, including Andros, Carystus, Chalcis, Eretria, Naxos, and Paros.

At its peak, the League could boast 200 members. Over time, Athens gradually gained a more hegemonic position over the other members of the league, leading to what became known as the Athenian Empire.

The Spartan king Leotychides had proposed the mass migration of all Greeks from Asia to Europe as the only way to liberate them from Persian rule; Xanthippus passionately opposed this on the grounds that the Ionian cities had been Athenian colonies, and the Athenians would surely stand by them.

The 470s BCE were largely taken up with campaigning in Thrace and the Aegean to eradicate the remaining Persian garrisons. Eion saw the first conflict, in 476 BCE. Cimon, son of Miltiades, was given the commander's role and was tasked with taking Eion, the strongest Persian stronghold west of the Hellespont and under the command of a determined Boges. Cimon defeated the army and began his siege; he offered the inhabitants the chance to leave the city but an obdurate Boges destroyed the treasure, murdered his wife, family, and entourage, threw the corpses onto a burning pyre, and jumped into the flames himself. Cimon, equally unyielding, diverted the River Strymon against the mud brick city walls, which collapsed. The inhabitants were enslaved.[3]

The Athenians then attacked the island of Skyros to wipe out the piracy that was flourishing thereabouts. This Athenian purging action liberated the Aegean; colonists were sent to the island to prevent any relapse into piracy.

Unsurprisingly, all was not always well with League. Naxos withdrew in 471 BCE and had their city walls torn down in retribution; it surrendered its fleet and its voting rights in the League.

In 465 BCE, Athens sent settlers to found a colony called Ennea Hodoi ('the nine ways') at what was later to be the site of Amphipolis on the Strymon river, a move that caused Thasos much anxiety over her economic future. She saw it as such a serious threat to her interests in the silver mines of Mt Pangaion that she defected from the League to Persia. Thasos called on Sparta for help; Sparta made a clandestine promise to invade Attica to support the Thasians but had to renege when an earthquake sparked a huge helot rebellion. Thucydides saw the Thasian crisis as a pivotal moment in the pentecontaetia (πεντηκονταετία), 'the period of fifty years' between Plataea in 479 BCE and the beginning of the Peloponnesian War in 431 BCE.[4] It was indicative of the transformation of the Delian League into an Athenian empire, which in turn demonstrated the growing existence of a robust militaristic party, anticipating growing tensions between Sparta and Athens and conflict in the First Peloponnesian War.

The Athenians won an opening battle then besieged the city. The Thasians were nothing if not determined: anyone suggesting surrender was executed; Polyaenus describes how the women of Thasos cut off their hair so that it could be used as roping in siege machinery, *mechanemata* (probably torsion catapults).[5] In 463 BCE, the Thasians were at last forced to surrender. The Athenians were in no mood for clemency and forced Thasos to renounce its claims to territories on the mainland (the mines), demolished its walls, requisitioned its fleet, and imposed indemnities and tribute; at first this was three talents per year, but in the 440s BCE, it was reassessed to a punitive thirty talents.[6]

The Persians would not lie down. The Battle of the River Eurymedon around 468 BCE was both a sea and a land battle between the Delian League and the Persians under Xerxes I. The year before, the Persians began amassing a large army and navy at Aspendos (at the mouth of the Eurymedon) for a major offensive against the Greeks. The plan was to advance up the coast of Asia Minor from Eurymedon, capturing each city and restoring the Asiatic Greek regions to Persian control, and, at the same time, furnishing the Persians with naval bases from which to launch further expeditions into the Aegean. Cimon's reaction was to sail with 200 triremes from Cnidus to Phaselis in Pamphylia. Initially, Phaselis refused him entry so Cimon devastated the land; the Phaselians eventually saw sense and agreed to join the Delian League; Cimon thus confounded the Persian strategy at birth, denying them their first targeted naval base. As retribution, Phaselis was forced to contribute troops to the expedition, and to pay the Athenians ten talents.

Cimon then executed a pre-emptive strike against the Persians at the Eurymedon where they were waiting for eighty Phoenician ships to arrive from Cyprus. Cimon routed the fleet gathered there. He then deployed the Greek marines to attack the Persian army, which he also routed.[7] The Greeks took the Persian camp along with numerous prisoners; as a *coup de grâce*, he destroyed 200 beached Persian triremes. Quite naturally, the Persians were thoroughly demoralised by this and were effectively out of action until at least 451 BCE. Plutarch tells us that Cimon was not satisfied even after his double victory, 'though like a powerful athlete he had brought down two contests in one day ... Cimon still went on competing against his own victories.' He sailed the Greek fleet swiftly to intercept the eighty Phoenician ships at Syedra on the Ciliccian coast on the way from Cyprus; with the advantage of surprise, he either captured or destroyed the whole fleet and their crews.[8] Nevertheless, it would appear that the Delian League states failed to press home their victories.

Simonides (*c.* 556–468 BCE) captures the spirit of Eurymedon in this epigram, *On Those Who Fell at Eurymedon*:

> *These by the streams of famed Eurymedon*
> *Their short but brilliant race of life have run;*
> *In winged ships and on the embattled field*
> *Alike, they forced the Median bows to yield,*
> *Breaking their foremost ranks. Now here they lie,*
> *Their names inscribed on rolls of victory.*[9]

Major change was afoot. In 461 BCE, Cimon was ostracised and succeeded by democrats Ephialtes and Pericles, who snubbed the Spartans and forged alliances with Argos and Thessaly, enemies of Sparta. Megara left the Spartan-led Peloponnesian League and allied herself with Athens. Crucially, this led to the construction of a double line of walls across the Isthmus of Corinth protecting Athens from attack.[10] The Athenians then built the 4.5-mile Long Walls connecting the city to the Piraeus, rendering Athens invulnerable to attack by land.

As sensible and militarily astute as these precautions were, Athenian policy towards the contemporaneous revolt in an ever-volatile Egypt was somewhat less judicious. Turmoil reigned in Persia when Xerxes was murdered in 465 BCE; around 460 BCE, the Persian satrapy in Egypt was rocked again (there had been a revolt in 486 BCE) by insurrection. The culprit was Inaros, a Libyan king settled on the border with Egypt. His rebellion spread like wildfire throughout the country, and Inaros was soon in control of much of the land.[11] Inaros now appealed to the Delian League to reinforce his conflict against the Persians. As it happened, the League had a fleet of 200 ships battling in Cyprus, which the Athenians diverted to Egypt to support the revolt.[12]

Why did the Athenians adopt such a seemingly reckless policy? First, it was probably seen as a chance to further damage Persia and her interests in Egypt; second, it may have satisfied a need for Athenian naval bases in the region; third, it gave access to Egypt's prodigious grain resources; and fourth, it might build ongoing lucrative trading links with Egypt.

Whatever, the Athenians sailed up the Nile to rendezvous with Inaros's forces. Yet they had not reckoned with the Persian king Artaxerxes I's reaction: he had assembled an army to crush the revolt, under his uncle Achaemenes. Diodorus and Ctesias assess this force at an exaggerated 300,000 and 400,000 respectively.

Diodorus reports that the Persians made their camp near the Nile at Pampremis. Herodotus writes that he 'saw too the skulls of those Persians at Papremis who were killed with Darius' son Achaemenes by Inaros the Libyan'.[13] The two sides joined battle with the Persians' superior numbers initially getting the upper hand. The Athenians, nevertheless, broke through the Persian line and routed the Persian army. Some of the few survivors took refuge in the citadel of Memphis (the 'White Castle') where they obstinately remained for some four years.[14]

The siege of Memphis (459–455 BCE) led a frustrated Artaxerxes to send the general Megabazus to bribe the Spartans into invading Attica, to divert the besieging Athenian forces from Egypt. This failed, so he gathered a large army (300,000 according to Diodorus) under Megabyzus (another Achaemenid Persian general, son of Zopyrus, satrap of Babylonia) and posted it to Egypt.[15] Moving from Persia to Cilicia, Megabyzus assembled a fleet of 300 triremes from the Cilicians, Phoenicians, and Cypriots, and proceeded to train their men for a year, after which they set sail for Egypt. Here, he soon lifted the siege at Memphis, defeated the Egyptians, and drove the Athenians out of Memphis.[16]

In 455 BCE, the Athenians retreated to the island of Prosopitis in the Nile delta only to be besieged there by Megabyzus for eighteen months; in the end, he drained the river from around the island by digging canals, thus, in the words of Thucydides 'joining the island to the mainland'. The Persians were now able to cross over to the former island and capture it. Only a few of the Athenians survived to return to Athens. Diodorus adds that the draining of the river caused the Egyptians to defect to the Persians. The ignominious defeat of the Egyptian expedition caused panic in Athens and prompted the relocation of the Delian treasury from Delos to Athens as a precaution. Inaros was captured and taken to Susa where he was crucified in 454 BCE.

Finally, Thucydides records the fate of a flotilla of fifty triremes sent out in a bid to relieve the siege of Prosopitis. Oblivious to the fact that the Athenians had succumbed, the Athenian ships put in at Mendesium in the mouth of the Nile, where it was immediately attacked from the land, and from the sea by the Phoenician navy. Most of the ships were destroyed, with only a few surviving to escape and return to Athens.[17]

The Egyptian fiasco led the Athenians to sign a five-year truce with Sparta in 451 BCE, which freed them up from fighting in Greece, and allowed the League to dispatch a fleet to campaign in Cyprus that same year, under the recently rehabilitated Cimon.[18]

As we have seen, Cimon was fighting in Cyprus with a fleet of 200 ships supplied by the Athenians and their allies. Sixty of these were diverted to Egypt at the request of Amyrtaeus, the so-called 'King of the Marshes'. The rest besieged Kition in Cyprus; during the siege, Cimon died either of sickness or from a wound. As the Athenians were running short of provisions, and on instructions from the dying Cimon, the Athenians retreated towards Cypriot Salamis.[19]

News of Cimon's death was kept secret from the Athenian army for reasons of morale. Not long after leaving Kition, the Athenians, while sailing off Salamis, and their allies were assaulted by a Persian army comprising Cilicians, Phoenicians, and Cypriots. A land and sea battle saw the Persians off; the Athenians sailed back to Greece. Diodorus controversially states that the 'Peace of Callias' was signed with the Persians.[20]

Pericles, Parthenon, and Athenian Power

We have noted how in 454 BCE, Pericles (*c.* 495–429 BCE) relocated the Delian League's treasury from Delos to Athens, on the pretext, perhaps, of keeping it safe from Persian hands. However, Plutarch insinuates that many of Pericles's rivals viewed the transfer to Athens as a means to finance local building projects. Athens also made the decision not to accept ships, men and weapons as League dues, only accepting money. Indeed, Pericles used the tribute paid by League members to build the Parthenon on the Acropolis—a clear indication that the Delian League was moving from being an alliance towards being an empire.

If there is one truly iconic symbol of ancient Greece, it is the Acropolis and the magnificent Parthenon, which dominated both Athens and western civilisation. It was an unmistakable symbol of Athenian power. Acropolis comes from the Greek ἄκρον ('edge' or 'extremity') and πόλις (*polis*, 'city'). The Acropolis was rebuilt in white marble from 449 BCE; work on the Parthenon began in 447 BCE and was completed in 438 BCE. It was dedicated to Athena Nike (patron goddess of the city) and houses a huge statue of the goddess. The Erechtheum, with its caryatids (marble female figures) supporting the roof, and the Temple of Athena Nike, were built on the Acropolis at the same time. Pericles was largely responsible for much of the construction on the Acropolis. Access was through the Propylaea, a large gateway building (437–432 BCE). The city was connected to the port of Piraeus by the parallel Long Walls, which formed a corridor that was 550 feet wide.

What we see today was not, of course, the first and only construction on the Acropolis. There was a Doric temple to Athena Polias from around 570–550 BCE referred to as the Hekatompedon or Ur-Parthenon ('original Parthenon'). The

Pisistratids built another temple between 529–520 BCE—the Old Temple of Athena. Around 500 BCE, the Ur-Parthenon was dismantled to make place for the 'Older Parthenon' (the Pre-Parthenon). This was still under construction when the Persians sacked the city in 480 BCE. After their victory at Eurymedon in 468 BCE, Cimon and Themistocles commissioned the reconstruction of the southern and northern walls of the Acropolis. Most of the major temples, including the Parthenon, were rebuilt under Pericles during what is called the Golden Age of Athens (460–430 BCE). Phidias, Ictinus, and Callicrates were responsible for this reconstruction.

Thucydides called Pericles 'the first citizen of Athens' and indeed, he did much to confirm Athens as the cultural centre of the ancient Greek world with his energetic promotion of the written word and the visual arts, sculpture and architecture, including the Parthenon. Politically, Pericles turned the Delian League into an Athenian empire, and led Athenian fighting during the first two years of the Peloponnesian War.

In 463 BCE, Cimon, who believed that democracy had run its course, was accused of neglecting Athenian interests in Macedon; Pericles was the chief prosecutor and although Cimon was acquitted this time, Pericles was instrumental in his ostracism two years later for betraying Athens by supporting Sparta. The leader of the pro-democratic party and Pericles's mentor, Ephialtes, had proposed a watering down of the powers of the Areopagus which the Ecclesia adopted, ushering in a new age of radical democracy.

Ephialtes was assassinated in 461 BCE, allowing Pericles to take over as ruler of Athens. Pericles now launched his populist social policy; he introduced a decree allowing the poor to attend the theatre free of charge with the state footing the bill; he lowered the property requirement for the archonship in 457 BCE (thus permitting poorer people) and paid wages to all jurymen in the Heliaia from around after 454 BCE. His law of 451 BCE restricted Athenian citizenship to those people who could prove Athenian parentage on both sides.

Pericles showed his military mettle when he led Athens in the First Peloponnesian War in 454 BCE. In line with Athenian tradition, he married a close relative, with whom he had two sons, Paralus and Xanthippus. In 445 BCE, Pericles divorced this wife for the woman whom he really loved: Aspasia of Miletus.

Pericles's enduring legacy is the stunning architecture which stands today on the Athenian acropolis, the peerless literature and philosophy of his age, and the Funeral Oration recorded by Thucydides, which stands as an emblem for the struggle for Athenian power, democracy, civic pride, and patriotism.

The Persians were not the only thorns in the side of an increasingly expansionist Athens. Carthaginians and Etruscans were also making nuisances of themselves.

Greek and Carthaginian rivalry for Sicily began in mid-eighth century BCE when the Greeks established their first colonies on the island and the Carthaginians arrived from North Africa to exert their claims and establish their presence there. The Greek city of Himera, founded around 648 BCE, was pivotal in this rivalry. Himera was a highly strategic city commanding not only the sea lanes along the north coast of Sicily but also a major land artery leading south across the island. In the early fifth century BCE, the competition to dominate Sicily reached a high point. Gelon, king of Syracuse and Theron, tyrant of Akragas formed an alliance not only to counter Carthage, but also to wrest Himera from their fellow Greeks. This they soon achieved in 483 BCE, exiling the city's Greek ruler, Terrilus, tyrant of Himera, who then turned to Carthage for help. The stage was set for the battle of Himera. This was a golden opportunity for the Carthaginian Hamilcar the Magonid, who mobilised his forces put at an exaggerated 300,000 with men recruited from Iberia, Sardinia, Corsica, Italy, Gaul, and Africa. These were complemented with chariots, 200 warships, and 3,000 transports.[21] The Syracusan army at Himera is alleged to have numbered 50,000 foot and 5,000 horses. *En route* to Sicily, however, a storm played havoc with the Punic fleet causing severe losses, particularly among the ships carrying the chariots and horses. After landing at Ziz (the Punic name for Panormus, today's Palermo), Hamilcar was decisively beaten by Gelon.

Hamilcar had set up two camps outside Himera: one for the army, one for the navy. Smart use of intelligence was his downfall when a message he had sent to Selinus, a Punic dependency on the south-west of the island, was intercepted by Gelon. The message requested Selinian cavalry to reinforce Hamilcar's naval camp; Gelon was only too pleased to oblige, sending in a disguised force of Syracusans who proceeded to burn the Carthaginian ships. Gelon then arrived on the scene and attacked the land camp. Some 150,000 Carthaginians apparently died in the battle. Hamilcar was either slain in the battle or he committed suicide out of shame for his defeat by leaping into the flames of a sacrifice he was making at the altar of Poseidon.[22]

The defeat had serious ramifications for Carthage. The entrenched nobility was ejected to be replaced by the Carthaginian Republic, in which most power was invested in the Council of Elders. Carthage paid 2,000 talents in reparations to the Greeks and languished in the cold in Sicily for the next seventy years. The battle resulted in no transfer of territory. Syracuse did not attack the cities allied to Carthage (Rhegion and Selinus) but booty from the war helped to finance a public building program in Sicily, which allowed Greek culture to flourish on the island. Likewise, Greek trade grew. Gelon died in 478 BCE and over the next twenty years the Greek tyrants were usurped while the Syracuse-Akragas alliance degenerated into eleven feuding oligarchies and democracies. The internecine turmoil and expansionism concluded with the Second Sicilian war beginning in 410 BCE.

For the past sixteen or so years, Stefano Vassallo of the Archaeological Superintendency of Palermo has been excavating at the site of ancient Himera. His fascinating, painstaking discoveries have helped pinpoint the battle's exact location, unravelled the ancient historians' accounts, and literally unearthed new evidence regarding how classical Greek soldiers fought and died. For example, in 2008, Vassallo's team excavated part of Himera's western necropolis to reveal eighteen extremely rare horse burials dating to the early fifth century BCE. They tally with Diodorus's account of the cavalry strategy the Greeks used against Hamilcar.

By the following summer, Vassallo had laid bare more than 2,000 graves dating from the mid-sixth to the late fifth centuries BCE, notable among which were seven communal graves, dating to the early fifth century containing at least sixty-five skeletons in total. 'The dead, who were interred in a respectful and orderly manner, were all males over the age of 18'. Thoughts that these were victims of an epidemic were soon dispelled when it was realised that the bodies were all male and that many of them exhibited signs of violent trauma. Given the date of the graves, these could be the remains of men killed in the battle of Himera in of 480 BCE and could be crucial in reconstructing the battle of Himera.

John W. W. Lee takes up the story:

> Their placement in the western necropolis strongly suggests that the main clash between the Greek and Carthaginian armies took place near the western walls of the city. Since bodies are heavy to move, it's likely they were buried in the cemetery closest to the battlefield, especially if there were many dead to dispose of ... They were probably not Carthaginians, for the defeated enemy would have received little respect. Dead Himeran soldiers would likely have been collected by their families for burial. Instead, Vassallo believes many or all of the dead were allied Greeks from Syracuse or Akragas. These warriors, who died far from home, could not be taken back to their native soil for burial. Instead, they were honored in Himera's cemetery for their role in defending the city.[23]

As Lee points out, the literary evidence, from Homer to Diodorus and beyond tends to focus on kings and generals, leaving the ordinary soldier and sailor fighting and dying out in the cold. Until Vassallo's work, only a small number of mass graves from Greek battles— for example, those at Chaeronea, where Philip of Macedon defeated the Greeks in 338 BCE—had been excavated and these graves were discovered and uncovered before the development of modern archaeological and forensic techniques available to Vassallo's team. It seems that the Himera graves are the best archaeological source found so far for classical Greek warfare.

The discoveries also throw up unique information on the soldiers' ages, health, and nutrition. Bone abnormalities enable us to identify the men's military specialties: for example, archers typically develop asymmetrical bone growths on their right shoulder joints and left elbows. Some of the men clearly suffered impact trauma to their skulls, while the bones of others exhibit sword hacks and arrow impacts. Some of the soldiers were buried with iron spearheads still lodged in their bodies; one man still has the weapon that killed him stuck between his vertebrae. Analyses determine whether the men fell in hand-to-hand close combat or from missiles, while advancing or in flight. The arrowheads and spearheads tell us the origin of some of the combatants as they would have brought their weaponry from their homelands.

The Carthaginians were not alone in coveting Greek colonies. As we have seen, the Etruscans too had designs on a Greek outpost on the Italian peninsula, which persisted into the 470s BCE. Once again, Cumae was the target in 474 BCE when the Etruscans dispatched a fleet and, at the same time, appealed to Hieron, tyrant of Syracuse for military assistance. Hieron responded by dispatching a fleet of triremes. The Etruscan threat to colonies in Magna Graecia was over.

The Peloponnesian Wars (460–404 BCE)

At the close of the seventh century BCE, Sparta was the most powerful *polis* in the Peloponnese; next came Argos. The city-states of Corinth and Elis allied with Sparta—the one because Sparta rid Corinth of her tyrants and the other because Sparta endowed Elis with the venue for the prestigious Olympic Games. The origins of the Peloponnesian League (*summachia*) can be seen around 550 BCE, according to Plutarch, when Sparta saw the need to protect itself against a potential revolt by Sparta's helots and attack from Sparta's rivals Argos.[1]

The League was never a league in the true sense of the word and it was never entirely or exclusively Peloponnesian. Sparta was always the leader, the *hegemon*; she controlled the council of allies, which comprised the assembly of Spartiates and the Congress of Allies. Each state had one vote regardless of size or power. Payment of tribute was paid only during wartime, when one third of the military capability of a member could be appropriated. Only Sparta could negotiate alliances with outsiders. The Peloponnesian League was different from other confederacies such as the contemporary Delian League in that it had had no single binding agreement but was more a collection of *poleis* each having negotiated their own terms independently with Sparta; member states were even at liberty to wage war against each other. The Peloponnesian League was designed to provide self preservation and prosperity for Sparta, and to give power and protection to its members. A perfect combination of self-interest engineered through altruism.

One of the League's earliest members was Tegea (Elis was another), which was coerced into collaboration by 530 BCE, during the reign of king Anaxandridas II. Tegea was militarily and commercially important: it controlled a large territory, 385 km² split into nine demes; it lay on routes leading to Argos and Sparta; Tegea minted its own coinage; and it could boast fortifications, which included five gates and several towers.

By 510 BCE, the League took in all of the Peloponnese under Cleomenes I. By deploying a judicious amount of old Greek hospitality (*xenia*), it spread wider afield to embrace such cities as Megara and parts of Attica. In 494 BCE, Argos was defeated but was never to become a member; according to Thucydides, the League's membership extended further to include cities in Phocis and Boeotia over the next half century.[2] Soon after the wars with Persia had ended in 473 BCE, Argos, Sparta's arch rival, allied with Arcadian Tegea in what was seen as a confrontational act; but Sparta, under Cleomenes, defeated them both in a battle outside Tegea. Two years later, in 471 BCE, all the Arcadian states, with the exception of Mantinea, joined together against Sparta. Sparta crushed them all at Dipaea.[3] Other Peloponnesian states joined up until only Argos and Achaea remained outside of the Peloponnesian League.

Tegea was pivotal to Spartan hegemony and formed a template of sorts for membership and members' obligations; every Peloponnesian city and town now had to make a critical choice between siding with Sparta or with Argos. Tegea sacrificed some of its autonomy in foreign affairs in return for Spartan protection.

The balance of power between Argos and Sparta soon tipped in favour of the latter to make Sparta the undisputed power in the Peloponnese. Crucially, the League's armed forces were always led by a Spartan—either one of the two Spartan kings or a senior Spartan commander.

After the Persian Wars, the Delian League crumbled and developed into the Hellenic League to include Athens and other states. It was led by Pausanias and, later, by a rehabilitated Cimon. Sparta then pulled out to reform the Peloponnesian League with its original allies. What remained of the Hellenic League then became the Athenian-led Delian League. The two Leagues, of course, were to clash in the Peloponnesian War. Thucydides saw it all coming: 'The growth of the power of Athens, and the alarm which this inspired in Lacedaemon [Sparta], made war inevitable.'

Major Athenian historian, political philosopher and general (*strategos*), Thucydides is famous for his *History of the Peloponnesian War*, a defining work of history which has led to him being called the father of 'scientific history' because of his rigorous research, reliance on eye-witness accounts, lucid evidence-gathering, and analysis of cause and effect. Unlike the work of Herodotus, Thucydides's history is devoid of interventions by the gods. He omits the arts, literature, or the social circumstances in which the events take place, focusing instead on actual events, excluding what he may have seen as frivolous or irrelevant.

Anger at the building of the Athenian Long Walls, Megara's defection from the Peloponnesian to the Delian League, and the envy and anxiety felt by Sparta at the growth of the Athenian Empire all contributed to the outbreak of what is called the First Peloponnesian War in 460 BCE. In 460 BCE, Argos, supported by Athens and Thessaly, rose against Sparta, who dispatched a small force to subdue the revolt. A combined force of Athenians and Argives defeated the Spartans at Oenoe. The next year, a spat between Megara and Corinth led to Megara walking out of the Peloponnesian League and joining Athens in the Delian League. The benefit to Athens of this new alliance was only matched by the depth of insult and disadvantage to Corinth and Sparta. What were effectively the first exchanges in the First Peloponnesian War were delivered when Athens sent a fleet to Haleis on the Gulf of Argolis; Diodorus tells us how Corinthian and Epidaurian forces dispatched to oppose the Athenians were defeated. Thucydides, however, reports the opposite.

Whatever, we do know for sure that the Athenians were victorious in a naval engagement that same year in 459 BCE against a Peloponnesian fleet off the island of Cecryphalea in the Saronic Gulf. This drew the island of Aegina into the hostilities and a battle ensued in which the Athenians besieged the town of Aegina.[4] Things got more complicated in 458 BCE when, in a bid to relieve the siege at Aegina, the Corinthians invaded Megara in the hope that the Athenians would be diverted there and away from Aegina. Yet this was only hope: the wily Athenians quickly raised an *ad hoc* army comprised of the too old and the too young to fight in the regular forces and dispatched them to the defence of Megara under Myronides. An inconclusive battle was claimed by the Athenians who erected a trophy to confirm this; the Corinthians, excited by the taunts of the old men of Athens, came out to put up their own trophy, at which point the Athenians attacked again and really did defeat them this time. Diodorus mentions a further two battles, at Cimolia, at which the Athenians came out victorious.[5]

In 457 BCE, the Athenian allies, the Phocians, joined in the war by attacking Doris; the Spartans went to their assistance with an army of 12,000 men led by Nicomedes. The Spartans won the battle but their return journey was problematic: the Athenians controlled both routes—through the Megarid and on the open sea. The decision was taken to march east towards Athens. The Long Walls were not completed at this time. The Athenians reacted with a 14,000-strong army sent out to meet the Spartans; the Spartans defeated their enemy at the battle of Tanagra, allowing the Spartans to return through the Megarid. Two months later, the Athenians, under Myronides, invaded Boeotia, and defeated the Boeotians at the battle of Oenophyta. This gave the Athenians Boeotia and Phocis, indeed control over the whole country with the exception of Thebes.[6]

The Athenians were uplifted by these victories and, in 453 BCE, set out, under Tolmides, on an audacious offensive expedition around the Peloponnese in which they set the Spartan dockyards on fire and captured Chalcis, an ally of Corinth. They landed at Sicyon, north-west of Corinth in northern Argolis, and defeated the Sicyonians but failed to take their city. Pericles led a second expedition but he too was unable to take Sicyon.[7]

Pericles saw the need to consolidate Athenian control over what can now be described as an empire. In 450 BCE, he established more *kleruchiai*—special colonies bound to Athens, which acted as regional garrisons. He created a number of official positions: *proxenoi*, public relations officials who promoted good relations between Athens and League members; *episkopoi* and *archontes*, who managed the collection of tribute; and *hellenotamiai*, ten magistrates appointed by the Athenians tasked to receive the contributions of the allied states. They have been called the chief financial officers of the Delian League.[8]

Things started to go wrong for the Athenians in 447 BCE. Locrians, Euboeans, and Boeotian exiles seized the Boeotian cities of Orchomenus and Chaeronea and delivered them from Athenian rule; the Athenians under Tolmides responded with an attack by 1,000 hoplites which won back Chaeronia for them. A garrison was left behind. However, while marching home, the Athenians were assailed by exiles from Orchomenos and Chaeronia; Tolmides was killed and many of the hoplites were taken prisoner. The price of freedom for these prisoners of war was a treaty in which the Athenians were compelled to relinquish Boeotia.[9] The defeat fomented revolts on Euboea and in Megara, causing further conflict with Sparta in the run up to the Peloponnesian War.

In 446 BCE, the Athenians and the Spartans signed the Thirty Years' Peace, designed to prevent further outbreak of war. Athens gave up all of her possessions in the Peloponnese including Boeotia and the Megarian ports of Nisaea and Pegae with Troezen and Achaea in Argolis; the Spartans allowed the Athenians to keep Naupactus. The peace ruled out armed conflict between Sparta and Athens if at least one of the two parties was willing to arbitrate. Athens and Sparta agreed not to attempt to seduce the other state's allies. Neutral *poleis* could join Sparta or Athens; Athens and Sparta would keep all other territories pending arbitration. It also recognised both the Delian and Peloponnesian Leagues as legitimate.

All the while during the peace the Athenians worked at undermining the truce. Athens got involved in the dispute over Epidamnus and Corcyra in 435 BCE, which angered the Corinthians, who were allies of Sparta. Athens introduced severe trade sanctions against Megara, again, allies of Sparta, because of its participation in the Corinthian-Corcyran dispute and allegations that the Megarians had desecrated the Hiera Orgas by cultivating it—a circular, fertile area of land sacred to the Eleusinian goddesses, Demeter and Persephone.[10] These sanctions were contained in an Athenian decree, issued in 433–432 BCE, and known as the Megarian Decree. This barred Megarians from ports and marketplaces throughout the Athenian Empire, thus destroying the Megarian economy and the economies of Megara's allies and trading partners. It would have been interpreted as a move by Athens to weaken her rivals and extend her influence. The Megarian Decree was akin to a modern trade embargo, which, at the time, was known in the ancient Near East, but was unheard of in the Greek world.

The decree and its consequences are skirted over by Thucydides, perhaps because he believed that these were mere pretexts, and not the real reasons, for war.[11] Aristophanes refers to it in *The Acharnians*, remarking how the decree left the Megarians 'slowly starving' and causing them to appeal to the Spartans for help. Diodorus, relying on Ephorus of Cyme, is much more direct:

When the Athenians voted to exclude the Megarians from both their market and harbours, the Megarians turned to the Spartans for aid. And the Spartans... dispatched ambassadors..., ordering the Athenians to rescind the action against the Megarians and threatening, if they did not accede, to wage war upon them together with the forces of their allies. When the [Athenian] Assembly convened to consider the matter, Pericles, who far excelled all his fellow citizens in skill of oratory, persuaded the Athenians not to rescind the action, saying that for them to accede to the demands of the Spartans, contrary to their own interests, would be the first step toward slavery.[12]

Sparta consulted her allies and demanded concessions from Athens including the immediate expulsion of the Alcmaeonidae family, Pericles included, and the retraction of the Megarian Decree. War was the only outcome if the demands were not met. In 432 BCE, as we shall see, Athens attacked Potidaea, an ally and a Corinthian colony. The Spartans claimed that the Athenians had violated the treaty and so declared war. The Thirty Years' Peace was null and void and the Second Peloponnesian War, often known just as the Peloponnesian War, began.

When Samos, an ally of Athens, attacked Miletus, the Miletians asked Athens for help; Athens responded by sailing to Samos and establishing a democracy there. They left the usual garrison and sailed home. However, a number of Samians remained displeased and sailed to the mainland where they recruited a mercenary army. This army then attacked Samos and turned the democratic government and the garrison over to the Persians. The Athenians sailed against Samos with a fleet of sixty ships under Pericles; forty-four of these faced a Samian fleet of seventy ships at Tragia. The Athenians, although inferior in number, pulled off a victory allowing Pericles to take the harbour and lay siege to the city by land and by sea.[13]

The next year, in 439 BCE, reinforcements arrived for Pericles in the shape of forty ships from Athens and twenty-five from Chios and Lesbos. Pericles deployed sixty vessels from his total fleet of 125 to ward off an attack by Phoenicians intent on helping Samos. In his absence, however, the Samians launched a surprise assault on the Athenian camp, supported by a naval attack on the Athenian fleet offshore. The Samians held sway for two weeks when Pericles arrived back on the scene and resumed his siege. After nine months Samos fell to the Athenians.[14]

The Corinth–Corcyra War (435–431 BCE)

In the spring of 435 BCE, there was a little local difficulty in Epidamnus on the Illyrian coast when the democrats expelled the aristocrats. The aristocrats were colluding with the local Taulantians (from around modern Albania) and made a number of piratical attacks on the city. The democrats and the autocrats both appealed to the Corcyraeans, Epidamnus being a colony of Corcyra (modern Corfu), for help. Corcyra possessed the second largest navy in Greece at the time. The appeal was denied to the democrats but the exiled aristocrats had more luck. They were able to point to the tombs of their ancestors in Corcyra, and soon won the support of the mother city. The democrats consulted the oracle at Delphi, which directed them to Corinth as Corinthians had originally founded the city. The oracle added that they should hand their city over to the Corinthians, a gift that the Corinthians could hardly refuse. A force of colonists from Corinth, Ambracia, and Leucas soon reached Epidamnus.

Corinth and Corcyra were long-standing enemies. Corinth dispatched an army by land; the Corcyraeans dispatched a fleet of forty ships which proceeded to lay siege to Epidamnus when the inhabitants rejected Corcyraean demands. A relief force of seventy-five ships were then launched by the Corinthians and her allies along with 5,000 hoplites—all aiming to lift the siege at Epidamnus. Diplomacy failed when demands were countered with counter demands. Corinth declared war, backing it up with the mobilisation of a seventy-five-ship fleet crowded with 2,000 hoplites. The Corcyraeans responded by launching an eighty-ship fleet; the two fleets met between the mouth of the Ambracian Gulf (the site of the battle of Actium) and Cape Leucimme at the southern end of Corcyra, having sunk fifteen of the enemy vessels. Epidamnus surrendered that same day; the Corcyraeans erected a trophy at the Leucimme Promontory. All prisoners were murdered, apart from the Corinthians, who were enslaved.[15] The victory handed Corcyra control of the seas around the western coast of Greece and enabled them to launch raids on Corinth and her allies for the next year or so.

Despite their defeat, the Corinthians embarked on a programme of shipbuilding in preparation for taking the fight back to the Corcyraeans. In the summer of 434 BCE, the Corinthians took up fortified positions around Actium, while the Corcyraeans faced them off Leucimme. This stalemate lasted until the winter of 434–433 BCE when both fleets returned home.

Until then, Corcyra had taken a neutral stance with regards to the affairs of mainland Greece, avoiding both the Delian and Peloponnesian Leagues. However, they decided that now would be a good time to try and join the Athenian League. Corinth did likewise and sent representatives to Athens as well. The Corcyraeans pleaded that they now needed help to preserve their freedom in the face of a powerful threat and with their mighty naval capability would prove a potent ally in any future struggle against Sparta; furthermore, Corcyra was a vital staging post on the sea routes to Italy and Sicily, both major sources of grain for Athens. The Corcyraeans also pointed out the ramifications of Corinth possessing their powerful fleet: Athens would have to face the combined fleets of Corinth, Corcyra, and the Peloponnese. The Corinthians naturally denigrated the Corcyraean claims concluding that if Athens did allow Corcyra into their league then war between Corinth and Athens would be inevitable.

The Athenians decided to accommodate the Corcyraeans in a deal in which both sides were obliged to come to the aid of the other in any war, but in a defensive capacity. A squadron of ten Athenian ships sailed to Corcyra, with orders to avoid battle unless the Corinthians attempted to invade Corcyra.

In 433 BCE, a massive sea battle took place off the isles of Sybota between Corcyra and Corinth. Like Leucimme, it was one of the catalysts for the next stage of the Peloponnesian Wars. The two fleets faced each other at the southern tip of Corcyra—the Corinthian fleet anchored at Chimerium comprised 150 ships and was under the command of Xenoclides; the Corcyraean fleet of 110 ships and their ten Athenian ally vessels were further north off the Sybota islands. The Corcyran fleet was under Miciades, Aisimides, and Eurybatus; the Athenian commanders—Lacedaimonius (the son of Cimon), Diotimus, and Proteas—sailed with them. The Corcyraeans had the Athenians on the right and their own ships making up the rest of the line in three squadrons. The Corinthian ships had the Megarans and Ambraciots on the right, and the other allies in the centre. Both sides deployed hoplites with archers and javelin-throwers.[16] Instead of the usual ramming and sinking tactic, both parties attempted to board their opponents' ships and fight what was in essence a land battle at sea.[17] The Athenian ships, of course, did not initially join battle, as the Corinthians had not attempted to invade.

The Corinthians destroyed seventy enemy ships, the Corcyraeans only thirty. The Corcyraeans and Athenians returned to Corcyra to defend the island. They were followed by the Corinthians, who immediately withdrew when they learnt that twenty Athenian reinforcements under Glaucon were on their way. The next day, these reinforcements threatened a second battle should the Corinthians attempt to land on Corcyra. The Corinthians retreated completely rather than risk another battle. Both Corinth and Corcyra claimed victory. When the Peloponnesian War resumed, Corcyra sided with Athens and Corinth with Sparta.

Before that, however, the Athenians had to deal with an insurrection in Potidaea in 432 BCE. The battle of Potidaea, between Athens and a combined army from Corinth and Potidaea, was another trigger for the Peloponnesian War. Paradoxically, Potidaea, while a member of the Delian League, was a colony of Corinth's situated on the Chalcidice peninsula. Following the battle of Sybota, Athens was anxious that Potidaea might revolt due to Corinthians or Macedonian pressure and influences— Perdiccas II of Macedon was fomenting unrest among Athens's other allies in Thrace. Consequently, Athens made some exacting demands; they insisted that Potidaea pull down its walls, expel all Corinthian ambassadors and send hostages to Athens.[18]

The Corinthians, naturally, were incandescent and encouraged Potidaea to revolt with the assurance that they would side with them. All the while, the Corinthians were secretly aiding Potidaea by planting contingents of men into the besieged city to help with its defence. This was a direct violation of the Thirty Years' Peace, which stipulated that the Delian League and the Peloponnesian League would respect each other's autonomy and internal affairs.

Things escalated very quickly. Athens assembled a thirty-ship fleet manned by 1,000 hoplites under the command of Archestratus; this fleet was originally destined to attack Perdiccas in Macedonia but was diverted to Potidaea to quell any revolt. The Potidaeans tried diplomacy and sent ambassadors to Athens and Sparta. Their efforts were in vain and when negotiations broke down in Athens, Sparta agreed to help Potidaea secede from Athens. When the Athenian fleet arrived at Potidaea, Archestratus attacked the Macedonians since the Potidaeans had already revolted and joined Perdiccas. Corinth embroiled herself by posting 1,600 hoplites and 400 light troops to Potidaea, under the command of Aristeus; these were nominally 'volunteers', flagging to Athens that Corinth was reluctant to provoke a full-scale war. Athens was unimpressed and sent out another 2,000 hoplites and forty more ships under Callias. The Athenians engaged Perdiccas and then sailed to Potidaea, where they landed. Perdiccas and 200 of the cavalry joined up with Aristeus and marched to Potidaea to confront Archestratus.

Aristeus's Corinthian troops enjoyed some success when they subdued part of the Athenian line; overall, though, the Athenians were victorious. A reserve force of Potidaeans, from nearby Olynthus, made an attempt to relieve Aristeus, but they too were defeated. The Corinthians and Potidaeans lost about 300 men, and the Athenians about 150, including Callias. The Athenians camped outside Potidaea and were reinforced by another 1,600 hoplites under the command of Phormio. Walls and counter walls were erected by both sides: the Athenians cut off Potidaea from the sea with a naval blockade. Aristeus was convinced that the besieged city could not hold out and so he advised the citizens to evacuate by sea as soon as possible, leaving a garrison of 500 men to defend the city. His advice was ignored; Aristeus escaped and tried to help the defenders from the outside with the assistance of the Chalcidians and the Peloponnese.

In the summer of 430 BCE, the largest Athenian army yet was sent against Potidaea—a force of 4,000 hoplites, 300 cavalrymen, 100 triremes and fifty ships from Lesbos and Chios commanded by Hagnon. By 430 BCE, the worst possible thing happened—plague had beset Athens, and Hagnon's army spread it to Potidaia, where it infected the troops maintaining the siege; the plague killed 1,050 of his 4,000 men. After spending at least a month outside Potidaea, Hagnon gave up and returned to Athens.

Starvation finally ended the siege. By the winter of 430–429 BCE, cases of cannibalism were recorded in the city. The Athenians were clearly increasingly impatient with the siege, which was swiftly depleting their treasury, and had already cost them 2,000 talents and forced them to maintain a large and costly army in the northern Aegean. The lenient surrender terms reflect this antipathy: the Potidaeans, their wives and children, and auxiliary troops were allowed to leave the city as free people; each woman was allowed to take two garments with her, each man a single garment, as well as a fixed sum of money for the journey. The Athenians kept Potidaea, eventually resettling the city with their own colonists.[19]

This is the battle in which Socrates is alleged to have saved the life of Alcibiades:

When he was very young, Alcibiades was a soldier in the expedition against Potidaea, where Socrates camped in the same tent with him, and stood next to him in battle. Once there was a sharp skirmish, in which they both behaved with notable bravery. When Alcibiades was wounded, Socrates threw himself in front of him to protect him, and beyond any question saved him and his weapons from the enemy, and so in all justice might have challenged the prize of valour. But the generals seemed keen to adjudge the honour to Alcibiades, because of his rank; Socrates, who desired to increase his thirst after glory of a noble kind, was the first to give evidence for him, and pressed them to crown him, and to decree to him the complete suit of armour.[20]

Indeed, Socrates was something of a veteran, serving as an Athenian hoplite, and distinguishing himself in a number of decisive battles during the Peloponnesian war. Socrates's military service is described in Plato's dialogues and in Diogenes Laertius's chapters on Socrates and Xenophon in *Lives and Opinions*. Xenophon's *Memorabilia* and Aristophanes's *The Clouds* caricatures Socrates and alludes to the battle of Delium in which Socrates fought.[21]

Plato's *Apology* has Socrates himself cite his service as a hoplite in the Athenian army during the siege of Potidaea, the Athenian attack on Delium (424 BCE), and the expedition to defend the Athenian colony of Amphipolis (422 BCE). In Plato's *Laches*, the eponymous general gives an eyewitness account of Socrates's valour in the battle of Delium.[22] In Plato's *Symposium*, Alcibiades describes Socrates's courage in the battles of Potidaea and Delium.[23] Xenophon describes Socrates during the siege of Athens in his *Apology*.[24] Elsewhere, Socrates expatiates authoritatively on military training and tactics. Socrates, then, was clearly an authority on military matters.

The Corinthians asked the Spartans to call a meeting of members of the Peloponnesian League in 432 BCE to give an opportunity for those states nursing grievances with Athens to voice their complaints in the Spartan assembly. Athens sent an uninvited delegation, which also held the floor at one point. Thucydides tells us that the Corinthians condemned Sparta's inertia, warning them that if they continued to remain inactive while the Athenians were active, they would soon find themselves without allies.[25] The Athenians, for their part, reminded the Spartans of their record against Persia, encouraging Sparta to seek arbitration within the provisions of the Thirty Years' Peace.[26] Notwithstanding, a majority of the Spartan assembly voted that the Athenians had broken the peace, making what was essentially a declaration of war.

Despite it all, the king of Sparta, Archidamus II (r. 476–427 BCE), kept trying to deflect a war. He dispatched a new delegation to Athens with a brief to get the Athenians to submit to Sparta's demands. The delegation, however, was refused entry to Athens.[27] A frustrated Archidamus now invaded Attica only to find the place devoid of Athenians. Pericles had anticipated Archidamus's plans for devastation and evacuated the entire population of the region inside the walls of Athens.[28] It is easy to underestimate just how huge a life-changing move this was for the farmers and landowners around Athens. They had to leave everything, and to leave everything to the prey of the Spartans in exchange for a new life in a packed urban Athens; not surprisingly, there was much discontent.[29]

In an attempt to placate the opposition, Pericles posted a fleet of 100 ships to plunder the coasts of the Peloponnese and tasked his cavalry with protecting the devastated farms closest to the walls of the city.[30]

We can divide the resumption of the Peloponnesian War in 429 BCE into three phases: the first phase, the Archidamian War (Thucydides's 'ten-year war'), saw Sparta repeatedly invade the region of Attica around Athens, while Pericles's strategy was to reciprocate by having Athens's navy launch raid after raid on the coast of the Peloponnese.[31] Strabo goes further when he calls the first part of the Archidamian War 'the Pachetian War' after the Athenian General Paches and the revolt of Mytilene.[32]

It was Archidamus who, in 446 BCE, negotiated with Pericles on the Thirty Years' Peace, bringing the First Peloponnesian War to an end. It seems Archidamus strove to find a diplomatic solution and prevent or delay the war. However, his wise words—'If we begin the war in haste, we'll have many delays before we end it, owing to our lack of preparation'—were ignored by the Spartan war party; Archidamus was taking a longer view than his opponents when he predicted 'they would bequeath [the conflict] to their children'. Other Spartans, including the ephor Sthenelaedas, saw war as inevitable and argued for an immediate Spartan attack; Athens, it was said, could be subdued if the Spartans lay waste the countryside around Athens.

Archidamus invaded Attica in command of the Peloponnesian forces in the summers of 431 BCE, 430 BCE, and 428 BCE; in 429 BCE, he also besieged Plataea. Archidamus was succeeded on the Spartan throne by his son, Agis II.

These invasions, of course, were not much more than short incursions. The Spartans had to return home to bring in the harvests and the disaffected helots could not be left to their own devices for too long. The longest Spartan invasion, in 430 BCE, lasted a mere forty days.

Pericles strategy was to avoid, wherever possible, open battle with the highly trained Spartans and their superior hoplite numbers, and to deploy the superior Athenian fleet to burn Peloponnesian agriculture and sack cities. On the other hand, Archidamus duly deprived Athens of the productive, fertile land around their city; crucially, though, the city still had access to the sea as a vital lifeline. Nevertheless, many citizens abandoned their farms and, fatally, moved inside the Long Walls, which now connected Athens to its port of Piraeus and Phalerum. The city of Athens was now very seriously overcrowded. The devastation of Athenian farmlands put severe strain on the city's treasury, burdened by paying for the naval expeditions and grain imports.

The Long Walls (6 kilometres in length) were critical to Athenian strategy. They gave Athens a link to the sea and prevented it from being besieged by land. The walls had been finally completed in the mid-fifth century BCE in the aftermath of the Athenian defeat at Tanagra, wrecked by the Spartans in 403 BCE after the defeat of Athens in the Peloponnesian War, and rebuilt again with the support of the Persians during the Corinthian War. With the walls completed, Athens was now effectively an island within the mainland; to capture it, any enemy would need an effective navy as well as an army.

The walls continued to serve the Athenians well throughout the early part of the Peloponnesian War, until the seizure of Spartan hostages in 425 BCE, during the Athenian success at Pylos. After Pylos, the Spartans had to suspend their annual incursions until 413 BCE: Spartan invasion would spell the execution of Spartan hostages.

In 413 BCE, the Spartans took possession of a fort at Decelea; the resulting garrison force there constituted a constant threat to Athens who now could only supply the city by sea. Athens was still smarting from the disastrous outcome of the Sicilian Expedition and so modified their walls; they abandoned the Athens–Phaleron Wall for the two Piraeus Walls. Quite simply, the Long Walls, and the access to Piraeus, were the only thing protecting Athens from defeat. Sparta finally woke up to the reality that they could not subjugate Athens with an army alone and so built a navy with which to defeat the Athenians at sea. This strategy was successfully realised at Aegospotami, where they severed the Athenian lines of supply and forced them to surrender. Significantly, one of the crucial terms of this surrender was the destruction of the Long Walls in 404 BCE. The peace treaty that was negotiated saw the end of Athenian naval superiority. Xenophon reports much jubilation to the accompaniment of flute girls as the walls came down.

At the end of the first year of the war, Pericles delivered his famous Funeral Oration (431 BCE). It stands as an emblem for the struggle for democracy, civic pride, and patriotism. It is to this day widely studied in political theory, history, and classical studies and formed the basis for Abraham Lincoln's Gettysburg Address during the American Civil War, in 1863.[33]

Our constitution does not copy the laws of neighbouring states; we are rather a pattern to others than imitators ourselves. Its administration favours the many instead of the few; this is why it is called a democracy. If we look to the laws, they afford equal justice to all in their private differences; if no social standing, advancement in public life falls to reputation for capacity, class considerations not being allowed to interfere with merit; nor again does poverty bar the way, if a man is able to serve the state, he is not hindered by the obscurity of his condition. The freedom which we enjoy in our government extends also to our ordinary life … But all this ease in our private relations does not make us lawless as citizens. Against this fear is our chief safeguard, teaching us to obey the magistrates and the laws, particularly such as regard the protection of the injured, whether they are actually on the statute book, or belong to that code which, although unwritten, yet cannot be broken without acknowledged disgrace.

Further, we provide plenty of means for the mind to refresh itself from business. We celebrate games and sacrifices all the year round, and the elegance of our private establishments forms a daily source of pleasure and helps to banish the spleen; while the magnitude of our city draws the produce of the world into our harbour, so that to the Athenian the fruits of other countries are as familiar a luxury as those of his own …

In short, I say that as a city we are the school of Hellas, while I doubt if the world can produce a man who, where he has only himself to depend upon, is equal to so many emergencies, and graced by so happy a versatility, as the Athenian … For Athens alone of her contemporaries is found when tested to be greater than her reputation, and alone gives no occasion to her assailants to blush at the antagonist by whom they have been worsted, or to her subjects to question her title by merit to rule. Rather, the admiration of the present and succeeding ages will be ours, since we have not left our power without witness, but have shown it by mighty proofs; and far from needing a Homer for our panegyrist, or other of his craft whose verses might charm for the moment only for the impression which they gave to melt at the touch of fact, we have forced every sea and land to be the highway of our daring, and everywhere, whether for evil or for good, have left imperishable monuments behind us. Such is the Athens for which these men, in the assertion of their resolve not to lose her, nobly fought and died; and well may every one of their survivors be ready to suffer in her cause.

Thucydides, *Peloponnesian War*, 2.34–36 trans. Paul Halsall

The funeral speech as part of a public funeral in honour the war dead was an established Athenian practice by the late fifth century.[34] The remains of the dead were kept in tents for three days so that offerings could be made. The bodies were cremated soon after death but the bones were kept for the funeral at the end of the year. A funeral procession took place, with ten cypress coffins carrying the remains, one for each of the Athenian tribes, and another for the remains that could not be identified. Finally, they were buried at a public grave at Kerameikos and a suitably solemn speech was delivered by a leading Athenian citizen.

Several funeral orations from classical Athens survive, which would confirm Thucydides's statement that this was a regular feature of Athenian funerary custom in wartime. They are the funeral orations of Lysias, Demosthenes, and Hyperides; Plato was the author of a satirical version of a funeral oration, the *Menexenus*.

The speech eulogises Athens and glorifies Athenian achievements; its purpose was to boost morale among the military and citizenry alike in a city at war. In his speech, Pericles urges the citizens to go on backing war, reminding them that the fallen soldiers gave their lives in the protection of Athens, its citizens, and its freedom. Moreover, he pointed out that Athens was different from everywhere else, not least because of its democratic institutions. Fighting for one's country was a great honour; he extols the soldiers for their unstinting and selfless pursuit of their duty.

If Pericles's stirring speech was a force for the good in war-torn Athens, then what was to follow the next year had completely the opposite effect. What no one—Spartan or Athenian—could have predicted was the devastating impact an outbreak of plague had on the course of the war. In 430 BCE, plague struck Athens, spreading relentlessly and remorselessly through the packed city. This plague was a major contributory factor in Athens's defeat: it exterminated over 30,000 citizens, sailors, and soldiers, including Pericles and his sons, Paralus and Xanthippus. Between one-third and two-thirds of the Athenian population died. Athenian manpower was drastically depleted and even foreign mercenaries refused to hire themselves out to a city reduced to its knees with plague. Sparta abandoned its planned invasion of Attica for fear of contagion.

Thucydides's description of the plague in Athens is a shockingly realistic and vivid account of a human disaster, the like of which the city had never suffered before.[35] Its appearance so soon after the stirring and patriotic Funeral Oration lends it even more realism and horror in its description of the frailty of human life; symptoms included the following:

people in good health were all of a sudden attacked by violent heats in the head, and redness and inflammation in the eyes, the inward parts, such as the throat or tongue, becoming bloody and emitting an unnatural and fetid breath … followed by sneezing and hoarseness, after which the pain soon reached the chest, and produced a hard cough. When it fixed in the stomach, it upset it; and discharges of bile of every kind named by physicians ensued … In most cases also an ineffectual retching followed.

Though many lay unburied, birds and beasts would not touch them, or died after tasting them [...]. The bodies of dying men lay one upon another, and half-dead creatures reeled about the streets and gathered round all the fountains in their longing for water. The sacred places also in which they had quartered themselves were full of corpses of persons who had died there, just as they were; for, as the disaster passed all bounds, men, not knowing what was to become of them, became equally contemptuous of the gods' property and the gods' dues. All the burial rites before in use were entirely upset, and they buried the bodies as best they could. Many from want of the proper appliances, through so many of their friends having died already, had recourse to the most shameless sepultures: sometimes getting the start of those who had raised a pile, they threw their own dead body upon the stranger's pyre and ignited it; sometimes they tossed the corpse which they were carrying on the top of another that was burning, and so went off.

There have been various suggestions as to what the plague actually was, including ebola haemorrhagic fever, glanders, typhus, typhoid, anthrax, measles, and toxic shock syndrome or smallpox.[36] These theories are, however, pointless as Thucydides himself declares:

All speculation as to its origin and its causes, if causes can be found adequate to produce so great a disturbance, I leave to other writers, whether lay or professional; for myself, I shall simply set down its nature, and explain the symptoms by which perhaps it may be recognized by the student, if it should ever break out again. This I can the better do, as I had the disease myself, and watched its operation in the case of others.

Thucydides 2, 48

Thucydides describes the collapse of social morality saying that people stopped obeying the law since they were already living under a death sentence. Similarly, people started spending money indiscriminately. Generally, the Athenians elected not to behave honorably because most did not expect to live long enough to be rewarded for having done so. To some extent, Pericles was blamed for the plague too; he was relieved of his command temporarily and fined between fifteen and fifty talents.[37]

The untimely death of Pericles saw a change in Athenian strategy: gone was Pericles's conservative and cautious approach to be replaced by a more aggressive strategy, which entailed taking the war to Sparta and its allies. The hawkish Cleon was a key player in this change, supported by the general Demosthenes. The naval assaults on the Peloponnese continued apace.

The first shot across the Spartan bows was at the battle of Spartolus in Chaldicice in Thrace to the north-west of Potidaea, where in 429 BCE, the Athenians advanced with an army of 2,000 hoplites and 200 cavalrymen under the command of Xenophon; these were complemented by a force of hoplites and auxiliary troops from Olynthus, along with peltasts from Chusis, and some troops from Spartolus itself. The Athenians were aided by a pro-Athenian faction within Spartolus. The defenders clashed with the Athenians who defeated the hoplites and auxiliaries from Olynthus and forced them back into the city. The Athenians were still very much in the battle. Reinforcement peltasts arrived from Olynthus and the light troops from Spartolus launched a new attack on the Athenians, who were forced to retreat back to their baggage train. Things started to go badly wrong for the Athenians—whenever the Athenian hoplites attacked their opponents, the agile peltasts simply melted away; whenever the Athenians then retreated the enemy javelins rained down on them and the enemy cavalry charged them. The Athenians broke formation, and survivors fled in disarray to Potidaea. The Athenians suffered 430 casualties and all of their generals were slain.[38]

That same summer, the tables were turned at the battle of Stratus when the Spartans, encouraged by their allies in the north-west of Greece—the Ambraciots (colonists of Corinth) and the Chaonians—tried to expel the Athenians from Acarnania, at the north-west of the entrance to the Gulf of Corinth. The plan was for a joint land and naval operation in which the Spartans and their allies were to invade Acarnania from the Gulf of Ambracia to the north, while their fleet would patrol off the coast in order to prevent the Acarnanians from attacking. The allied army came together at Leucas, an island outside the gulf of Ambracia; it comprised 1,000 Peloponnesians and a further 2,000 allies: Greek troops from Ambracia, Leucas and Anactorium, and non-Greek soldiers from the Chaonian, Paravaean, and Orestian tribes—all commanded by the Spartan admiral Cnemus. The Acarnanians appealed to Athenian Phormio for help, but he was unwilling to leave Naupactus undefended.

Cnemus moved south from Argos, sacked the village of Limnaea, and then assailed Stratus. His plan was to negotiate a settlement and for his three divisions to camp close together near the city, but the impetuous Chaonians in the central division tried to capture Stratus in a surprise attack. The defenders of Stratus, seeing a chance of victory because of this split within the enemy, set a trap in which the Chaonians were attacked from the town and ambushed from the wings. The Chaonians broke and fled. The more lightly equipped Acarnanias refused to be drawn against the hoplites, preferring to pelt them from a distance. Cnemus was forced to retreat back to the Anapus river, 9 miles outside Stratus from where he negotiated an armistice to collect the bodies of the fallen, and then retreated back north. To make matters worse, elements of Cnemus's fleet were defeated at Chalcis.[39]

The Peloponnesians tracked westward along the south coast of the Gulf of Corinth with the Athenian fleet following them on the northern shore. The Peloponnesians, with forty-seven ships, disregarded the twenty Athenian vessels on the other side of the gulf; that night they sailed through the strait between Rhium and Cape Antirrhium, hoping to elude the Athenians. The Athenians, however, gave chase and caught the Peloponnesians in the open waters of the Gulf of Patras.

The next battle that summer was the Battle of Rhium (also known as the battle of Chalcis), a naval engagement between an Athenian fleet led by Phormio, based at Naupactus, and a Peloponnesian fleet made up of contingents from various allied states, each with their own commanders. The Peloponnesian fleet of forty-seven triremes was attacked by Phormio when attempting to cross over to the northern shore of the Gulf of Patras to attack Acarnania in an offensive in northwestern Greece. The smaller numbers of the Athenian fleet (twenty ships) was more than compensated by their vastly more experienced crews and by the fact that they were led by a single commander.

The real problem, though, for the Peloponnesians was that many of their vessels were transports rather than warships. Their strategy was to circle round together for defence, prows facing out, but Phormio sailed around the Peloponnesians, forcing them closer and closer together until their oars clashed, immobilising them. When a favourable wind blew up, the Athenians attacked, picking off the Peloponnesians and capturing twelve of their ships.[40]

Sparta's naval debut had not gone well. Nevertheless, the Spartans responded by putting together a larger fleet of seventy-seven triremes; meanwhile, Athens dispatched twenty ships to reinforce Phormio via Crete, where they were held up for some time with orders to attack Cydonia; Phormio had to fight the next battle with the same twenty ships as he had in the first.[41] One week later, the two navies confronted each other again, this time at the Messenian city of Naupactus.[42]

The surviving Peloponnesian ships had escaped west to Cyllene, at the north-western extremity of the Peloponnese, where the fleet that had taken part in the unsuccessful invasion of Acarnania joined them. Further reinforcements arrived, bringing the numbers up to seventy-seven warships. They were accompanied by a commission sent out from Sparta to offer advice; it included the famous general Brasidas.

The two fleets weighed anchored on opposite sides of the Gulf of Rhium, with the twenty Athenian ships on the northern side of the gulf and the Peloponnesians on the Peloponnesian side. The two navies spent the next six or seven days facing each other off with less than a mile of sea separating them. Phormio vowed not to fight in the narrow waters of the Gulf of Rhium, where the enemy's superior numbers might well be decisive.

However, the Peloponnesians forced Phormio to sail straight into those straits, teasing the Athenians out from their anchorage at Antirrhium by sailing into the Gulf of Corinth, manoeuvring as if they were about to attack the undefended Athenian base at Naupactus. Phormio's dilemma was that if he failed to respond to the Peloponnesian move, he would expose Naupactus to capture; on the other hand, if he did react, he would be forced into the narrow waters. Phormio chose to save Naupactus and the Athenian fleet sailed east in single file with their Messenian hoplites shadowing them on the coast.

With both fleets in the Gulf of Rhium the Peloponnesian commanders sprung their trap, racing across the gulf at the Athenians, hoping to pin the entire Athenian fleet against the northern shore of the gulf. However, eleven of the twenty Athenian ships escaped into the wider waters of the Gulf of Corinth; the nine others were forced onto the shore where some of the crews were killed. One ship was captured with its entire crew, others had been abandoned and were towed away, while some were rescued by the Messenians on the northern shore.

The twenty swiftest Peloponnesian ships sailed in hot pursuit of the surviving eleven Athenian ships. Ten reached Naupactus. The last Athenian ship was almost in the harbour with the Peloponnesians pursuing it closely when it came alongside a merchant ship anchored outside the harbour. The clever captain used the merchant ship to protect his flanks while he turned, spinning his ship 270 degrees, ramming the first of the pursuers in the side, and sinking it. This single piece of naval brilliance greatly shook the Peloponnesians while it emboldened the Athenians and turned the tide of the battle. Confusion overcame the Peloponnesians; some rowers dropped their oars to allow the main body to catch up, thus becoming immobile and vulnerable; other ships ran aground. The ten Athenian ships in the harbour sped out and joined the attack. The Athenians chased the Peloponnesians, capturing six of them with their crews, and liberating all but one of the ships they had lost earlier in the battle. Both sides claimed victory; however, the thoroughly demoralised Peloponnesians took refuge in Corinth. The twenty Athenian ships that had been sent as reinforcements via Crete then arrived; the Athenians controlled the Gulf of Corinth, for the time being at least. The Athenian victory at Naupactus ended Sparta's attempt to challenge Athens in the Corinthian gulf and the North-west, securing Athenian naval superiority in the region.

In 428 BCE, Mytilene and most of the other towns on the island of Lesbos revolted against the Athenians. The Spartans were never far away, stirring things up in the background. Boeotia was involved; the aim of the Mytileneans was to unite Lesbos against Athens. The outcome was the siege of Mytiline (428–427 BCE) and two debates on the most appropriate punishment to be meted out to the rebels.

Lesbos was a member of the Athenian alliance, but not of the Athenian Empire; the cities and towns on the island had retained their independence, paid no taxes to Athens as empire members did but were obliged to furnish contingents to the fleet and the army. The inhabitants of Lesbos had harboured desires to revolt before the outbreak of the Peloponnesian War, but relented when support from Sparta was not forthcoming.

Mytilene made careful and comprehensive plans to prepare their city for the revolt and the inevitable war. The fortifications were strenghtened and new warships were built; supplies were imported and mercenaries enlisted from Pontus. Although support this time was guaranteed from Sparta and from Boeotia, there was opposition to the revolt on the island itself from Methymna and from the nearby island of Tenedos who both remained loyal to Athens. They warned the Athenians that the Mytilenians were preparing to revolt.[43]

This unwelcome news arrived in Athens while the city was beset by the plague, and so there was some procrastination. The Athenians were determined not to allow their loyal ally Methymna to be subdued by the Mytileneans, and so the Athenian fleet blockaded Mytilene by sea, hoping to surprise the Mytilenians unawares while in the throes of celebrating the feast of the Malean Apollo. However, the Mytilenians got wind of this plan and were able to face the enemy fleet who were at readiness for battle. One short naval skirmish outside the harbour later, the Athenian commanders settled on an armistice, and a Mytilenian delegation was sent to Athens with the brief to convince the Athenians to withdraw from Lesbos. A second delegation was simultaneously dispatched to Sparta. The embassy to Athens was unsuccessful because Athens as leaders of their empire could not desert Methymna. Athens and Lesbos were now at war.

The Mytilenians struck first when they attacked the Athenians who were camped nearby. Mytilene won but retreated back within the walls.[44] When reinforcements arrived for the Athenians, they were able to construct two fortified camps, which between them blocked the two harbours of Mytilene; the land side of the city, however, was still open.

While the embassy to Athens failed, that to Sparta was successful. The Spartans eventually agreed to support Mytilene and raised a large fleet: the strategy was to open a second front by invading Attica while the Athenians were busy at Lesbos.[45] In response, the Athenians raised a new fleet of 100 warships, which deterred the Peloponnesian fleet from taking further naval action.

The siege of Mytilene began in the autumn of 428 BCE, but the Mytileneans pressed on with campaigning on the island and made an unsuccessful attempt to capture Methymna. A counterattack by Methymna against Antissa also failed. Athens now tightned the screw on Mytilene by posting 1,000 hoplites under Paches to prosecute the siege. Paches built a single wall around the city, with forts; the harbour was blockaded; and the siege was firmly in place.

The only real hope the Mytilenians had was Alcidas's fleet of forty-two Spartan ships, but this delayed setting sail until the summer of 427 BCE; it was the only effective help they received from Sparta, made even less useful by taking a slow and circuitous route around the Peloponnesian coast. The Mytilenians however had been encouraged, groundlessly it turned out, when the Spartan Salaethus slipped through the Athenian lines in a trireme to let them know that the Spartans were coming.[46] He took over in the city and, with food running low, he opted for a mass breakout.[47] Accordingly, hoplite armour and weaponry was issued to all the citizens, most of whom had only ever served as light troops. The citizens refused to comply and demanded that the authorities distribute any remaining food supplies; if not, they would negotiate terms with the Athenians independently of the government. Consequently, the Mytilenians were forced to surrender and began negotiations with the Athenians. Paches agreed to hold off executing, imprisoning, or enslaving anyone until the Athenian people had decided what to do. The Mytilenians were allowed to send envoys to Athens to plead their case, on the condition that they then agreed to comply to whatever punishment the Athenians decided on.

Athens herself was under increasing financial strain, having to pay the expenses for the siege; the desperate situation required desperate fiscal remedies: they introduced an *eisphora*, direct tax, on their own citizens—anathema to the Greek in the street; then they increased the tribute payable by its subjects, and twelve ships were sent out to collect, a measure made all the more unpopular by attempting to collect several months early. One of the generals commanding these ships was murdered in Caria.[48]

Two crucial debates followed, showing Athens acting in a much more aggressive and punitive light. The first was angry and vindictive with the Athenian *ecclesia* voting to exterminate the entire population of Mytilene. A trireme was dispatched to the seemingly doomed city for the ghastly task.

Salaethus was captured and sent to Athens with the Mytilenaean rebels. When the captives arrived at Athens the Athenians instantly put Salaethus to death, although he made various offers, and among other things promised to procure the withdrawal of the Peloponnesians from Plataea, which was still blockaded. A discussion was held concerning the other captives, and in their indignation, the Athenians determined to put to death not only the men then at Athens, but all the grown-up citizens of Mytilene, and to enslave the women and children; the act of the Mytilenaeans appeared inexcusable, because they were not subjects like the other states that had revolted, but free.[49]

Having slept on it, though, the *ecclesia*'s anger had subsided to some degree when they resumed the debate the following day. Cleon, son of Cleaenetus, spoke for the hardliners while Deodotus, son of Eucrates, took a more moderate line. Cleon proposed a reign of terror, to instil fear in Athens's allies by demonstrating the reprisals and death squads that awaited any others contemplating revolt. Diodotus reasoned that this would be counterproductive: future rebels in a siege situation would see that nothing was to be gained from surrendering early, encouraging them to hold out and fight on to the death—costly in terms of money and lives. Diodotus won the day in a close vote and a second trireme was hastily dispatched to convey the change of plan to the crew of the first trireme. Speed was of the essence; it was guaranteed when a handsome reward was promised to the crew of the second ship if it was able to catch the first. Meanwhile, in Mytilene, the orders for the mass execution were delivered, but the second trireme arrived just in time to overturn the execution order before it was carried out in all its horror.

Although the ethnic cleansing originally proposed was now not an option, the new reprisals were robust and repressive enough: they stipulated that 1,000 (probably more like thirty in reality) or so of the leading rebels be executed. The Mytilenean navy was requisitioned and the city walls were levelled. The island of Lesbos, apart from territory held by Methymna, was carved up into 3,000 *kleroi*, 300 of which were to be kept sacred to the gods, while the rest were redistributed by lot to *klerouchs* who were sent to the island and then sub-let the land to the locals at an annual rate of two minae; the locals were then required to work their lands.[50] Athens also took over the Mytilenian possessions on the Ionian coast.

Above: Assyrian warship, 700–692 BCE. From Nineveh in the British Museum. This ship was by Sennacherib. It is a bireme with two levels of oars. Shields are fastened around the superstructure, just like on the fortifications of some city walls. The pointed bow is a ram for barging into enemy ships. It was probably built by Phoenicians.

Right: Detail from the Archers' Frieze in Darius's palace in Susa. Glazed siliceous bricks, *c.* 510 BCE. From the Louvre Museum.

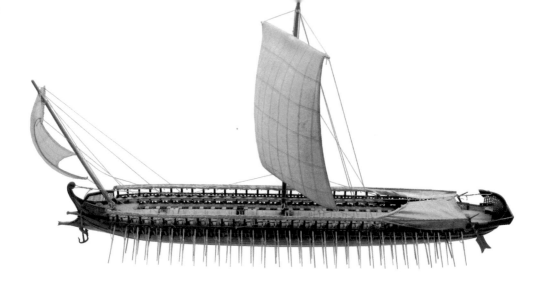

Above: Model of a Greek trireme in the Deutsches Museum, Munich.

Below left: Greek iron swords. The one on the right is double-edged with a hilt in the shape of a bird's head.

Below right: Weapons found on the battlefield at Marathon, including a small dagger with a bone hilt and the bone scabbard; bronze arrowheads; and a lead sling shot stamped with a thunderbolt and the name Zoilos. All from the British Museum.

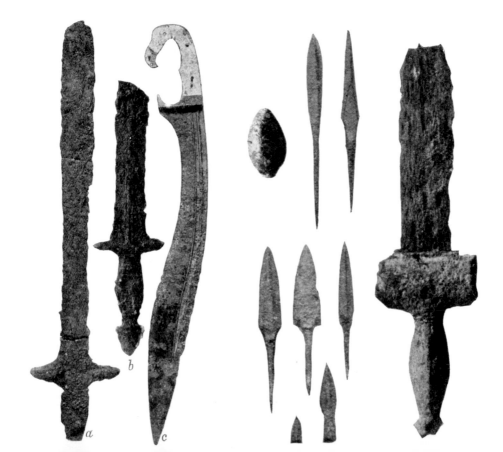

Above: Fallow Deer Painter: Phalanx. An Attic black-figure Tyrrhenic amphora, *c.* 560 BCE. Staatliche Antikensammlungen, Munich.

Right: Four-horse fighting chariot on a small scent jar (*lekythos*); Athenian, from the second half of the sixth century BCE. Il Museo Eoliano di Lipari.

Above: Ancient Greek helmets. Top, from left to right: Illyrian type helmet, Corinthian helmet. Bottom, from left to right: Phrygian type helmet, Pileus, Chalcidian helmet. Staatliche Antikensammlungen, Munich.

Below: Hoplites fighting. From the Louvre.

Above: Rider Painter: Achilles watching out for Troilus or Cadmus fighting the Theban dragon. Laconian black-figure cup, *c.* 550–540 BCE. Louvre Museum, Department of Greek, Etruscan and Roman Antiquities.

Below: Detail from the Chigi-vase. Hoplites go to battle to the accompaniment of music. From the seventh century BCE.

Above: Dionysos (left) with ivy crown, and thyrsos attacking a Giant, Attic red-figure pelike, *c.* 475–425 BCE. From Nola.

Below: Soldiers marching off to war while a woman waves goodbye, painted on the 'Warrior Vase' crater of Mycenae. Late Bronze Age, twelfth century BCE, National Archaeological Museum of Athens.

Above: Kneeling warrior with unsheathed sword: Achilles waiting for Troilus? Tondo of an Attic black-figure kylix, *c.* 560 BCE. Staatliche Antikensammlungen, Munich.

Below: Achilles Lamenting the Death of Patroclus (1734) by Gavin Hamilton (1723–1798). National Gallery of Scotland, Edinburgh. Achilles refuses the comfort of his Greek comrades as he grieves over the dead body of his devoted friend, Patroclus, who was killed by the Trojan Hector. The huge size of the painting—227.30 × 391.20 cm (framed: 286.30 × 424.20 × 11.50 cm)—conveys his ambition to depict episodes from Homer's *Iliad* in an epic mode. Hamilton painted six *Iliad* canvases, each commissioned by a different patron.

Above: Le soldat de Marathon: Pheidippides giving word of victory after the Battle of Marathon (1869) by Luc-Olivier Merson (1846–1920).

Below: Léonidas aux Thermopyles (1814) by Jacques-Louis David (1748–1825), Louvre Museum. Nearly fifteen years in the painting, it depicts the sacrifice of Leonidas and 300 Spartans who were massacred resisting the Persian armies when they invaded Greece. We see Leonidas centre stage, naked, and getting ready for combat. On the left, a soldier carves on the wall of rock the famous phrase, 'Go, passer-by, to Sparta tell/Obedient to her law we fell'. Soldiers embrace before meeting their death, while others equip themselves with weapons or shields. In the background, you can see the ships of the Persian army.

Above: View of the Thermopylae Pass at the Phocian Wall. In ancient times, the coastline was where the modern road lies, or even closer to the mountain, 15 March 2011. (*Fkerasar*)

Below: Essay on the Battle of Plataea for the Travels of Anacharsis (1784) by Jean-Denis Barbié du Bocage (1760–1825): a colour map showing the Battle of Plataea fought between an alliance of the Greek city-states, including Sparta, Athens, Corinth, and Megara, and the Persian Empire of Xerxes I. The map shows Mount Cithaeron, where the tide of the battle turned. It also indicates the camp of Mardonius, the Temple of Ceres, Road to Thespiae, Temple of Apollo, and other important landmarks. Prepared by de Bocage in 1786 to illustrate the *Travels of Anarcharsis*.

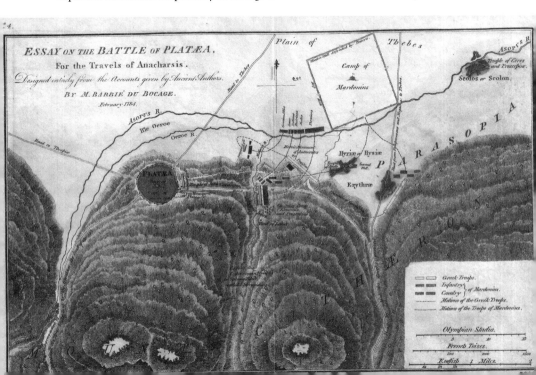

Above: Idealised bust of Pericles. Roman copy of the second century CE after a Greek original of between 440 and 430 BCE by Kresilas. British Museum. From the Villa Adriana, Tivoli.

Right: Herma of Demosthenes. Copy of a statue in the agora of Athens; original work by Polyeuktos (*c.* 280 BCE). Height: 189 cm (74.4 inches). Glyptothek, Munich. Found in 1825 in Circus of Maxentius.

Title page from *Eight bookes of the Peloponnesian Warre written by Thucydides the sonne of Olorus*. 'Interpreted with faith and diligence immediately out of the Greeke by Thomas Hobbes secretary to ye late Earle of Deuonshire. Published: London, imprinted [at Eliot's Court Press] for Hen: Seile, and are to be sold at the Tigres Head in Paules Churchyard, 1629'. Houghton Library, Harvard University.

Death of Alcibiades (1839) by Michele De Napoli (1808–1892). Museo Archeologico Nazionale, Naples.

Above: Plague in an Ancient City (*c.* 1652) by Michael Sweerts (1618–1664). The painting is thought to be the plague of Athens. Los Angeles County Museum of Art. 'It depicts the appalling devastation of the plague. The cityscape derives from Sebastiano Serlio's design for a tragic stage from Book II of the Architettura (Paris, 1545). Sweerts's tragic theme is set in a piazza filled with figures in classical poses and drapery. The dead and dying are surrounded by figures kneeling in prayer, crying out in anguish, or awestruck with horror. The motifs of the infant suckling his dead mother, in the left foreground, and the man holding his nose, in the right middleground, derive from Marcantonio Raimondi's engraving after Raphael, known as Il Morbetto which was one of the most influential plague compositions in Italy. The woman on the far-left rests her head on her hand, in a pose traditionally associated with melancholy'. (worcesterart.org/Hope/sweerts_plague_detail.htm)

Below: Front view of an Attic black-figure lekythos, showing a hoplite preparing to leave home for battle with family members, 530–520 BCE. (*Ure Museum of Greek Archaeology, University of Reading*)

Above: Detail of a Greek warrior, on an Attic, black-figure lekythos showing '(Herakles) attacking a kneeling Amazon. This scene is flanked by two other battle scenes. On the left side, an Amazon is attacking a Greek. He is wearing a cuirass, helmet, he is holding his spear and his shield and he is shown ready to fall down. The Amazon has attacked him with her spear. She is wearing a helmet and a short chiton. On the right, an Amazon and a Greek are shown in profile running towards the left, projecting their spears. The Amazon is wearing a ahsort chiton and a helmet. She is holding her shield, covering large part of her body', 525–500 BCE. (*Ure Museum of Greek Archaeology*)

Below: Detail view of the exterior of a Euboean black-figure *lekanis* depicting a fight between three warriors with female onlookers, 550 BCE. (*Ure Museum of Greek Archaeology*)

Above: Warriors on the west pediment on the temple at Aegina, now in the Staatliche Antikensammlungen, Munich. It shows two warriors fighting over a fallen comrade on either side of Athena.

Left: Black-figure amphora in the British Museum depicting a combat scene, 540–530 BCE. Signed by Exekias. Made in Athens and found at Vulci, Etruria (Lazio).

Opposite above: Amazon mosaic from Paphos found in the Orpheus House. Note the exposed right breast, the Phrygian cap, and the double-headed axe. Some believe that this is Hippolyta in the ninth labour of Hercules.

Below: A Spartan Woman Giving a Shield to Her Son (1805) by Jean Jacques François Lebarbier. A Spartan woman bidding her husband farewell in the traditional manner: 'Return carrying your shield or on it'. All elements of the painting reinforce its message of civil duty. The children playing with the warrior's lance allude to Spartan military training, which began in infancy. The simplicity of the stone-walled interior underscores the austerity of Spartan existence, while the dog is both a symbol of fidelity and a reference to the famed dogs of Sparta. (*The Portland Art Museum, Ohio*)

Spartan helmet on display
at the British Museum. The
helmet has been damaged
and the top has sustained a
blow, presumably in battle.

*Artemisia Prepares to Drink
the Ashes of her Husband,
Mausolus* (*c.* 1630),
attributed to Francesco
Furini (1604–1646). Yale
University Art Gallery.

The Mytilenean debate is one of the most celebrated debates in the history of Athenian democracy, and one of only two occasions in which Thucydides records the content, and perhaps the actual words of the speeches in the assembly.

In 427 BCE, Athens became embroiled in a revolution in Corcyra. Cocyraeans who had been taken captive by the Corinthians were allowed to return home on strict conditions, namely that they convince Corcyra to sever its ties with Athens and join the Corinthians. Furthermore, they brought Peithias, a pro-Athenian leader, to trial on charges of 'enslaving Corcyra to Athens'.[51] He was acquitted and took his revenge by prosecuting five of the accusers. However, the accused men burst in to the council and killed Peithias and sixty other people.

Street fighting broke out in the city between the democrats (assisted by the slaves) and the oligarchs, who hired mercenaries; the oligarchs were annhilated. Efforts to bring about a peaceful settlement were made by the Athenian general, Nicostratus, by way of an alliance between Corcyra and Athens. He had arrived from Naupactus with twelve of his ships. Nicostratus agreed to leave five Athenian ships to defend Corcyra while he sailed with five Corcyraean ships. The people tried to get their enemies to crew these departing ships; fearing for their lives, they took refuge as suppliants to Hera.

Four or five days later, fifty-three Peloponnesian ships under Alcidas turned up and engaged the Athenian and sixty hopelessly disorganised Corcyraean vessels. Desertions and 'blue on blue' were the order of the day. The Peloponnesians drove off the Athenian and Corcyraean ships, thirteen of which were captured, devastated the surrounding country, but did not attack the city itself. Chaos and panic reigned.

The Peloponnesians departed south on the rumour that a larger Athenian fleet was on its way. The democrats wreaked carnage, killing as many of their enemies as they could, including, iconoclastically, those taking refuge with Hera. Others committed suicide or killed each other.

> The Corcyraeans butchered [hundreds] of their fellow-citizens whom they regarded as their enemies: and although the crime imputed was that of attempting to put down the democracy, some were slain also for private hatred, others by their debtors because of the monies owed to them.[52]

The following summer, 426 BCE, the Athenians attacked the island of Melos with sixty ships and 2,000 hoplites under the generalship of Nicias. Their crime was to decline an invitation to join the Delian League after enduring some plundering by the Athenians. The operation, however, was inconclusive, so the Athenians continued to Oropus in Attica and thence over the border into Boeotia and the town of Tanagra. They rendezvoused with the main Athenian army *en route* from Athens under Hipponicus and Eurymedon. More pillage followed; the next day the Athenians overcame a combined Tanagran and Theban army, then returned victorious to Athens.[53]

Athenian aspirations in Aetolia ended in defeat at the battle of Aegitium in 426 BCE and ignominy for Demosthenes, the commander of the campaign. It started when a flotilla of thirty warships under Demosthenes was sent around the Peloponnese to operate in the north-west of Greece and the Corinthian Gulf. On arrival, Demosthenes assembled a strong allied army, with a fifteen-ship flotilla from Corcyra, Cephalonia, and Zacynthos as well as from the Acarnanians on the mainland. Much to the delight of the Acarnanians, he then blockaded the island of Leucas, a Spartan ally on an isthmus close to the entrance to the Gulf of Ambracia. The Acarnanians provided Demosthenes with reinforcements.

The large number of Messenian hoplites in his force persuaded Demosthenes to attack Aetolia, a predominantly mountainous region inland from the northern coast of the Gulf of Corinth, which had been a constant menace to them. Demosthenes found this plan attractive, firstly because it would extinguish the Aetolian threat to the Athenian naval base at Naupactus, and partly because it would facilitate his invasion of Boeotia, thus eliminating another major threat to the Athenians. The Acarnanians and Corcyraeans were not impressed by this *volte face* and refused to take part in the plan leaving Demosthenes with a force comprising Cephallenians, Messenians, Zacynthians, and 300 Athenians. He elected to launch his invasion before a contingent of light javelin-armed troops from Locris arrived, a decision with serious consequences.

Demosthenes raised his siege of Leucas and sailed east to Oeneon in Locris and then marched north-west into Aetolia, taking Potidania on the first day and Crocylium on the second day before turning west to take Tichium on the third and then shipping the booty back to Athens. The Aetolians, however, had seen it all coming and were massing their army against Demosthenes, who, undeterred, continued with his invasion, marching east to take Aegitium, 9 miles north of Oeneon.

The inhabitants of Aegitium escaped from the town and joined up with the main Aetolian army on higher ground. Demosthenes's force was, of course, deficient in javelin-armed soldiers but he did have archers. The Aetolian army, on the other hand, was almost entirely made up of lightly armoured and agile javelin-throwers who made running attacks from the hills against the Athenians and their heavy troops, retreating whenever the Athenians advanced or when they came under attack by the archers.

The turning point in the battle came when the captain of the archers was killed. The Athenians scattered and many were slain including Demosthenes's Messenian guide Chromon, which left the Athenians with no local knowledge, causing them to flee into dried-up water-courses, where they became trapped between the high, dry banks. Others rushed into a forest that was torched around them. According to Thucydides, 120 of the 300 Athenian hoplites were killed, along with Procles, the co-commander of the army. Demosthenes stayed away from Athens, shamed by his defeat.[54] The battle was a significant morale booster for Sparta and her allies in the region; Athenian interests were only salvaged by some tactical wizardry in the later defense of Naupactus and Acarnania, which helped restore Demosthenes's military reputation.

That same summer, Syracuse and Leontini were at war with each other. Leontini asked Athens for help; the Athenians sent twenty ships, ostensibly on the basis of mutual friendship: the real reason, though was to stop the supply of corn to the Peloponnesians from the west and gathering intelligence for a future invasion. The Athenian flotilla under Laches with 1,600 hoplites and eighty archers set sail for Locri, a colony of Syracuse on the toe of Italy where Laches took five Locrian ships; he then crossed to Mylae, a colony of Messana on the eastern part of the north coast of Sicily. They were met with an unsuccessful ambush laid by the two battalions of Messianans there amounting to 1,200 hoplites and 300 *psiloi*. The Messanians suffered heavy losses and lost Mylae to the Athenians who went on to take Messana unopposed.[55]

Later that year, in the winter, the Athenians marched on Inessa (Aetna), a Sicilian town garrisoned by the Syracusans.[56] When the attack failed and the Athenians withdrew, the Syracusans sallied forth and routed their attackers. About the same time, the Athenian victory at the battle of Olpae in Epirus brought an end to the Spartan campaign aimed at the conquest of Acarnania and Amfilochia. When the Spartans were defeated at Naupactus, the Spartan commander Eurylochus then adopted a plan for an invasion of Acarnania and Amphilochia as proposed by the Ambraciots, the inhabitants of the Corinthian colony of Ambracia, a city 7 miles to the north of the Gulf of Ambracia. Acarnania was between the Gulf of Corinth and the Gulf of Ambracia; Amphilochia was the region around Amphilochian Argos, a city at the south-eastern end of the Gulf of Ambracia. For their part, the Ambraciots promised to attack Amphilochian Argos; the Spartans took up a position at Proschium, in the south-west of Aetolia.

The Ambraciots advanced around the Gulf of Ambracia with 3,000 hoplites occupying a position at the fortress of Olpae; the Acarnanians moved most of their army to relieve Amphilochian Argos. One division of the army went straight to the city while the rest took up a position at Crenae, on the route that the Spartans were expected to take. Demosthenes was asked to take command of their army, and help was requested from the twenty Athenian triremes then cruising around the Peloponnese under the command of Aristotle and Hierophon.

However, Eurylochus and his Peloponnesian army took an unconventional route to Orpae. Demosthenes arrived with the twenty triremes, 200 Messenian hoplites, and sixty Athenian archers who moved towards Olpae, camping on the opposite side of a ravine from the Peloponnesian army. They stayed here for five days before coming out of their camps on the sixth day and preparing to do battle.

Demosthenes set a trap for the Peloponnesians, concealing a force of 400 hoplites and Acarnanian light troops in trees and bushes. Initially, the battle went well for Eurylochus. He soon outflanked Demosthenes and was about to surround him when Demosthenes sprang his ambush: the 400 hidden troops attacked the Peloponnesian rear, which was reduced to chaos, causing a disorderly retreat. Eurylochus was killed. The Acarnanians attacked them as they tried to retreat to Olpae and inflicted heavy casualties. Demosthenes lost about 300 men.

The replacement Peloponnesian commander, Menedaius, asked permission from Demosthenes to recover his dead and requested a truce to allow the defeated army to retreat to safety. Demosthenes granted the first request but refused the second. However, he and Menedaius secretly agreed a deal in which Menedaius, the Mantineans and the more important among the Peloponnesians were allowed to leave.[57] By doing this, he would not only weaken the Ambraciot army but would also smear the Spartans by showing how, with some clever psychological warfare, they had no qualms about deserting their allies in defeat. In the words of Thucydides. Demosthenes was able 'to discredit the Lacedaemonians and Peloponnesians with the Hellenes in those parts, as traitors and self-seekers'.[58] The select Peloponnesians retreated as agreed but their Ambraciot allies tried to join them; the Acarnanians pursued them and killed about 200 of the Ambraciots.[59]

The next day, Demosthenes discovered that a second Ambracian army was advancing to relieve Olpae, blithely unaware of the previous day's reverse. They set up camp on the lower of two steep hills on the road to the fort at Idomene, not far to the north. Demosthenes surprised them with a night attack while they slept, pretending to be the other Ambraciot army. He killed the majority; the rest fled to the hills or waded into the sea where they were captured by the twenty Athenian ships. In total, the Ambraciots lost about 1,000 men over the two days.[60] Thucydides describes this as: 'The greatest disaster to strike a single city in an equal number of days in this war.'

These two victories went some way to restoring Demosthenes's reputation back in Athens; he felt safe enough now to return to the city, taking 300 suits of enemy armour with him as a trophy. Demosthenes could easily have taken Ambracia but did not; his allies were nervous about a strong Athenian presence in the region and so the Acarnanians and Ambraciots signed a 100-year peace treaty in which each side promised to support the other against any invasion with the proviso that neither the Athenians nor Peloponnesians were involved.[61]

Meanwhile, in Sicily, the Syracusans had completed the rebuilding of their fleet and posted it to guard Messana from attack by Rhegium over the straits on the Italian mainland. With the Athenians preoccupied elsewhere, the Syracusans decided to test the waters and try for naval superiority with their thirty ships. Sixteen Athenian and eight Rhegian vessels defeated them and sank one of their ships in what has become known as the battle of the Straits of Messina.[62]

In the meantime, the Messanians attacked the Chalcidian colony of Naxos (near modern Taormina), forcing the inhabitants to take refuge within their city walls. Other Sicels came to the aid of the Naxians, which encouraged them to successfully attack the Messanians and defeat them decisively, slaying 1,000 or so in the attack and more stragglers.[63]

The Leontinians observed the turmoil the Mesanians were now in and took the opportunity to attack Messana, supported by the Athenians. However, the Messanians rallied and routed their aggressors; the Athenians disembarked from their ships in the harbour and chased the Messanians back inside their city.[64]

The battle of Pylos in 425 BCE was the first element in a two-part battle most celebrated for the unpredicatable surrender of a detachment of Spartan hoplites trapped on the island of Sphacteria. The occupation of Pylos by Demosthenes was not really the result of official Athenian foreign policy. When Messana revolted that year against Athens, the Athenians responded by sending a fleet to Sicily to quell the insurrection; forty ships under Sophocles and Eurymedom made up the complement. They were also detailed to assist Athenian democratic allies at Corcyra. Demosthenes, although not one of the official commanders, was given leave to go along in an advisory capacity; he was *strategos*-elect for the Hellenic year beginning midsummer 425.

Demosthenes, though, had already conceived a plan: he wanted to occupy the rocky headland of Pylos in the south-west of the Peloponnese, build a fort, and use it as a base from which to raid Spartan territory. The headland was in territory that had once belonged Messania. Demosthenes was sure that the Messenians would provide the garrison; furthermore, it was close to a natural harbour and well-provisioned with building materials.

Not surprisingly, when Demosthenes raised this plan with the commanders, it was flatly rejected: the generals had other, more pressing, priorities. Yet bad weather intervened on Demosthenes's behalf and the fleet had no choice but to shelter at Pylos. Demosthenes reiterated his plan, which again was officially rejected. Thucydides tells us, however, that the plan was taken up inependently by the Athenian soldiers, who of their own volition, set about fortifying the headland, largely out of boredom caused by the delay, caused by the weather. Once the fortifications were complete, the generals relented and donated Demosthenes five triremes and their crews for his garrison; these were reinforced with forty hoplites from a passing Messenian ship that stopped at Pylos. The rest of the Athenians sailed away to deal with the job in hand at Corcyra. In total, Demosthenes had 600 or so men, only ninety of whom were hoplites.

Obviously, Demosthenes was never going to get away with this cavalier and belligerent action. His occupation of Pylos took place during the annual Peloponnesian invasion of Attica. When the bad news reached the Spartan king Agis, he had no hesitation in terminating the invasion after only fifteen days, turning his armies' attention towards Pylos. The decision was made easier because his troops were short of provisions and hampered by unseasonably wet weather. Agis sent a detachment of Spartans to Pylos with his army following close behind. A Spartan fleet of forty-three ships based further north at Corcyra was also deployed and slipped past an Athenian squadron based on Zakynthos. It was clear to Demosthenes that he was about to be besieged so he summoned the fleet from Zakynthos.

The Spartans formulated two plans: plan 'A' was to attack the Athenian fortifications, which they believed would fall without too much trouble. Plan 'B' was more sophisticated and took cognizance of the fact that the headland at Pylos was at one end of Pylos Bay, which is interrupted by the island of Sphacteria running nearly 3 miles long north–south across the mouth of the bay. Although this created a good harbour, it also had the effect of restricting access to the narrow channels at either end of the island: the northern channel could accommodate only two passing ships at one time; the southern had room for eight or nine. The Spartans elected for plan 'B' and moored their ships in rows to block these two channels, with prows projecting outwards. In addition, elements of their army would blockade the Athenians on the mainland while others were stationed on Sphacteria to prevent any amphibious Athenian landings there.

Fortuitously (or was it shrewd behind the scenes planning on the part of Demosthenes?), Pylos, meanwhile, was reinforced by a privateer with a cargo of arms, and by a Messenian pinnace, which brought forty more hoplites. Demosthenes left most of his troops up in the fort but led sixty hoplites with some archers down to the beach to defend the place he considered to be the Spartans' most likely intended beachhead: the south-west corner of the peninsula where the defensive wall was weakest. Demosthenes guessed right: the Spartans attacked exactly where Demosthenes had expected with a fleet comprising the forty-three ships led by Thrasymelidas, son of Cratesciles. However, because the beach was not big enough to take them all at once, the ships could only attack in small numbers at any one time. Despite the efforts of Brasidas, the Spartans failed to establish a foothold on the beach; the attacks against the fort also failed, and after two days, the Spartans resorted to building siege engines.

In the meantime, the Athenian fleet of fifty ships was on its way while the Spartan fleet was beached inside the bay of Pylos at the mercy of the Athenians. The ensuing Athenian naval victory left the last detachment of 420 Spartan hoplites marooned on Sphacteria. Under the command of Epitades, son of Molobrus, the island was soon under attack. The only problem was that 120 of these marooned hoplites were Spartiates—crack troops who were the cream of the Spartan army and, in contrast to their peerless military reputation as elite soldiers, chose to surrender rather than fight to the death.[65]

The Spartan government was thrown into panic and envoys were sent to Sphacteria to negotiate an immediate armistice. The Spartans were allowed to take food to the men on the island; as a guarantee for good conduct, the Spartan fleet was surrendered to the Athenians, and ambassadors were sent to Athens to obtain a permanent peace. Athens threatened to execute its prestigious prisoners if Sparta invaded Attica, so the annual incursions stopped. The negotiations failed when Cleon insisted on more stringent terms than the Spartans were willing to concede: the obdurate Athenians retained the Spartan fleet and settled in to besiege the hoplites on Sphacteria. The fighting continued, but it was now evident that Sparta was not at all averse to stopping fighting when its own elite people were in danger, and with no regard for its allies. The myth of Spartan invincibility had been shattered.

The Spartans continued to attack the Athenians on Pylos, while the Athenians resumed the naval blockade of Sphacteria. For the Spartans, it was essential to get provisions to their troops. Volunteers were offered a cash reward and helots their freedom if they managed to smuggle supplies through; damaged or lost boats would be compensated. Some men sailed headlong at the beaches, damaging their boats but winning the reward. Others swam in under water, with supplies protected by skins. There was only one source of fresh water for the whole force. Winter was fast approaching and the Athenians were concerned lest they would be forced to raise the siege.

Back in Athens, the people were getting restless; the siege was dragging and Cleon was attracting more and more unpopularity, especially when he blamed Nicias (personal enemy and that year's *strategos*) for failing to take the island. Nicias responded by offering to stand down, inviting Cleon to get on with it. In the end, Cleon had no option but to go himself to Sphacteria with Demosthenes as his co-commander. He boasted that he would subdue the island in twenty days, with no additional Athenian troops.

As it happened, Demosthenes had declined to chance a landing on the island because it was all thick woodland, with no paths. Yet just before Cleon arrived, many of the trees were accidentally burnt down, revealing a number of viable landing points. That was the good news; the bad news was that there were clearly more Spartans on the island than was previously thought. Putting a positive spin on it though, the more Spartans, the bigger the prize.

Attempts at diplomacy failed when the Spartans, under Epitadas, were invited to surrender on generous terms and refused. The Athenians then launched a surprise attack on the Spartans who were now in three separate locations by embarking their 800 hoplites onto the ships undercover of darkness. The ships sailed off, giving the impression that this was just another routine daily patrol, but then instead landed on the island. The 800 hoplites were followed by some 2,000 *psiloi* and archers, and 8,000 rowers from the ships. Demosthenes's tactics ensured that the Spartans would be trapped: if they attempted to attack any part of the Athenian line, they would be exposed to attack from the rear.

Stalemate ensued, but this was finally broken by Comon, the commander of the Messinian contingent who, enlisting archers and light troops, worked his way around the rocky coastline and took up position on some high ground behind the fort causing the Spartans to flee.

Cleon and Demosthenes repeated their offer of surrender terms. The Spartans had lost Epitadas; their second in command, Hippagretas was critically wounded; and the third in command, Styphon, son of Pharax, was now in charge. When the herald made his announcement, most of the Spartans lowered their shields to indicate that they wished to surrender leading Styphon to enter into surrender negotiations. The advice that came back to him from the Spartans comrades on the mainland was not particularly helpful: 'make your own decision about yourselves, but do not do anything dishonourable'; Styphon surrendered.

Traditionally, Spartans did not do surrender. It is no surprise then that this mass capitulation, which, as noted, included 120 elite Spartiates, sent tremors resounding through the Greek world, plunged the Spartans into unmitigated gloom and precipitated a number of hasty peace offers. Of the 440 hoplites who had been trapped on the island, 292 were captured and taken to Athens. Athenians could farm their crops securely for the first time for many a year. A Messenian garrison was installed at Pylos, which launched guerilla raids that were extremely damaging to the Spartans and caused numerous helots to desert. Cleon was fêted in Athens as the man of the hour.

The prisoners were still a major bargaining factor four years later in the negotiations surrounding the Peace of Nicias in 421 BCE.[66]

Corinth also came under attack from the Athenians in 425 BCE; the Athenians dispatched an expedition to raid the eastern shores of the Isthmus of Corinth with 2,000 hoplites and 200 cavalrymen conveyed on eighty ships; they were commanded by Nicias. The Athenians had the support of allied forces.

The Corinthians got wind of this and assembled a reception committee in the Isthmus. Yet the Athenians wrong-footed the Corinthians when they sailed by night and landed on a beach under the hill of Solygia. The Corinthians opted for a three-pronged attack: half of the army stayed to protect Cenchriae; one company from the other half under Battus occupied Solygia; and the main part of this half, under Lycophron, faced the Athenians. The Corinthians were pushed back and retired up a slope. They unsuccessfully charged the Athenian line again. Reinforcements arrived pushing the Athenians back to their boats; however, the Corinthians were still unable to break through.

Eventually, the Athenian cavalry prevailed and the Corinthians retreated in disarray onto the hill at Solygia. Lycophron was killed along with many others. The Athenians collected their dead and plundered the Corinthian dead. The Athenians lost fifty or so men, the Corinthian 112. In the meantime, the other half of the Corinthian army approached from the north, and reinforcements from Corinth from the west. The Athenians saw them and took them for reinforcements from the Peloponnese at which point they retreated, sailed along the coast, raiding Crommyon before moving south-east to capture and fortify the peninsula of Methana. A garrison was left in Methana while the rest of the fleet returned to Athens.[67]

In the summer of 424 BCE, the Athenians attacked the strategically important island of Cythera, with sixty ships, 2,000 hoplites, and allied support. They were under the command of Nicias and two other generals. The inhabitants of Cythera lined up to confront the Athenians but they were routed, the survivors fleeing back into the city where they submitted.[68]

The battle of Delium later in 424 BCE ended the Athenian run of victories. It was an expensive defeat after an unsuccessful attempt to take Boeotia. That summer, Demosthenes had been busy currying favour with Boeotian rebels disaffected by the Boeotian League led by Thebes. The plan that emerged was for the rebels to seize Siphae, on the southern coast of Boeotia and Chaeronea, to the west. These would then be handed over to the Athenians, who were to capture Delium, at the east edge of Boeotian and the site of a temple to Apollo. The idea was that this would incite democratic revolts across Boeotia, and that the newly democratised cities would go over to Athens.

The plan, though, was doomed to failure from the start. The Spartans discovered the plot and told the Boeotians, so the element of surprise evaporated. The Athenians bungled their operation when Demosthenes's fleet reached Siphae only to find it occupied by a strong Boeotian army. The rebels initially decided not to act and Demosthenes was forced to retreat without having achieved anything.

The Athenian army, under the command of Hippocrates, turned up only after Demosthenes had left the scene. However, the temple at Delium was captured, and the Athenians set to work with the fortifications there which were completed in five days. Bizarrely, Hippocrates left a garrison and then marched the rest of his army back to Athens. His army comprised 7,000 Athenian hoplites, cavalrymen, and a large motley force of light troops. One mile into the march, the hoplites stopped to rest, but the light troops carried on.

The Boeotians mustered at Tanagra, near to Delium with 7,000 hoplites, 1,000 cavalrymen, 500 peltasts, and 10,000 light troops. The Boeotians were led by eleven generals—two from Thebes and nine from the other major members of the League. Only one, Pagondas of Thebes, son of Aeolidas, was in favour of doing battle, but he managed to convince his ten colleagues to fight, mindful of the fact Athenians would surely return and use Delium as a springboard for further incursions. The Boeotian army then advanced unexpectedly while Hippocrates was addressing his men and the two lines of hoplites clashed. The Boeotian left flank was surrounded and almost finished off; only the Thespian forces stood their ground.

Some of the Athenian hoplites fought with and killed one another when they met at the other end, mistaking their compatriots for the enemy. The battle of Delium is one of history's first documented incidents of 'friendly fire' made worse in part because neither army bore 'state' shields, which would have identified friend and foe as uniforms later did. State shields did not come into general use until the 362 BCE Second Battle of Mantinea between the Thebans and the Spartans. 'Friendly fire', as we euphemistically call it, would have been very frequent in the head-on, close-quarter combat fighting of the tightly knit Greek fighting units. It would have been exacerbated by a number of factors: no distinctive or recognisable armour or uniforms and similar languages yelled out by enemies and allies in the heat of battle, to name but two. The general mayhem and turmoil would only have increased the chances of fighting your own men or raining arrows, spears, and sling-shot down on friends and allies. The consternation of the Athenian defeat at the night-time battle of Epipolae in 413 BCE is graphically described by Thucydides—a blueprint for 'blue on blue' battlefield confusion. He asks how anyone can possibly know what is really going on in the dark: 'many parts of the enemy ended by falling upon each other, friend against friend, citizen against citizen'.[69] This nightmare scenario must have been repeated endlessly down the years.

The Athenians panicked and took flight when they mistook Boeotian cavalry for reinforcements: some made for Delium, while others fled towards the mountains or the coast. Only nightfall saved the Athenians from annihilation. Negotiations were fraught and only after the temple had been recaptured did the Boeotians agree to let the Athenians recover the dead. The Athenians had lost almost 1,000 men, most of them citizen hoplites, including Hippocrates; this was to be one of the highest numbers of casualties suffered in any hoplite battle. The Boeotians lost around half that number.[70]

As noted, the philosopher Socrates fought in the battle; Plato has Alcibiades give the following account of the retreat of the Athenians at Delium, and Socrates's actions then:

Furthermore, men, it was worthwhile to behold Socrates when the army retreated in flight from Delium; for I happened to be there on horseback and he was a hoplite. The soldiers were then in rout, and while he and Laches were retreating together, I came upon them by chance. And as soon as I saw them, I at once urged the two of them to take heart, and I said I would not leave them behind. I had an even finer opportunity to observe Socrates there than I had had at Potidaea, for I was less in fear because I was on horseback. First of all, how much more sensible he was than Laches; and secondly, it was my opinion, Aristophanes (and this point is yours); that walking there just as he does here in Athens,'stalking like a pelican, his eyes darting from side to side,' quietly on the lookout for friends and foes, he made it plain to everyone even at a great distance that if one touches this real man, he will defend himself vigorously. Consequently, he went away safely, both he and his comrade; for when you behave in war as he did, then they just about do not even touch you; instead they pursue those who turn in headlong flight.[71]

After a short cessation of hostilities, the Boeotians were reinforced by 2,000 hoplites from Corinth, as well as other troops from other allies. Apart from Socrates's cameo appearance, the battle of Delium is famous also for the debut of the flamethrower as a weapon of destruction. According to Thucydides, the Boeotians used it to torch Delium and put the Athenians to flight.[72] Despite the ferocity of this formidable weapon, only about 200 Athenians were killed; the rest were allowed to escape.

Philosophers and the invention of innovative military equipment were not the only remarkable features of Delium. Pagondas was something of a gifted tactician who used the cavalry as a vital fighting force and made significantly different use of other military units. At Delium, Pagondas revolutionised the standard hoplite formation by arraying his Thebans twenty-five shields deep, rather than the standard eight, to give them more push and punch. This is the first recorded instance of any Greek general ever changing the standard depth of a hoplite unit; this and his deployment of reserve cavalry amounts to what many historians agree is the first recorded use of formal military tactics in military history. The deployment of a reserve cavalry force was unprecedented in the annals of Greek warfare. The innovations were to come to the fore and were fully exploited in later Theban victories led by Epaminondas in the battle of Leuctra, among others.

In 423 BCE, Scione revolted from Athens with support from the Spartans, resulting in the siege of the town which lasted for two years until 421 BCE, even though the two enemies had earlier agreed a temporary peace treaty. Ultimately, the defenders of the city were either executed or sold into slavery.

Scione is in Pallene, the western-most of the three narrow peninsulas that extend south from Chalcidice. The city of Potidaea, at the head of the Pallene peninsula, was Athenian country and for the first few years of the Peloponnesian War Scione was an Athenian ally. This all changed in 423 BCE, when, emboldened by the success of the Spartan general Brasidas in northern Greece, the people of Scione decided on revolution.

Brasidas made for Scione where he delivered a speech of support and left a garrison: Brasidas intended to use the city as a base for an attack on Potidaea. The timing of the revolt at Scione could not have been more controversial because the revolt came two days after a one-year-long armistice was agreed between Athens and Sparta: 'It is proposed that each side should remain in its own territory, holding what it now holds ... The armistice is to last for one year.'

The Athenian general, Laches, with the support of Nicias, had successfully moved in the Athenian Assembly in 423 BCE for an armistice with Sparta in order to check Brasidas. However, the 'Truce of Laches' as it became known was a failure: it had little impact on Brasidas and folded within the year. Brasidas captured Scione and Mende; Athens sent reinforcements under Nicias, who recaptured Mende. Cleon nullified the truce when he set out to rescue Amphipolis in Macedonia.

Brasidas stayed in Thrace while the truce was in force, campaigning in areas exempt from the truce. Brasidas claimed that the revolt had predated the armistice and the switch of allegiance was legal, but the Athenians argued the opposite—that Scione was governed by the ceasefire and prepared to besiege the city. Brasidas evacuated the women and children and made the necessary preparations, which included bringing in reinforcements: 500 Peloponnesian hoplites and 300 Chalcidian peltasts, all led by Polydamidas. Brasidas then left for his campaign in Macedonia.

The Athenians mobilised under the command of Nicias and Nicostratus with a fleet of fifty ships, 1,000 hoplites, 600 archers, 1,000 Thracian mercenaries, and a small squad of peltasts; they sailed down the peninsula, captured the town of Mende with the help of pro-Athenian inhabitants, and advanced on Scione where the defenders of Scione occupied a strong position on a hill outside the city. The Athenians took the hill and began to build walls of circumvallation around Scione, which were completed at the end of the summer of 423 BCE. The Athenians left a garrison to man their walls while the rest of the army returned home.

The following summer, in 422 BCE, after the year-long truce expired, Cleon was promoted to lead an army in Thrace. On his way there, he called in at Scione, but instead of helping to end the siege, he actually enlisted some of the besieging troops to reinforce his own army.

The siege dragged on into the summer of 421 BCE by which time the Peloponnesian War had been temporarily ended by the Peace of Nicias. Under the terms of this treaty, any men sent by Brasidas, Spartans, or allies of Sparta who were besieged in Scione were to be released by the Athenians, but not the inhabitants of the city. These defenders were met with the severity that was becoming the norm after sieges. All men of military age were executed, while the women and children were sold into slavery and probably raped. The city and its lands were gifted to the Plataeans, allies of Athens who had lost their own city after the siege of Plataea between 429 and 427 BCE.[73]

That winter, during the brief ceasefire, the battle of Laodocium saw the armies of Tegea (in the centre of the Peloponnese) and Mantinea (in the north-east of the Peloponnese) clash. Tegea was an ally of Sparta, while Mantinea had sided with Sparta earlier in the war, but then allied with Athens. The battle was inconclusive but both sides suffered heavy losses.[74]

It was not long after the end of the one-year truce before the Athenians and the Spartans resumed hostilities. Amphipolis was an important power base for the Athenians in Thrace and as such, it attracted the attentions of the Spartans. In 424 BCE, Brasidas captured the city while it was under the command of Eucles. Eucles called on Thucydides (then a general, later an historian), who was stationed at Thasos with seven Athenian ships, for help. Thucydides failed in his attempt.[75]

Before Thucydides arrived, Brasidas gave generous terms to the inhabitants: he offered to let everyone who wished to stay keep their property, and safe passage to those who wished to leave. Amphipolis surrendered, despite the best efforts of Eucles to dissuade them.[76] Thucydides arrived at the nearby port of Eion on that same day and defended it with help from those who had left Amphipolis. Meanwhile, Brasidas was busy mopping up more Thracian towns, as well forging an alliance with Perdiccas II of Macedon, and attacking other towns in the region, such as Torone. The Athenians were naturally anxious lest their other allies would capitulate.

Thucydides comes out of this badly and is considered to be responsible for the fall of Amphipolis. Some have even gone so far as to describe his actions as gross negligence; he was recalled to Athens where he was tried and exiled.[77]

Cleon arrived in Thrace in 422 BCE with thirty ships, 1,200 hoplites, and 300 cavalrymen, along with allied forces. He recaptured Torone and Scione, where the Spartan commander Pasitelidas was killed. He then took up position at Eion awaiting reinforcements while Brasidas was situated at Cerdylion on the right bank of the Strymon on high ground close to Amphipolis and with a good view of the Athenian position. Brasidas was waiting for a chance to attack the Athenians while they were still without reinforcements.

Brasidas could count on 2,000 hoplites, 300 Greek cavalrymen, 1,000 local peltasts, the army of Edon, and 1,500 Thracian mercenaries; however, despite his superiority in numbers, he was reluctant to join Cleon in a pitched battle. Nevertheless, Brasidas retreated back into Amphipolis and prepared his attack; Cleon retreated in disarray allowing Brasidas to deliver a victorious assault spearheaded by 150 of his best men in a surprise attack on the Athenian centre.

However, Brasidas was killed in the fray, as was Cleon when attacked by troops under the Spartan commander Clearidas. The Athenian army fled back to Eion, although about 600 of them were killed before they reached the port. Only seven other Spartans were killed. The Amphipolitans lauded Brasidas as a hero and the founder of Amphipolis. A churlish Thuycidides records that, seeing that the battle was lost, Cleon fled from the battlefield and was killed by a Myrcinian peltast. After the battle, both the Athenians and the Spartans lost their appetite for war; with Cleon and Brasidas gone, both sides had lost their most hawkish personalites. The Peace of Nicias was signed in 421 BCE.

Ch. Koukouli-Chrysanthaki has spent thirty or so years researching at Amphipolis and uncovering evidence of the recovery and identification of Brasidas's burial at the agora in ancient Amphipolis.[78]

Unsurprisingly, when we think of Thucydides, we think of a pre-eminent historian. However, as we learn from Thucydides himself and from the description of the battle of Amphipolis above, that the historian was also an army general. Thucydides tells us that he fought in the Peloponnesian War, caught the plague and was exiled by the democracy. He may have also been involved in suppressing the Samian Revolt.[79] When Eucles sent to Thucydides for help, Brasidas, only too well aware of Thucydides's presence on Thasos and his influence with the people of Amphipolis, was worried lest help should arrive by sea. So, he wasted no time in offering terms to the Amphipolitans for their surrender, which they accepted. When Thucydides arrived, Amphipolis was already under Spartan control.[80]

Amphipolis was strategically important to the Athenians so, when, news of its fall reached Athens, there was much dismay and great consternation. Thucydides, as noted above, got the blame although he claimed that he had simply been unable to reach Amphipolis in time.

> I lived through the whole of [the war], being of an age to comprehend events, and giving my attention to them in order to know the exact truth about them. It was also my fate to be an exile from my country for twenty years after my command at Amphipolis; and being present with both parties, and more especially with the Peloponnesians by reason of my exile, I had leisure to observe affairs somewhat particularly.

> Thucydides 5, 26, 5

The time spent in exile gave Thucydides the unique opportunity to write his history and, in doing so, to present events from both sides; being an exile, he was able to travel freely among the Peloponnesian allies and comment without fear of committing treason.

The Peace of Nicias

Thucydides's record of the Peace marked the end of the Archidamian War:

> [5.18.1] The Athenians, the Spartans and their allies made treaty and swore to it, city by city, as follows:
> [5.18.2] With regard to the Panhellenic temples, everyone who wishes, according to the customs of his country, to sacrifice in them, to travel to them, to consult the oracles, or to attend the games shall be guaranteed security in doing so, both by sea and by land. At Delphi the consecrated ground and the temple of Apollo and the Delphians themselves shall be governed by their own laws, taxed by their own state, and judged by their own judges, both the people and the territory, according to the custom of the place.

[5.18.3] The treaty is to be in force between the Athenians, with their allies, and the Spartans, with their allies, for fifty years without fraud or damage by land or sea.

[5.18.4] It shall not be lawful to take up arms with the intent to do injury either for the Spartans and their allies against the Athenians and their allies, or for the Athenians and their allies against the Spartans and their allies, in any way or by any means whatever. If any dispute should arise between them, they are to deal with it by law and by oath, as may be agreed between them.

[5.18.5] The Spartans and their allies are to give back Amphipolis to the Athenians. In the case of all cities given back by the Spartans to the Athenians, the inhabitants shall have the right to go where they please taking their property with them.

These cities are to pay the tribute fixed by Aristidesnote and are to be independent. So long as they pay the tribute, it shall not be lawful for the Athenians and their allies to take up arms against these cities, once the treaty has been made. The cities referred to are Argilus, Stagirus, Acanthus, Scolus, Olynthus, and Spartalus.note These cities are to be allied neither to Sparta nor to Athens. If, however, the Athenians persuade the cities to do so, it shall be lawful for the Athenians to make them their allies, provided that the cities themselves are willing.

[5.18.6] The Mecyberneans, the Sanaeans, and Singaeans shall inhabit their own cities, as shall the Olynthians and Acanthians.

[5.18.7] The Spartans and their allies shall give back Panactum to the Athenians.

The Athenians shall give back Coryphasium,note Cythera, Methana, Ptelium, and Atalanta to the Spartans; also all Spartans who are in prison in Athens or in any other prison in the Athenian dominions.

[5.18.8] The Athenians shall let go the Peloponnesians besieged in Scione and all others in Scione who are allies of Sparta, and those whom Brasidas sent in there, and any other allies of Sparta who are in prison in Athens or in any other prison in the Athenian dominions.

The Spartans shall and their allies shall in the same way give back all Athenians or allies of Athens whom they have in their hands. With regard to Scione, Torone, Sermyle, and any other cities in Athenian hands, the Athenians may act as they shall see fit.note

[5.18.9] The Athenians shall take an oath to the Spartans and their allies, city by city. The oath shall be the most binding one that exists in each city, and seventeen representatives on each side are to swear it. The words of the oath shall be these: 'I shall abide by the terms of the treaty honestly and sincerely.' In the same way, the Spartans and their allies shall take an oath to the Athenians. This oath is to be renewed annually by both sides.

[5.18.10] Pillars are to be set up at Olympia, Pythia, the Isthmus, in the Acropolis at Athens, and in the temple at Amyclae in Lacedaemon.

[5.18.11] If any point connected with any subject at all has been overlooked, alterations may be made, without any breach of oath, by mutual agreement and on due consideration by the two parties, the Athenians and the Spartans.

[5.19.1] The treaty comes into effect from the 27th day of the month of Artemisium at Sparta, Pleistolas holding the office of ephor; and at Athens from the 25th day of the month of Elaphebolium, in the archonship of Alcaeus.

[5.19.2] Those who took the oath and poured the libations were as follows:

For the Spartans: Pleistoanax, Agis, Pleistolas, Damagetus, Chionis, Metagenes, Acanthus, Daithus, Ischagoras, Philocharidas, Zeuxidas, Antiphus, Tellis, Alcindas, Empedias, Menas, and Laphilus.

For the Athenians: Lampon, Isthmonicus, Nicias, Laches, Euthydemus, Procles, Pythodorus, Hagnon, Myrtilus, Thrasycles, Theagenes, Aristocrates, Iolcius, Timocrates, Leon, Lamachus, and Demosthenes.

The Defensive Alliance

[5.23.1] Sparta and Athens shall be allies for fifty years, under the conditions to be set out.

In case of any enemy invasion of Spartan territory or hostile action against the Spartans themselves, the Athenians are to come to the aid of Sparta in the most effective way possible, according to their resources.

But if by this time the enemy enemy has laid waste the country and gone away, then that city shall be held to be in a state of war with both Sparta and Athens and shall be punished by them both. Peace shall be made by Sparta and Athens jointly and simultaneously. These provisions are to be carried out honestly, promptly, and sincerely.

[5.23.2] In case of any enemy invasion of Athenian territory or hostile action against the Athenians themselves, the Spartans are to come to the aid of Athens in the most effective way possible, according to their resources.

But if by this time the enemy enemy has laid waste the country and gone away, then that city shall be held to be in a state of war with both Sparta and Athens and shall be punished by them both. Peace shall be made by Sparta and Athens jointly and simultaneously. These provisions are to be carried out honestly, promptly, and sincerely.

[5.23.3] In case of a rising of the slaves, the Athenians are to come to the aid of Sparta with all their strength, according to their resources.

[5.23.4] This treaty shall be sworn to by the same people on either side who took the oath on the previous treaty. The oath shall be renewed every year by the Spartans going to Athens for the Dionysia and by the Athenians going to Sparta for the Hyacinthia.note

[5.23.5] Each party shall set up a pillar, the one at Sparta to be near the statue of Apollo at Amyclae, the one at Athens near the statue of Athena on the Acropolis.

[5.23.6] If the Spartans and the Athenians should wish to add or take away anything from the terms of this alliance, they may do it jointly together without any breach of oath.

[5.24.1] Those who took the oath for the Spartans were Pleistoanax, Agis, Pleistolas, Damagetus, Chionis, Metagenes, Acanthus, Daithus, Ischagoras, Philocharidas,

Zeuxidas, Antiphus, Tellis, Alcindas, Empedius, Menas, and Laphilus, and for the Athenians Lampon, Isthmonicus, Nicias, Laches, Euthydemus, Procles, Pythodorus, Hagnon, Myrtilus, Thrasycles, Theagenes, Aristocrates, Iolcius, Timocrates, Leon, Lamachus, and Demosthenes.[81]

The Spartiates imprisoned on Sphacteria were still a cause for concern. The threat of a helot insurrection was never far away. War loomed on two fronts because the thirty-year truce between Sparta and neighbours and enemies Argos was due to expire with little prospect of renewal. Peace with Athens was, therefore, now an attractive option.

The hopes and intentions were for the Peace of Nicias to last for fifty years; however, it was violated after only eighteen months, and the war continued until 404 BCE. Apart from Athens being able to retain Nicaea and Sparta the city of Plataea, the treaty was designed to restore the geopolitical situation as it was before the war, and the Athenians would release the prisoners taken at Sphacteria.

From the start, there was disaffection and discontent. Amphipolis was not going to be returned to Athenian rule; this was Athens's chief objective, denied when Clearidas obtained from the Spartans a clause in the treaty rendering the transfer null and void. So, the treaty was strangled at birth. Several other states such as Thebes, the Corinthians, the Boeotians, Elis, and Megara refused to sign unless there were modifications to the terms. Corinth began a campaign of diplomacy against Sparta and Athens did not return Pylos.[82] The Athenians took Alcibiades's advice to join the coalition of the democratic states Argos, Mantinea, and Elis, giving her allies on the Peloponnese, and weakening the Peloponnesian League as a result. Astonishingly, Sparta and Athens signed an alliance with each other whereby both cities agreed to come to the other's aid if they were invaded and Athens agreed to support the Spartans in the event of a slave revolt.

Thucydides records the Peace as lasting for six years and ten months, but this refers to the time in which neither side invaded the other's territory. In actual fact, as stated, hostilities resumed after about a year and a half. In 418 BCE, Athens and Sparta confronted each other at Mantinea.

A cynical Thucydides took no prisoners when it came to establishing personal motives for going for peace. Nicias, he said was just motivated by the desire to end his military and political career free from the taint of disaster.

> While still happy and honoured, [Nicias] wished to secure his good fortune, to obtain a present release from trouble for himself and his countrymen, and hand down to posterity a name as an ever successful statesman, and thought the way to do this was to keep out of danger and commit himself as little as possible to fortune.[83]

Plutarch concurs that Nicias always took the safe and cautius option. King Pleistoanax of Sparta, who had been exiled for nineteen years before being reinstated as king, according to Thucydides, desired to distract attention from this in the hope that the repatriation of Spartan prisoners would achieve that.

It could be, and indeed has been, argued that the Peace of Nicias was a limited victory for Athens.[84] If its terms had been implemented, Athens would have achieved the objectives set forth by Pericles at the start of the war. Athens had clearly highlighted Sparta's inability to redress the grievances of her allies with the effect that the Peloponnesian League was on the brink of collapse when the Peace of Nicias was signed. On the other hand, Athens was unable to gain maximum advantage from her superior position in 421 BCE because her war strategy had weakened Sparta without inflicting similar damage on Sparta's allies, and it was these allies that would have delivered the most vital political and territorial concessions in Athens's favour. A weakened Sparta was unable to force her allies to comply with the terms of the peace, and her failure accelerated a movement toward a renewal of the war. The Peace clearly 'illustrates the difficulty of securing a lasting peace through negotiations when neither side holds a decisive military advantage, and especially when the war has involved coalitions of states whose vital interests and war fortunes may differ'.[85]

Nicias (*c.* 470–413 BCE), whose name is on the treaty, was a very rich man; of the Athenian aristocracy, he had inherited a large fortune from his father which he sank into the silver mines around Mt Laurium. His 1,000 or so slaves worked these mines. Nicias could afford to be extravagant but he was also a generous man donating much to charity and funding choruses for Athenian dramas, sporting events, public exhibitions, festivals, and underwriting new or restored statuary and temples. As a prominent politician on the aristocratic conservative side, Nicias became Cleon's rival, leader of the popular democratic party. Nicias was *strategos* in 427 BCE and 425 BCE: 'thanks to his cautious competence, he suffered no serious defeat and won no important victory'.[86]

War erupted again with the battle of Mantinea in 418 BCE—ultimately a Spartan victory over an alliance of Peloponnesian states led by Argos with the support of Athens. As we have seen, the Corinthians were uncomfortable with the Peace of Nicias and made no secret of their displeasure to Sparta, persuading the Argives to ally with them and thereby dilute Sparta's power. The alliance grew to include Mantinea, Elis, and most significantly Athens; meanwhile, the Corinthians lost their appetite for it and stayed loyal to Sparta.

In the summer of 418 BCE, the Argives attacked the Epidaurians, Spartan allies in Arcadia; both sides called on their allies and the two armies confronted each other outside Argos. However, the seemingly inevitable battle never materialised; instead, the leaders of the two sides parleyed and agreed not to fight. King Agis II returned home to a decidely hostile reception. Meanwhile, an Athenian contingent joined the Argives and convinced the allies to continue the fight. They captured Orchomenos and attacked Tegea, a Spartan ally but where a pro-Argive faction was standing by to turn the city over to the Argive alliance. Tegea was strategically vital: it controlled the exit route from Sparta and enemy control there would mean that the Spartans could not move freely out of their home city, effectively spelling the end of the Peloponnesian coalition.

Back in Sparta, Agis was censured for his lack of pugnacity; he was very nearly fined 100,000 drachmas and had his house flattened but managed to avoid all of this by promising to redeem himself with a victory elsewhere. The ephors agreed but henceforth, he had to seek approval from a committee of ten officers, *xymbouloi*, before he could lead an army from the city. He was saved from this humiliation by Tegea when it was declared that the city would change sides if the Spartan army did not make an appearance. Sparta was galvanised into action and Agis was soon leading out what was described by Thucydides as 'the best army ever assembled in Greece to that time'. Messages were sent to Corinth and to the Boeotians, Phocians, and Locrians calling them to Tegea, while Arcadians joined on the march from Sparta.

Agis, anxious to cancel out that earlier embarrassment, led the army towards Mantinea, laying waste the local countryside; the intention was to force a pitched battle with the Argives because he could not afford show any sign of avoiding battle again. The Argives drew up their battle lines with the support of 1,000 Athenians while Agis advanced to within javelin range. Again, battle looked inevitable but, at the last minute, Agis had a change of heart and the Spartans retreated into Tegean lands. According to Thucydides, his change of heart came about when 'one of the elder Spartans', the *xymboulos* Pharax, sagely advised Agis not to try to correct one error with another.[87, 88] The Spartans, therefore, retreated to find a way to get the Argive army to do battle. In the end, they diverted the Sarandapotamos river to the smaller Zanovistas river, and filled up the sinkholes into which Zanovistas flowed, in an effort to flood the Mantinean territory.

It did. The Argives formed their battle lines again. The Spartans, with 9,000 troops at their disposal including a *lochos* (battalion) of 600 Sciritae, an elite unit of of light infantry, were surprised to encounter it as they were returning to their own camp. The Spartans also had 2,000 *neodamodeis* (helots freed after a certain length of service as hoplites in the Spartan army) and Brasideans (veterans of Brasidas's armies) and about 3,000 Arcadians in their ranks. The Argives and their allies suffered heavy losses. The Argives and their allies lost 700 dead, the Mantineans 200, and the Athenians and Aeginentans 200, including both of their generals; Spartan losses were significantly lower, at just over 300. Later that year, 4,000 reinforcements supplemented the Argives and their allies—3,000 from Mantinean allies and 1,000 from Athens; they then attempted, unsuccessfully, to besiege the Spartans in Epidaurus.[89]

The Argives accepted a truce in which they renounced Orchomenus, gave up all their hostages and joined with the Spartans in expelling the Athenians from Epidaurus. They also repudiated their alliance with Elis and Athens. After deposing the democratic government in Sicyon, the Argive Thousand staged a coup against the democratic rule of a despondent Argos. Obviously, the battle provided a significant boost to Spartan morale and prestige, which had been at a low since the disaster at Pylos. Mantinea reasserted the prodigious military skills and reputation of the Spartans in hoplite combat.

The anti-Spartan alliance collapsed. Interestingly, although Athens and Sparta had confronted each other in battle, they were still officially at peace; the terms of the Peace of Nicias had not been broken.

Melos is a small island, founded by Spartans, which remained neutral in the war, or at least tried to. Thucydides tells us how the Athenians wanted to change this and offered the Melians a stark choice: join or be conquered.[90] The plucky Melians chose to remain independent and to resist whatever Athens threw at them. Their town was besieged and taken; the men were put to the sword and the women sold into slavery, presumably raped along the way. They then settled 500 of their own colonists on the island.

The most significant thing to come out of the siege of Melos is the Melian Dialogue, a pivotal work of international relations theory based on political realism, interpolated by Thucydides into the invasion of Melos by Athens and dramatising the negotiations between the Athenians and the Melians. The Athenians on the one hand insisted that Melos submit and pay tribute, or be destroyed, appealing to the Melians' pragmatism, emphasising the overwhelming odds they were up against. The Melians, on the other hand, appealed to the Athenians' sense of fair play and their fear of the gods. The Dialogue demonstrates the foolishness of pride and hope, and that self-interest and pragmatic concerns are the engines that drive war. The result was stalemate and Athens proceeded with the promised atrocity.

In 426 BCE, Athens had dispatched an army of 2,000 men led by Nicias to raid the Melian countryside, but the Melians refused to be drawn to battle and the Athenians had little appetite for a siege.[91] In 425 BCE, Athens formally demanded a tribute of fifteen talents of silver (about 390 kg) from Melos—an amount that would have paid the wages of a trireme crew for fifteen months, or bought 540 tonnes of wheat, enough to feed over 2,000 men for a year.[92] Melos was clearly a prosperous and attractive island; they had never paid tribute to Athens before, and they were unwilling to do so now.

Melos was strategically important and a valuable prize for that reason. Contemporary warships of the era, triremes, had little room for supplies, and so it was necessary to have a network of friendly and neutral ports where food and other necessities could be bought on a regular basis. Even though Melos was nominally neutral, Peloponnesian and allied ships could freely stop and resupply there. A captured Athenian Melos would reduce the 'combat radius' of the enemy's navy.[93]

In the summer of 416 BCE, during that truce with Sparta, Athens sent an army of 3,400 men to conquer Melos: 1,600 heavy infantrymen, 300 archers, and twenty mounted archers from Athens, plus 1,500 heavy infantrymen from other Delian League cities. Their transport fleet comprised thirty ships from Athens, six from Chios, and two from Lesbos and was led by Cleomedes and Tisias. During the siege, the Melians made a number of sorties, even taking a section of the Athenians' lines; however, the siege remained solid and Athens consolidated its forces with reinforcements under the command of Philocrates. The Athenians were also helped by traitors within Melos.[94] Melos surrendered in the winter of 416 or 415 BCE. A decade or so later, in 405 BCE, the Spartan General Lysander expelled the Athenian settlers from Melos and resettled the survivors of the original Dorian colony on the island.[95] The fiercely independent Melos had become a Spartan territory with a Spartan garrison and military governor (*harmost*).

Here is a summary of the Dialogue:

The Athenians deliver an ultimatum to the Melians: surrender and pay tribute to Athens, or be destroyed. The Athenians have no interest in arguing over the morality of the situation, because in practice might makes right—or 'the strong do what they can and the weak suffer what they must'.

The Melians argue that they are a neutral city and not an enemy, so there no need to subdue them. The Athenians respond that if they accept Melos' neutrality and independence as reasons for doing nothing, they would look weak: Athenians they were not strong enough to conquer Melos.

The Melians argue that an invasion of Melos will send shock waves to other neutral Greek states, who will become hostile to Athens for fear of being invaded themselves. The Athenians repy that Greek states on the mainland are unlikely to act this way. It is the independent island states and the disaffected subjects that Athens has already conquered that are more likely to revolt against Athens.

The Melians argue that submitting without a fight would be shameful and cowardly. The Athenians argue that it is only shameful to give in to an opponent where there is a reasonable chance of defeating them. There is no shame in submitting to an overwhelmingly superior opponent like Athens.

The Melians concede that the Athenians are far stronger yet there remains a slim chance that the Melians could win, and they will have no qualms over trying their luck. The Athenians condemn that counter that as emotional and short-sighted. If the Melians lose, which is highly likely, they will bitterly regret their foolish optimism.

The Melians believe that they have the gods on their side because their position is morally just. The Athenians respond that the gods will not intervene because it is natural for the strong to dominate the weak.

The Melians argue that their Spartan relations will come and help them. The Athenians retort that the Spartan pragmatism will ensure that they will not put themselves at risk when their interests are not at stake; rescuing Melos would be especially risky since Athens has the stronger navy.

The Melians remain adamant and politely dismiss the envoys.[96]

At Mytilene, we saw how the Athenians were not averse to meting out atrocities where they believed the perpetrators deserved it and where Athenian security was in peril. Even so, the savage events on Melos were seen as exceptional. Euripides's *The Trojan Women* is a commentary on the razing of Melos. Xenophon wrote that in 405 BCE, after the conclusive battle of Aegospotami with the Spartan army closing in on Athens, the citizens of Athens were understandably worried that the Spartans would treat them with the same violence that the Athenian army had shown the Melians.[97] Isocrates, proud patriot that he was, agreed that the razing of Melos was a stain on Athens's history.[98] He says in the *Panegyricus*:

Now up to this point I am sure that all men would acknowledge that our city has been the author of the greatest number of blessings, and that she should in fairness be entitled to the hegemony. But from this point on some take us to task, urging that after we succeeded to the sovereignty of the sea we brought many evils upon the Hellenes; and, in these speeches of theirs, they cast it in our teeth that we enslaved the Melians and destroyed the people of Scione.

Then, in the *Panathenaicus*, he describes:

[The Spartans] dwell on the cruelties suffered at [Athens's] hands by the Melians and the Scionians and the Toronians, thinking by these reproaches to sully the benefactions of Athens which I have just described.

Just as stigmatic for the Athenians was that 'Melian hunger' became synonymous with extreme enforced starvation in sieges. The earliest known reference to the starvation suffered by the Melians comes in Aristophanes's *The Birds*, first performed in 414 BCE. It continued to be used well into the Byzantine era and is mentioned in the *Suda*, the tenth-century Byzantine encyclopedia.[99]

The Sicilian Expedition was the second phase of the war. In 415 BCE, Athens dispatched a mighty expeditionary force to assail Syracuse; the attack culminated in a calamity for Athens when the entire force was destroyed in 413 BCE. The expedition was plagued with problems from the start: unclear objectives; muddled aims and scope, confusing command structure, and political machinations in Athens which bloated a minor force of twenty ships into a massive armada. Alcibiades, the expedition's champion, was recalled from command to stand trial even before the ships had reached Sicily. His decamping to the Spartans remains one of history's outstanding defections.

Up until now, Sicily for the Athenians was something of an afterthought, but it was by no means a backwater. There was a treaty with Segesta sometime around 458 BCE and a treaty with Leontini was renewed in 433 BCE, having been struck originally between 460 and 439 BCE. Most small Sicilian cities regarded Athens as a potential counterweight to the brooding power of Syracuse down in the south east of their island, strong enough as she was to dominate all comers. The Athenians now increasingly saw Sicily as a threat, a source of grain or military assistance to the Peloponnesians—as well as a target for future Athenian conquests.[100]

In 427 BCE, Athens had sent twenty ships, under Laches, following an appeal for help from Leontini. That fleet, operating from their base at Rhegium, remained on station for a number of years, sporadically fighting with Athens's allies and fighting alongside Rhegium, Leontini, Naxos, Kamarina, and various Sicel tribes, against the Syracusans and their allies, without any significant successes. However, in 426 BCE, Athenian forces captured the strategically important city of Messina on the straits between Sicily and the mainland. Syracuse, whose allies included Locris, Gela, and other cities, regained the initiative in 425 BCE, recaptured Messina, and threatened several other Athenian allies.

In 425 BCE, plans to bolster the Athenian fleet with an additional forty triremes came to nothing because the reinforcements got embroiled in the battle of Pylos *en route*. War weariness set in. Kamarina and Gela took the initiative; although traditional allies, they found themselves on opposing sides: while Gela was an ally of Syracuse, Kamarina was most definitely not. Notwithstanding, the two cities signed an armistice in the late summer of 425 BCE. Seeing that this would not last while the rest of the island was at loggerheads, the two cities convened all the belligerents to discuss peace terms. The Congress of Gela saw the Sicilian cities make peace on a ticket of 'Sicily for the Sicilians', and the Athenian fleet went back to Athens.[101]

However, the peace established at Gela was short-lived and evaporated as soon as Syracuse intervened on the side of the oligarchs in the civil strife which ignited between the democratic and oligarchic parties in Leontini. Fear of foreign domination had brought the Leontinians together, and the two erstwhile enemies united in war against Syracuse. Athens saw her chance and sent envoys to Sicily in 422 BCE to test the appetite locally for resuming the war against Syracuse, but it came to nothing.[102] However, in 416 BCE, another opportunity arose with another Sicilian conflict: the city of Segesta (an Athenian ally) declared war against Selinus and, after losing an open battle, appealed to Athens for help. Duplicitously, in order to secure that support, the Segestaeans offered to finance the lion's share of the cost of sending a fleet (sixty talents of uncoined silver up front), fooling the Athenian ambassadors into thinking that the city was wealthier than it actually was.[103]

The Segestaean ambassadors went to Athens to present their case before the assembly, where the debate soon degenerated into the usual party bickering. The assembly finally voted an expedition of sixty triremes, but with no hoplites, led by a reluctant Nicias, Alcibiades, and Lamachus; all were given the equal status of *strategoi autokratores* (unlimited power). Five days later, a second assembly was held to organise the logistics; here, Nicias took the opportunity to dissuade the assembly and overturn its earlier decision to send the expedition. Nicias reasoned that the Athenians would be leaving powerful enemies behind them if they sent a force to Sicily; he warned that they would be fighting formidable enemies too difficult and numerous to conquer and rule. He denigrated Alcibiades, calling into question his dubious experience and being only too ready to drag Athens into a war for his own selfish ends.[104]

Alcibiades responded by shrugging off the personal attack, reminding the Athenians of their obligation to their Sicilian allies, appealing to the Athenian vim and verve that had won this city her empire, and indicating that many Sicilian states would surely support Athens.[105]

When Nicias realised that the assembly was inclining towards Alcibiades, he changed tactics completely and argued that, in fact, a much larger expedition would be needed, in the hope that the cost of such an armada would deter the assembly. However, no doubt to his horror, quite the opposite reaction saw the assembly enthusiastically approving his proposal: they passed a motion allowing the generals to assemble a force of over 100 ships and 5,000 hoplites. Nicias had badly misread the situation; now, whereas the loss of sixty ships might have been just about tolerable, the loss of 100, plus hoplites, would constitute a trauma of some considerable magnitude.[106]

Trauma of a hugely symbolic kind was inflicted on the male genitalia in 415 BCE, just before the launching of the expedition. All over Athens at the time, at people's front doors, at crossroads, at one corner of the Agora, for example, there were edifices called Hermai, lifesize or larger stone apotropaic pillars with the head of the messenger god, Hermes, carved at the top with genitals at the front. The night before the expedition was due to sail, a person or persons mutilated many of these Hermai, defacing and castrating them. This iconoclasm, known as the Mutilation of the Hermai, remains unsolved to this day.

Hermes was originally a phallic god, associated with fertility, liminality, luck, roads, and borders. The Hermai would habitually be rubbed or anointed with olive oil and adorned with garlands. Such superstition persists today, for example with the Porcellino bronze boar of Florence where the nose is rubbed shiny from being constantly touched in the quest for good luck or fertility. George Grote struggled to 'comprehend the intensity of mingled dismay, terror, and wrath, which beset the public mind on the morning after this nocturnal sacrilege, alike unforeseen and unparalleled ... This was, the mutilation of the Herma, one of the most extraordinary events in all Grecian History'.[107]

Many believed the sacrilege compromised the success of the expedition, suggesting it was the work of saboteurs or revolutionaries who were intent on undermining or overthrowing the government, either from Syracuse or Spartan sympathisers in Athens itself; one suspect was the historian Xenophon. Enemies of Alcibiades, notably Androcles, took this opportunity to accuse him of other acts of impiety, including mutilations of other sacred objects and deriding performances of religious mystery ceremonies. Alcibiades volunteered to be put on trial under penalty of death in order to prove his innocence, anxious as he was to avoid his enemies charging him, in his absence, with more false information, but he was refused.

Notwithstanding, Alcibiades was a popular general who had earned the support of the army; he had also gained the backing of Argos and Mantinea. As soon as he had left on the expedition, he was sentenced to death, both for the mutilation of the Hermai, and for profaning the Eleusinian Mysteries at a symposium. His opponents had slyly waited for the army, his main source of support, to leave so that what was left of his supporters would be outnumbered in the vote.

We know that Nicias erred on the side of diplomacy rather than belligerence and that Alcibiades was much more bellicose. Lamachus, perhaps, was enlisted as a career soldier who, though something of a risk-taker and blessed with a short fuse, could provide balance and experience. He is, of course, most famous for his part in *The Acharnians* in which Aristophanes remorselessly lampoons him. Paradoxically, Lamachus proposed that the Athenians should attack immediately, taking the Sicilians by surprise and forcing a quick surrender; Nicias, ever cautious, proposed that the fleet should sail to Selinus and coerce Selinus and Segesta to come to terms and then show the flag around Sicily. Alcibiades, who recommended mustering allies first before attacking Selinus and Syracuse, won the day when Lamachus came down on his side.[108] Perhaps if the Athenians had gone with Lamachus's strategy they would have scored that early victory and avoided the disaster that was about to unfold?

Confusion and paranoia reigned in Syracuse where many believed that the Athenians were coming specifically to get them, and that the show of assistance to Segesta was just a pretence. Accordingly, the Syracusan general Hermocrates recommended that they request help from other Sicilian cities, and from Carthage even, adding his preference to confront the Athenian fleet in the open waters of the Ionian Sea. His opponents argued that Athens was no threat to Syracuse, indeed that there was not even a fleet: why would Athens be so foolish as to attack them and open a second front while they were already waging a war with Sparta? Athenagoras accused Hermocrates and others of stirring up fear in the minds of the people in a bid to overthrow the government.

Corcyra was the Athenian fleet's first port of call where they picked up allies and divided into three sections, one for each of the commanders. Three ships were sent ahead to seek out more allies in Sicily. At this juncture, the armada comprised 134 triremes (100 of which were from Athens), 5,100 hoplites (of which 2,200 were Athenians), 480 archers, 700 slingers, 120 other light troops, and thirty cavalrymen; in addition, there were 130 other supply ships, trireme crews, and other non-combatants.[109]

All that those three advance ships brought back to the fleet was no allies and the disappointing news that Segesta did not have the money it had promised after all. Nicias saw an opportunity to cut losses by making a show of force and then returning home. As before, the commanders differed in their strategies: Alcibiades was all for fomenting revolts against Syracuse, enlisting allies (not least Messenia) and then attacking Syracuse and Selinus; Lamachus proposed an immediate attack on Syracuse and laying siege before the city could stock up with provisions. Once again, Alcibiades got his way but alliances at Messenia and Catana (modern Catania) were not forthcoming and the Athenians were refused entry to both harbours; the Athenians then sent ten ships into the Great Harbour of Syracuse on reconnaissance to check out the defences there before returning to Catana. This time, they were permitted to enter the port and gained their first ally.

More bad news, for some at least, awaited the fleet when it arrived at Catana. An Athenian ship docked to inform Alcibiades that he was under arrest, not only for the desecration of the *hermai*, but also for profaning the Eleusinian Mysteries. Alcibiades complied and agreed to return to Athens in his ship; however, when they called in at Thurii in southern Italy he jumped ship and sought asylum in Sparta. Athens passed a death sentence on him *in absentia*: Alcibiades was found guilty on all counts without the inconvenience of a tedious and bothersome trial. In Sparta, the condemned Alcibiades naturally proved a fruitful source of intelligence about the Athenian forces.

Another problem for the Athenian expeditionary force was that it was comparatively weak in cavalry, while, with 1,200 horsemen, cavalry was one of Syracuse's strengths;

consequently, land operations for the Athenians were difficult, to say the least, without adequate cavalry protection. Nullifying Syracuse's advantage here then was a priority and it fell to Nicias to solve the problem. He sent a double agent from Catana to Syracuse who let it be known that the Athenians slept some distance from their armour and weaponry. If the Syracusan army were to attack Catana, support factions in the city would see to it that the weapons remained out of reach, thus gifting the Syracusans an easy victory. In actual fact, the Syracusan military would vacate their city, leaving it exposed to Athenian attack in which they would take up position at the southern end of the Grand Harbour, where the Syracusan cavalry was rendered redundant.

It worked. The Syracusans fell for it and marched on Catana. The Athenians sailed south, landed as planned at the Olympeium at the southern end of the Grand Harbour and took up position between the coast and the temple of Zeus; protection was afforded by steep slopes on their left and the sea on their right. They built a fort behind their lines to protect their rear.

When the Syracusans reached Catana, they found that the Athenians had all gone, so they turned back to Syracuse where they found the Athenians lined up for battle in a formidable defensive position. The two enemies camped for the night ready for the next day's battle.

A furious and hard-fought fight ensued, but the Athenians then broke the centre of the Syracusan line; the Argives pushed back the Syracusan left wing, causing the rest to flee. Thanks to the Syracusan cavalry, the Athenians were prevented from chasing them, thereby averting a catastrophe for the Syracusans, who lost about 260 men, and the Athenians about fifty.[110] The fall of Syracuse should have been next. It was at this point, though, that Nicias made two catastrophic strategic miscalculations.

After the battle the Syracusans occupied the Epipolae, the hill on which the Temple of Zeus stood, close as it was to the left flank of the Athenians. Nicias had decided not to use the hill, perhaps out of religious superstition. Then, instead of besieging the city straight away when the inhabitants were still vunerable after defeat, he retreated to Catana to winter with a view to resuming the siege in the spring of 414 BCE. Obviously, this gave the Syracusans ample time to recover from their defeat and to provision for a siege. Worse still, the bungling encouraged the Spartans to declare war on Athens in 414 BCE, with not a little help from Alcibiades.

The winter of 415–414 BCE was fraught with activity on both sides. Hermocrates agued for an overhaul and streamlining of the Syracusan army by reducing the number of generals from fifteen to three—Hermocrates, Heraclides, and Sicanus. Hermocrates sent for help from Corinth and Sparta while the Athenians also sent home for more money and cavalry.

Camarina on the southern coast (near the modern town of Scoglitti) was the focus of attention from both the Athenians and the Syracusans as they each tried to form an alliance with the city. While Hermocrates wanted Camarina and the other cities to unite with Syracuse against Athens, Euphemus, for the Athenians, pronounced that Syracuse only wanted to dominate Camarina, and they should ally with Athens if they valued their freedom. The Camarinans sat firmly on the fence, although they secretly sent aid to the Syracusans because they were nearer and potentially more of a threat.

The shuttle diplomacy continued apace with Athens spreading their diplomatic net ever wider by sending for help from the Carthaginians and Etruscans, with both Athens and Syracuse trying for military aid from the Magna Graecia cities in Italy. In Corinth, Alcibiades was busy weaving his web of deception on behalf of his new friends, the Spartans. Representatives from Syracuse met with him there and he told the Spartans that there would be an invasion of the Peloponnese by Athens were Sicily to be subdued and that they should send military aid to Syracuse and fortify Decelea, a vitally important town very near Athens.

The occupation of Decelea was the Athenians' worst nightmare. Herodotus reports that Decelea enjoyed a special relationship with Sparta.[111] The Spartans did indeed fortify Decelea, giving them control of rural Attica and thereby denying the Athenians use of and benefit from this productive land, as well as severing the main land arteries for food imports, forcing all supplies to be brought in by sea at greatly increased expense. Moreover, the lucrative silver, copper, and lead mines at nearby Laurium, approximately 50 km south of Athens, were totally disrupted, and 20,000 Athenian slaves were liberated by the Spartan hoplites. Treasury and emergency reserve funds estimated at 1,000 talents were steadly being salted away, compelling the Athenians to exact even more tribute from her subject allies, increasing tensions and the threat of more rebellion. Altogether, Decelea was a devastating blow of some considerable magnitude for Athens.[112]

Be that as it may, the spring of 414 BCE saw reinforcements arrive from Athens, consisting of 250 much-needed cavalrymen, thirty mounted archers, and 300 talents of silver used to pay for 400 additional cavalrymen from their Sicilian allies. In the summer, they scaled the Epipolae, the heights above Syracuse, which was defended by Domilius and 600 Syracusans. In the attack, Domilius and 300 of his men were slain.

Meanwhile, Syracusan envoys were in Corinth seeking military assistance which the Corinthians agreed on, providing troops, and interceding to persuade the Spartans to come on board too. However, the Spartans only sent a small force, under Gylippus, a '*mothax*' rather than a full 'Spartiate' (Spartiate lite).[113]

The Athenians duly began the Siege of Syracuse in the spring of 414 BCE. The same day that the Athenians marched onto the Epipolae via the pass of Euryalus, the Syracusans coincidentally sent a force to occupy the very same place. Their rushed attempt to drive the Athenians off the heights failed. The victorious Athenians marched to Syracuse to offer battle, but the defenders declined to come out and fight.

The Athenian plan was to erect a wall with which to blockade Syracuse by land, running from the coast at Trogilus, across the heights and down into the city, before reaching the sea again in the middle of the Great Harbour. They built a fort at Labdalum for provisions then proceeded to Syce where they built a fort called 'the Circle' in the middle of their blockading wall.

The Syracusans for their part now responded by coming out to offer battle, but the indiscipline of the Syracusan infantry caused their generals to withdraw the army back into the city, leaving a cavalry unit to harass the Athenians. The now reinforced Athenian cavalry, with support from a squad of hoplites, prevailed to win a second victory.

The Syracusans reacted by building their own wall running south-west from the city and crossing the Athenian wall running from the Circle to the Great Harbour. The Athenians launched a counterattack with 300 hoplites and heavily armoured light troops who captured the stockade protecting the counter wall. The Syracusans retreated to the city, pursued by the Athenians who wrecked the first counter wall.[114]

Not to be deterred, the Syracusans set about building a second counter wall with ditch and palisade over the marshes of Lysimileia; once again, the Athenians assaulted the builders, and at the same time sailed their fleet into the Grand Harbour. This was the spark for another battle in which the Athenians, despite an initial success, were routed by the Syracusan cavalry who went on to attack the Athenian right wing and delivered a second rout. Lamachus was cut off and killed. When the main part of the Athenian army turned up, the Syracusans fell back.[115]

Morale in the city remained high despite the reverses. Some of the troops in there attacked the main Athenian force; others assaulted the poorly guarded Circle, destroying around 1,000 feet of the Athenian wall on the heights. The fort itself was saved by Nicias who ordered the timber supplies around the fort to be set on fire, so stopping the Syracusan advance.

The Athenians finally extended their wall to the sea, completely blockading Syracuse by land while their fleet sailed in to the harbour to blockade them from sea. The Syracusans responded by sacking Hermocrates and Sicanus as generals and replacing them with Heraclides, Eucles, and Tellias.

Morale in the city then plunged to an all time low: peace terms were now on the agenda. However, the city was saved by Gylippus and his small squadron of two Spartan and two Corinthian ships, closely followed by a Corinthian fleet of fourteen.[116] Gylippus originally thought that the walls and the blockade were complete and so toured the cities of Magna Graecia in Italy to ensure that they did not ally with the Athenians. It was here that he learned that Syracuse was not yet totally blockaded so he proceeded to Himera on the east coast of Sicily and march overland to Syracuse. Much local support was forthcoming and his modest force of 700 men soon swelled to a more impressive 2,800: 700 marines, 1,000 hoplites, 100 cavalrymen, and 1,000 Sicilians. While Gylippus was making for Syracuse by land, the Corinthian commander Gongylus eluded the Athenians and entered Syracuse where he was just in time to forestall the discussion of peace terms, convincing the Syracusans to work with Gylippus.

As Nicias failed to defend the pass of Euryalus, Gylippus could lead his men onto the heights and join up with the Syracusans; here, they offered battle, but Nicias stayed within the shelter of the walls; Gylippus camped just outside Syracuse. The next day, he took the Athenian fort at Labdalum and although he failed with an attack on a vulnerable part of the Athenian line, the momentum on land had definitely shifted from the Athenians to the Syracusans and their allies. The Syracusans began to build another counter wall, across Epipolae towards Labdalum, traversing the last major gap in the Athenian lines. Yet they were repulsed by the Athenians; in a second battle, however, Gylippus defeated the Athenians by making better use of his cavalry and javelin-throwers. The Syracusans completed their counter wall, rendering the Athenian wall redundant. The Corinthian fleet arrived, under the command of Erasinides.

Nicias now turned his attention to the naval war, fortifying Plemmyrium at the southern entrance to the Great Harbour and basing his fleet there. Another land battle, between the two walls, saw the Athenians victorious. Gylippus reacted and offered battle again; the Athenian left was routed by the Syracusan cavalry and javelin throwers and the whole army had no option but to retreat, thus allowing the defenders to extend their wall across the line of the Athenian wall.

Significantly, this marked the beginning of a serious decline in the morale of the Athenian army. Also, the naval blockade was coming apart—twelve Syracusan ships were able to enter the harbour without challenge from any Athenian vessel, and Gylippus was able to slip out on an ally recruitment trip around the island, where he succeeded in gathering new support. The Syracusans began to train their fleet and were sufficiently confident to send envoys to Sparta and Corinth requesting more military aid.

Nicias piled on the despondency in the winter of 414–413 BCE when he sent a bleak message back to Athens describing the precariousness of his position with a weak fleet and a next to useless army. 'Reinforce me or recall me' was the clear message. Any prospect of winning that longed for recall for the expedition were well and truly dashed when, on the contrary, the Athenians voted to send a second army, just as large, to reinforce Nicias. Eurymedon, a general with experience of Sicily, and Demosthenes were the commanders of this new relief army.

Gylippus returned to Syracuse in the spring of 413 BCE with reinforcements and then persuaded the Syracusans to chance a naval attack on the Athenians, while he simultaneously attacked Plemmyrium by land. The naval attack ended in defeat: the Syracusan fleet was divided in two with thirty-five triremes attacking from the Great Harbour and fifty-five from the smaller harbour (on the eastern, sea-ward side of the city). The Athenians sent twenty-five and thirty-five Athenian ships respectively and were successful, losing only three ships to the Syracusans' eleven. Gylippus had more luck at Plemmyrium where he captured all three forts—a major setback for the Athenians as they were full of provisions and protected inbound convoys.[117] Gylippus pulled off a diplomatic coup when he convinced all the neutral cities on Sicily to join him with the exception of Acragas (Agrigento); allies of Athens killed 800 Corinthians, including all but one of the Corinthian ambassadors.

The Athenian fleet was now virtually trapped inside the Great Harbour, and supply convoys were forced to battle their way in. Morale in the army remained at an all time low. The Syracusans launched another naval attack under Diphilus at Erineus before Athenian reinforcements arrived; they had wisely fitted their ships with stronger prows to improve their ramming power and capability. In the end seven Athenian ships were sunk with more put out of action and their crews captured and killed. By contrast, the Syracusans lost only three ships.[118] Yet the Syracusan elation over this victory was short-lived. Demosthenes finally arrived with his fleet plus 1,200 Athenian hoplites, 3,800 allied hoplites, sixty-five triremes, and a large contingent of javelin troops and slingers. Athenian morale rose; Syracusan morale plumbed new depths.[119]

Demosthenes, anxious for a swift victory, planned to retake Epipolea in a night attack, but another disaster loomed. Things went well initially when the Athenians occupied and destroyed part of the Syracusan counter wall. Yet a force of Boeotians in the Spartan contingent rallied causing the unwieldy Athenian force to retreat. Many Athenians fell off the cliff to their deaths, and others were killed as they fled pell mell down the slope. The retreat was a calamity and it was the turn of the Athenians to lose confidence.[120]

At the highest level, there was disagreement over how to proceed. Demosthenes had had enough and proposed abandoning the expedition, returning to Athens to defend Attica against the Spartan incursion that had captured Decelea. Nicias intimated that he was privy to discussions by factions in Syracuse who were ready to surrender. Demosthenes suggested the Athenians leave Syracuse and establish a base elsewhere from which to prosecute the war. It all ended in stalemate and nothing changed.

Superstition then intervened. With Gylippus's reinforcements very much in mind, the Athenians were about to sail away when there was an eclipse of the moon. To the soothsayers, this was a bad omen and they demanded that the army wait twenty-seven days before moving on. A very superstitious Nicias and many of the soldiers were happy to comply. Unfortunately for them, this of course gave the Syracusans time to make preparations to stop them from leaving.

The delay proved fatal to the Athenians. The Syracusans attacked. On day one, they successfully assailed the Athenian walls; on day two, seventy-six Syracusan ships confronted eighty-six Athenian ships and won the naval battle despite the odds. Eurymedon was killed and many of the Athenian ships were pushed on to the shore, where Gylippus was waiting. He killed some of the crews and captured eighteen beached ships, but a squad of Athenians and Etruscans repulsed Gylippus, sending his forces into the marshes.[121]

The Syracusans now had hopes of capturing the entire Athenian force and built on their success by blocking the Athenians inside the harbour with triremes and merchant ships; the Athenians were besieged inside the Great Harbour, with no prospect of getting fresh supplies. Outside Syracuse, the Athenians built a smaller, walled enclosure to hospitalise their sick and injured, and embarked everyone else on their ships for one final battle, on 9 September. Demosthenes, Menander, and Euthydemus were the new commanders; the Syracusan fleet was led by Sicanus and Agatharchus of Syracuse on the wings and Pythen from Corinth in the centre. Javelins and arrows rained down from both sides; the Syracusans were able to neutralise Athenian grappling irons by covering their decks with animal hides.

The Athenians deployed their heavily laden ships as stepping stones by which to board the enemy triremes and fight what was effectively a hand-to-hand close combat land battle at sea with 200 ships involved. The Athenians lost and the army's only hope was to escape overland. This of course exposed them to the Syracusan cavalry; moreover, food supplies were perilously low. A decision to allow the soldiers time to pack gave the Syracusans the time they needed to post guards, blocking river crossings and passes.

The Athenians left their wounded and their dead unburied; the retreat to Catana with its 40,000 men was agonisingly slow and, after two running battles, food and water supplies were further depleted to dangerously low levels. Consequetly, Nicias and Demosthenes conceived a change of plan, and direction, and initiated a night march to Camarina or Gela on the south coast of Sicily. The night march was a shambles for Demosthenes: half of the army, who were in disarray and easy prey for the Syracusans, caught up with Demosthenes and attacked with a storm of javelins, forcing Demosthenes to surrender on generous and humane terms whereby none were to be executed, allowed to die in prison or to be starved. In all, 6,000 men surrendered, indicating that Demosthenes's army of around 20,000 had suffered heavy losses during the march from Syracuse.

Meanwhile, Nicias proceeded until he learnt the awful truth regarding his co-commander and the surrender of his army. Nicias offered to pay the entire cost of the war if the Syracusans and their allies would let his men return to Athens; the terms were rejected and they were subjected to an extensive missile bombardment instead. A last-ditch attempt to break out failed and further misery followed at the river Assinarus, where the soldiers, frantic with thirst, broke ranks, and were mercilessly attacked from both banks. Many Athenians were trampled to death and others were killed in fighting with fellow Athenians. The Athenians were nearly totally massacred in the worst defeat of the expedition in terms of lives lost. Nicias surrendered in person to Gylippus, hoping the Spartan would remember his role in the peace treaty of 421 BCE. The paltry few who escaped found refuge in Catana. Nicias and Demosthenes were both executed by the Syracusans, despite a reluctant Gylippus who appealed for clemency, and the surviving troops were incarcerated in a stone quarry near Syracuse.[122] After ten weeks, any who survived the atrocious inhuman conditions there were sold into slavery except the Athenians, Italians, and Sicilians. The Athenians were left to a slow death by disease and starvation in the quarry. Some survivors did manage to escape and found their way back to an incredulous and frantic Athens with their personal horror stories.

Plutarch, in his *Life of Nicias*, describes the incredulity:

It is said that the Athenians would not believe their loss, largely because of the person who first brought them news of it. For a stranger, it seems, arriving in Piraeus, and sitting in a barber's shop there, began to talk about what had happened, as if the Athenians already knew all about it. When the barber heard the story, before telling anybody else, he ran as fast as he could into the city, addressed himself to the Archons, and presently spread the news about in the agora. The result, as you can imagine, was widespread terror and consternation. The Archons summoned a general assembly and brought in the man and asked him how he came to know these things. Because he could not offer a plausible answer he was taken for a rumour-monger sowing unrest in the city. He was, therefore, fastened to the wheel and racked for a long time, till other messengers arrived who related the whole disaster in the same detail. That is how Nicias is believed to have suffered the calamity which he had so often predicted.[123]

When the truth and enormity of the disaster sank in, there was a general panic. Attica looked vulnerable and free for the taking, and the Spartans were hovering close by in Decelea. States hitherto neutral joined with Sparta, assuming that Athens was on the point of being defeated a second time. Many of Athens's allies in the Delian League also rose up, and although the city immediately began to rebuild its fleet, the disaster was seen worst in terms of the loss of the huge naval force dispatched to Sicily. Triremes were replacable, but the 30,000 experienced, professional oarsmen lost in Sicily could not be replaced and Athens was now dependant on inexperienced slaves to man her emergent new fleet.

In 411 BCE, things came to a head when the Athenian democracy was overthrown in favour of an oligarchy, and Persia joined the war on the Spartan side. However, it was not all doom: the oligarchy was soon overthrown, and Athens was victorious at the battle of Cynossema.

The Sicilian Expedition was, then, an unmitigated disaster for the Athenians and did irreperable damage to Athenian power with far reaching consequences to their military, political, and commercial status in the region. Thousands of men died, two fleets were lost, and a prodigious amount of money was dissipated with no benefit. Sparta (and Athens's other enemies) derived great pleasure and confidence from such an ignominious defeat of their enemy. Despite it all, though, the Athenians, astonishingly, clung on for another ten years.

The third part of the Peloponnesian War (also known as the Decelean or the Ionian War) is notable for the fact that Sparta was bolstered by support from Persia, rebellions among Athens's allies in the Aegean Sea and Ionia, and the loss of Athenian naval supremacy.[124] The Persian satraps Tissaphernes of Lydia and Pharnabazus of Hellespontine Phrygia offered money to Sparta in return for military support for the king's aims of expelling Athens from Persian territory. The war would effectively come to an end with the destruction of Athens's fleet at Aegospotami, after which Athens surrendered in 404 BCE. Aegospotami marked the end of Athens as a political and military force. Poverty was everywhere in the Peloponnese, while the once proud and magnificent city of Athens was devastated; civil war between *poleis* was endemic. Sparta, on the other hand, took on the mantle as the leading power in the region.

Encouraged by Sparta, *polis* after *polis* queued up to revolt against Athens; they included the Chians, the Lesbians, and the Erythreans. The Syracusans sent their fleet to the Peloponnesians, and the Persians, under Tissaphernes, came in to support the Spartans with money and ships. Insurrection threatened within Athens itself. Yet the Athenians were not for lying down: in 412 BCE, their Gulf of Corinth-based fleet of thirty-seven triremes tailed the thirty-nine trireme Spartan fleet under Alcamenes *en route* to rebellious Chios and drove them into the harbour at Spiraeum in Corinthia. Here, they attacked from ship and shore wrecking most of the enemy ships and killing Alcamanes. Soon after, though, the ships were repaired and the Spartans retaliated, ending the Athenian blockade and seizing four of their ships.[125]

Four further battles followed in quick succession the same year. From the new Athenian base at Samos, admirals Leon and Diomedon landed at Cardamyle and Bolissus in Chios and defeated the revolting Chians. Two further battles at Phanae Promontory and Leuconium saw two more Athenian victories after which a demoralised Chios gave the Athenians free reign to lay waste their lands, and gave up their resistance.[126]

Reinforcements came for the Athenians in the shape of forty-eight ships with 3,500 Athenian, Argive, and other allied hoplites. These all landed at Miletus to be confronted by 800 troops strengthened by Peloponnesians and mercenaries in the pay of Tissaphernes. The Spartans had signed their first treaty with king Darius II Nothus; Tissaphernes was to be the king's agent, but he believed that an unconditional alliance with Sparta was not in Persia's interests, so he withheld payments and threatened to negotiate with Athens on more than one occasion. Tissaphernes was there on the field, in person in command of his cavalry. The impetuous Argives lost 300 men due to their lack of discipline while the Athenians defeated the rest of the opposition, apart from the Milesians.[127] Alcibiades was present at the battle too.

The island of Syme (in the south-eastern Aegean) was the location for the next confrontation in January 412 BCE and was an early demonstration of the new concord between Sparta and Persia and of Persia's exploitation of Athens's current weakness. The alliance was struck by Therimenes, who handed the Spartan fleet over to Astyochus once the negotiations were concluded; Therimenes later drowned at sea. Astyochus sailed to Cnidus to rendezvous with twenty-seven ships from Caunus, originally equipped and intended for Pharnabazus—the satrap of Dascylium and ruler of Hellespontine Phrygia. Meanwhile, the Athenian navy at Samos under Charminus was aware that the Spartans were coming, from intelligence supplied by the Melians, and prepared to confront them at Syme.

A storm played havoc with the fleets and the only positive result was that Charminus, with twenty ships, attacked the Spartan left wing which was all that he could see through the driving rain. However, the rest of the Spartan fleet arrived on the scene and surrounded the Athenians. Charminus retreated to Halicarnassus with the loss of six ships. The rest of the Athenian fleet came out from Samos and sailed to Cnidus, but both sides had seemingly lost their appetite for another battle.[128]

The inexperienced Athenian commander, Phrynichus, failed to press home his victory. We hear next from Thucydides of a naval action at Rhodes where the islanders were persuaded by the Spartans to revolt from Athens. Leon and Diomedon were dispatched to deal with the Peloponnesians and the Rhodians whom they attacked and defeated on the shoreline.[129]

Despite repeated promises of military assistance from the Spartans over the years, nothing ever seemed to materialise until a Spartan commander called Leon arrived in Chios with twelve ships. Athens had been blockading Chios under the command of Strombichides so this was an opportunity to free the island. Augmenting Leon's twelve ships with twenty-four more ships, the Chians sailed out to attack the thirty-two blockading Athenian vessels. Chios eventually got its waters back.[130]

Alcibiades now returned to the scene. He told the Athenians that he could make the Persian king, through his sponsor Tissaphernes, change sides if he, Alcibiades, was taken back into the fold, and if Athens renounced its democracy.

At the same time, Peisander triggered a long simmering oligarchic coup in the city in 411 BCE, justified on the grounds that the democrats were failing in their handling of the Decelean War and that the oligarchs could manage foreign, fiscal, and war affairs better than the democrats had so far done. It was supported and led by a faction of prominent and wealthy Athenians, who also wielded power in the Athenian army at Samos in concert with Alcibiades. Both Thucydides and Aristotle believed that 'the revolution was provoked by defeat in Sicily'; in other words, the disaster of the Sicilian Expedition was the last straw for democracy.

The Constitution of the Athenians gives an account of the coup that took place both in Athens and in the garrison at Samos amid a climate of terror, but largely along constitutional lines. First, a law was passed to lift the ban on unconstitutional proposals; powers were then transferred to a group of oligarchs, called the Four Hundred, who would draft a new constitution for a moderate oligarchy, the Five Thousand. Antiphon was one of the leaders of the Four Hundred; he firmly believed that oligarchy was preferable to democracy; a general named Theramenes, son of Hagnon, argued that the suspension of democracy would bring with it Persian support and was, therefore, worth trying. Others joined because an oligarchy was a cheaper form of government and, given Athens's financial straits, this must be an option worth considering. The oligarchs, however, were divided.

Alcibiades's machinations certainly helped the coup, but Thucydides believed that it would have happened anyway. However, the oligarchs in Samos came unstuck when Samian pro-democratic leaders in the Athenian fleet deposed their generals and elected new ones to replace them. The new leaders recalled Alcibiades to Samos and declared their intention to proceed with the war against Sparta. The Five Thousand ruled for several months, until after the Athenian victory at Cyzicus in 410 BCE.

The Hellespontine Confederacy had survived Athens's calamity relatively intact but very soon after Chios Lampsacus and Abydos revolted. Strombichides was deployed to quash these insurrections; he was successful at Lampsacus but not at Abydos.[131] Disaster awaited at Eretria, however, later that year. When a Spartan flotilla approached Salamis, the Athenians were concerned about an attack on Piraeus; their fears were dispelled, though, when the Spartans sailed past and docked at Oropus. This was just as bad: nearby Euboea was now under threat. Euboea, of course, was now the principal source of most of Athens's supplies after the Spartans occupied Decelea. The Eretrians expelled the Athenians from Oropos with the help of the Boeotians. Thymochares set sail with thirty-six ships and poorly trained Athenian crews to Eretria where they fought immediately on arrival against Agesandridas and his forty-two vessels. Agesandridas won a convincing victory, capturing twenty-two of the Athenian ships. The whole of Euboea then revolted against Athens. Athenians who tried to take refuge in Eretria were killed by the town's inhabitants; only those who reached the Athenian fort in Eretria survived.[132]

These small naval battles were the direct consequence of Sparta's policy of fomenting revolt against a weakened Athens, largely through a small Spartan fleet commanded by Chalcideus, advised and assisted by Alcibiades, and of Tissaphernes's alliance with Sparta against Athens.[133] The Spartans were reluctant to fight the Athenians at sea, allowing the Athenians to recapture a number of cities and to besiege Chios. The rebellions just described at Rhodes and Euboea, and the threats to Abydos meant, however, that the Athenian forces had to be split to deal with these various menaces. The Spartan commander Clearchus tried to sail forty ships past the Athenian fleet in to the Hellespont but he was confounded by a storm; nevertheless, his comrade, the Megarian General Helixus, did reach the Hellespont with ten ships where he was able to incite revolts in Byzantium, Chalcedon and other key cities.[134]

Later, a newly appointed Spartan navarch, Mindarus, ditched Tissapharnes and entered into negotiations with Pharnabazus.[135] Mindarus set out from Miletus and managed to slip his entire fleet past the Athenians to join the Peloponnesian ships already operating in the Hellespont; he then established a base at Abydos, forcing the flight of the small Athenian fleet at Sestos, with losses, to Imbros and Lemnos.[136]

With a substantial Peloponnesian fleet now operating in the Hellespont, Athens's vital lifeline, the trade route through which her grain supply passed, was in peril, so the Athenian fleet was obliged to pursue Mindarus. Thrasybulus, the commander, sailed the fleet to Elaeus at the end of the Gallipoli peninsula and spent five days getting ready to confront the eighty-six Spartan ships at Abydos with his seventy-six. When the Athenian fleet rounded the point of Cynossema, the Spartans attacked. With the Athenians divided and much of their fleet incapacitated, a Spartan victory seemed definite.

Indiscipline, however, struck the Peloponnesians at this critical juncture; the Peloponnesian line collapsed as ships broke ranks to pursue individual Athenian vessels. Thrasybulus then suddenly turned his ships and attacked the Spartan left. After routing these, the Athenian right bore down on the Peloponnesian centre, and, catching them in total disarray, soon annihilated them as well. By the end of the battle, they had captured twenty-one Spartan ships to their earlier loss of fifteen in the early fighting. The Peloponnesians sailed back to Abydos; the Athenians docked at Sestos where they refitted their ships.[137]

They also sent a flotilla to Cyzicus, took the town, and captured eight ships. A trireme was sent to Athens with the express purpose of delivering the excellent news of the victory at Cynomessa.[138] As intended, this boosted the morale of the Athenians no end, restoring the people's belief in the war effort. The effect of the victory should not be underestimated; fighting on the enemies' terms with a ramshackle fleet, the Athenians carved out a hard-fought success that allowed them to continue fighting, with overall victory still a possibility.

The same year, the battle of Abydos gave Athens a second victory in the Hellespont; its importance lies in the fact that it helped secure Athens's food supplies and further lifted morale back home.

This is the first battle in the war for which we cannot rely on Thucydides as his history ends just before the battle begins; Xenophon and Diodorus Siculus are now our main sources. The battle of Abydos begins when Dorieus, son of Diagoras, a Rhodian serving with the Peloponnesians and commanding a fleet of thirteen or so ships from Rhodes, sailed into the Hellespont to aid Mindarus. The Athenians gave chase; the Rhodians were forced to the shore, where they were attacked. Mindarus sailed out with his fleet of eighty-four ships to save Dorieus and a major naval battle ensued. There was deadlock until Alcibiades, back working for the Athenians, arrived with reinforcements of between eighteen and twenty ships, at which the Peloponnesians made for the shore, and were saved from rout by Pharnabazus. The Athenians captured thirty Spartan ships and recovered the fifteen lost at Cynossema; they withdrew victorious again.[139]

The spring of 410 BCE saw a third Athenian victory consolidate the achievements won at Abydos and further raise morale in Athens. The battle of Cyzicus began with the fleets facing each other inside the Hellespont, with the Athenians at Sestus and the Peloponnesians at Abydus. In terms of numbers of ships, the Athenians still had the inferior force so, to avoid being trapped here, they sailed out of the Hellespont into the Aegean, around the northern shore of the Chersonese (the Gallipoli peninsula) to Cardia.

Mindarus had designs on the city of Cyzicus in the Propontis (modern Marmora) and set out to lay siege to the city with Pharnabazus; the city soon surrendered. The Athenian commanders (Alcibiades, Theramenes, and Thrasybulus) had by now arrived in the area and bore down on Cyzicus.

As the combined Athenian fleet approached the Peloponnesian fleet of sixty ships, the Peloponnesians sailed to the shore where they prepared for a naval battle. Alcibiades sailed past the Peloponnesians with twenty ships and landed; Mindarus followed, and a land battle ensued. Mindarus was killed and his men fled. The Syracusans in the Peloponnesian fleet burnt their ships, but the rest of the fleet was captured. Cyzicus itself fell to the Athenians the next day.

Diodorus's account differs somewhat but whichever is accurate, there is no doubting that the result was a significant Athenian victory. Athenian control of the Hellespontine region had been well and truly restored, the corn supply to Athens from the Black

Sea was secure, and morale in the city was the highest it had been for a long time. Unfortunately, this euphoria led to a Spartan offer of peace being rejected—a grave miscalculation of the situation, as we shall see.[140]

At Athens, the oligarchic government that had prevailed since 411 BCE yielded to a restored democracy soon after the battle. The Athenians eventually recaptured Byzantium and resumed collecting tribute from Chalcedon, but they failed to press home the military advantage won at Cyzicus and financial problems continued to restrict their options. Meanwhile, the Spartans, benefiting from Persian financial support, wasted no time in rebuilding their fleet.

The battle of Ephesus in 409 BCE was a significant reverse for the Athenians. Thrasyllus headed for Ephesus with a flotilla of thirty ships and a detachment of hoplites and cavalry. When he landed and disembarked his troops, the Ephesians attacked, killing 100 hoplites first and then a further 300.[141] In the same year, the Megareans took the Athenian owned port of Megara. The Athenians were furious and sent Leotrophides and Tiarchus with 1,000 hoplites to retake the port. At Cerata (the Horns), the Megarians drew up for battle. The Athenians won the day, despite their inferior numbers.

Meanwhile, far to the west in Sicily, the battle of Selinus, which took place early in 409 BCE, was the opening shot in the Second Sicilian War. Ten days of siege and battle was fought between the Carthaginian forces under Hannibal Mago and the Dorian Greeks living in Selinus. Selinus, the most western Greek colony in Sicily, had attacked the Elymian city of Segesta in 415 BCE over territorial and marital issues; Segesta appealed to Carthage but was denied; Athens, however, agreed to help and this was the catalyst for the Athenian invasion of Sicily the same year, which culminated in defeat for Athens in 413 BCE. When Selinus attacked Segesta again in 411 BCE, Carthage responded positively this time to appeals for military assistance by sending two expeditions: the first in 410 BCE, which expelled the Selinute army from Segestan territory, and the second, which extirpated Selinus after besieging the city in 409 BCE for nine days with an army of 100,000 men. They then levelled the city's walls. Some 16,000 Selininteans were butchered and 5,000 taken prisoner; however, only 2,600 of its inhabitants escaped as their offer of negotiations had been rejected by the Greeks. This was also an initial step in Hannibal's campaign to avenge his grandfather's defeat at the 480 BCE battle of Himera. Selinus was later rebuilt, but never regained her former glory and status.

The second battle of Himera was fought in 409 BCE, not far from location of the first battle where the Carthaginians were defeated in 480 BCE. The sequel was between the Carthaginians under Hannibal Mago and the Ionian Greeks of Himera with the support of an army and a fleet from Syracuse. Hannibal, as we have just seen, sacked and razed Selinus before turning his attention to Himera.

Carthage is said to have brought 120,000 men, including 4,000 cavalrymen, with them. Their forces were nothing if not cosmopolitan and reflect their wide orbit of military activity. Soldiers had been recruited from North Africa, Sardinia, and Spain and also included Sicilian Greeks. A more realistic estimate number is about 40,000 soldiers, reinforced after the battle of Selinus, with 20,000 Sicel and Elymian soldiers on the way over to Himera. The highly disciplined Libyans contributed both heavy and light infantry, and heavy, four-horse war chariots; Numidia brought crack light cavalry armed with javelins, riding bareback without bridle or saddle.

Rather than build a circumventing wall and lay on a full siege of the city, the Carthaginians scaled the walls using siege towers and battering rams. However, this was to no avail. Hannibal then deployed sappers, who dug tunnels under the walls and brought sections of it down by torching the wooden support beams. Carthaginian infantry then poured through the holes but the Himerans repulsed them and erected temporary walls to plug the gaps.

Later, the Himerans were reinforced by the Syracusan general Diocles with 3,000 hoplites, 1,000 troops from Akragas, and another 1,000 mercenaries to complement the 10,000 strong Himeran force. The determined Greeks then launched a surprise attack on the Carthaginians throwing them into confusion with considerable 'blue on blue'. The Punic army broke and fled with the loss of about 6,000 soldiers. Hannibal then made a counterattack with a force he had shrewdly kept in reserve, routed the Greeks, and pursued them back into Himera with the loss of 3,000 defending troops.[142] Some Himerans were evacuated when twenty-five Syracusan triremes arrived at Himera; the Carthaginian fleet was stationed at Motya, which gave the Greeks command of the sea around Himera. Diocles marched out of the city while the Syracusan fleet evacuated as many of the women and children as possible. However, the Carthaginians resumed their attack the next day; the city held out for one more day.

To be rid of the Syracusans, Hannibal made clever use of false imformation when he started the rumour that the Carthaginians were intent on attacking Syracuse, a city undefended while the main Syracusan army was at Himera. The Syracusans quite naturally headed for home. When the fleet got back within sight of Himera, the Carthaginians broke through and took the city.

Hannibal then sacrificed 3,000 Greek prisoners on the spot where Hamilcar, his grandfather and leader of the 480 BCE expedition, had died. The city of Himera was razed, including the temples; the women and children were enslaved. Hannibal paid off his army and left a garrison in the Punic territories. Hannibal had achieved what he set out to do: having won his revenge, he returned to Carthage laden with booty.[143] Himera was destined never to rise again: the survivors built a new city called Thermae nearby, home for Greeks and Phoenicians.

In the aftermath, Syracuse expanded her fleet and Akragas built up her army. Hermocrates, the Syracusan general, established a base at Selinus around 407 BCE from which he raided Motya and Panormus much to the annoyance of the Carthaginians. By 405 BCE, much of Sicily fell under Carthaginian sway.

The Declean War, meanwhile, continued apace when in the spring of 408 Chalcedon, opposite Byzantium, severed its ties with Athens and revolted. Theramanes, Alcibiades and Thrasyllus between them invested the city and built a stockade all the way around.

Hippocrates, the Spartan governor, however, led his forces out to engage the Athenians: Hippocrates and many of his men were killed for their trouble. Theramenes struck a deal whereby the city would be reprieved on payment of the tribute plus arrears. The support army brought by Pharnabazus was not required.[144]

Byzantium had followed suite by revolting as well, which led Alcibiades to lay siege that winter. A faction of Byzantians tried to do a deal with Alcibiades whereby they would betray their city to him if he agreed not to sack it. Alcibiades refused and proceeded to fox the inhabitants into believing that he had been called away. After pretending to depart, Alcibiades returned under cover of night, camping his army outside the walls he had thrown up earlier and forcing his navy into the harbour. The Peloponnesians, Boeotians, and Megarians went down to the harbour, engaged the naval forces, routed them, and forced the survivors back on board. When they then confronted the army, they were considerably less successful: the city was handed over to Alcibiades on condition that there were no reprisals. In a remarkable u-turn, given his earlier robust refusal of terms, Alcibiades agreed to this and no one was killed and no one was expelled.[145]

Alcibiades had not been back to Athens since his political rehabilitation, but now he returned a hero and was promoted to commander in chief of all Athenian forces and all things military. His next act was, in 407 BCE, to sail with a fleet of 100 to Andros. Andros had revolted; Alcibiades took the city of Gaurium.[146]

The following year, 406 BCE, saw the battle of Notium; this may have been a relatively insignificant Athenian naval defeat but the events which surrounded it had huge significance for Athens. One of the repercussions of the defeat was that Alcibiades was sent into exile for a second time by the Athenians, thus depriving themselves of one of the best commanders they ever had. At the same time, a thrusting and capable young Spartan naval commander burst onto the military stage; he was called Lysander and had a fleet of ninety ships based at Ephesus.

Alcibiades was up for a fight and took the Athenian fleet to Ephesus; Lysander, with his fleet of ninety ships, declined to fight so Alcibiades sailed to nearby Notium but soon left the scene with a few troopships to assist Thrasybulus in the siege of Phocaea. Alcibiades delegated the command of the fleet to Antiochus, his *kybernetes* (helmsman), with explicit orders not to attack Lysander. This decision was unconventional to say the last and contributed significantly to Alcibiades's downfall. Meanwhile, in Ephesus, Lysander was currying favour with Cyrus, a Persian prince who agreed to finance a pay increase from his own purse for Spartan rowers. This enabled Lysander to headhunt experienced rowers from the Athenian fleet.

Antiochus attacked Lysander. Diodorus records that Antiochus took only ten ships to confront Lysander who squared up with all his ships; Lysander then proceeded to sink Antiochus's ship, and pursued the other nine back to Notium. Antiochus was killed. However, Xenophon says that Antiochus took two ships into Ephesus, eventually teasing out Lysander's entire fleet.

From here on, the two accounts largely converge. When he heard about the unscheduled battle, Alcibiades lifted the siege of Phocaea and returned south to reinforce the fleet at Notium. Lysander was bearing down on the Athenian base at Notium. The Athenians had to rush to arms and could only fight in small contingents, as a result of which they were soundly beaten, losing between fifteen and twenty-two ships. A victorious Lysander then returned to Ephesus. The Athenians withdrew to Samos, where they were joined by Alcibiades, who sailed out to Ephesus with all his ships, but Lysander refused to fight.

Despite the lionisation of Alcibiades only the previous year, the general's popularity evaporated completely when the bad news surrounding Notium percolated back to a hostile Athens. Prudently, Alcibiades thought better of returning to the city in the current climate to avoid the risk of facing a trial. Instead, he went into self-imposed exile to property he owned in the Thracian Chersonese. Alcibiades was now, militarily speaking, a liminal figure—his army days numbered.[147].

After Notium, it was all change. As there was a restriction on how long navarchs could serve, Lysander was replaced by Callicratidas; Alcibiades brought down Thrasybulus and Theramenes with him and the overall command fell to Conon. The gifted Thrasybulus was a particularly serious loss; it was he who had devised the Athenian naval victories of 411 and 410 BCE. Unlike Lysander, Callicratidas was suspicious of the Persians and could not ask for Cyrus to support him. Consequently, Callicratidas had no choice but to fund his fleet with contributions from Sparta's allies; this got him some 140 triremes. Conon had problems too: the morale of his sailors was so low that he was able to crew only seventy of the 100 plus triremes he had at his disposal.[148]

The Siege of Mytilene in 406 BCE was a Peloponnesian attempt to capture this Athenian held city on the island of Lesbos. The siege ended when the Athenians were victorious at Arginusea, but, as with Notium, the significance lies in the impact and far reaching consequences of the aftermath.

The Peloponnesians enjoyed a run of successes, beginning with the capture of the Athenian fortress at Delphinium, in Chios. Next, Callicratidas attacked Teos and then besieged the Athenian garrison of Methymne on Lesbos. At Methymne, Callicratidas missed the opportunity to take the rest of Lesbos and the Hellespont, where he might have severed the Athenian grain supply route, all to defend Lesbos.

When Conon put in at one of the 'Hundred Isles', or Hecatonnesia (east of Lesbos), he inadvertently gave the Peloponnesians the opportunity to cut the Athenians off from their base on Samos. Taking advantage of this, Callicratidas, with a fleet of 170 ships, put to sea and headed for the Athenian position.

When the two fleets were within sight of each other Conon decided not to risk a battle against a fleet twice as large as his own, and tried to reach safety at Mytilene, an Athenian-held city on Lesbos. The Peloponnesians caught him and in the ensuing battle the Athenians lost thirty ships, although most of the crews escaped to shore. Callicratidas then set about besieging the city. According to Xenophon, Conon was besieged by land and sea, and was powerless to do anything.

He then had two of his ships dash through the Hellespont and on to Athens to collect much-needed supplies and bring reinforcements. Emergency measures were swiftly passed to build and man a relief force. Gilded statues of Nike were melted down to finance the building of the ships while slaves and metics were enlisted to crew the fleet. To make this attractive, the Athenians went so far as to extend citizenship to thousands of slaves who took to the oars. More than 100 ships soon came out of the shipyards, complemented by fifty allied ships. Unusually, the fleet was commanded by eight generals: Aristocrates, Aristogenes, Diomedon, Erasinides, Lysias, Pericles, Protomachus, and Thrasyllus.[149] The Athenian fleet sailed to Samos and then on to the Arginusae Islands.

Callicratidas led his fleet out to meet the Athenians with 140 ships; the Athenians had 150, having left fifty to monitor Conon at Mytilene. Uniquely, the Spartan crews and commanders were more experienced than their Athenian counterparts so the Athenians had to rely on some innovative tactics. First, the Athenian fleet was divided into eight divisions, one for each of the generals; then they orchestrated their fleet in a double line instead of the traditional single line in order to prevent the Spartans from using the *diekplous*.

Callicratidas led his fleet into battle but was killed when his ship rammed an opposing ship; the Athenians went on to win the day convincingly. The Spartans lost some seventy ships, and the Athenians twenty-five.

The people of Athens were initially jubilant at the news, going so far as to vote to grant citizenship to the slaves and metics who had fought in the battle. However, inclement weather had prevented the rescue of many survivors of the twenty-five damaged or sunken Athenian triremes and many sailors drowned. This caused uproar in Athens: the trierarchs Thrasybulus and Theramenes first took the blame but then the finger pointed at the generals; all six were executed.[150] As it happened Socrates, holding public office for the one and only time, was *epistates* (chairman) on the day that the generals were tried. He pronounced that he would 'do nothing that was contrary to the law'.[151] Socrates would not call a vote but in the end, a vote was taken, and all six generals were found guilty. A more self-damaging and short-sighted act of so-called justice would be hard to find: the ruthless cull left Athens devoid of any experienced commanders in 405 BCE, which was sure to have a deleterious effect on Athens's naval capability. Later, when the Athenians had had time to reflect, they came to regret their decision and charges were levelled against the instigators of the executions. The accused escaped before they could be brought to trial, but one, Callixeinus, did return to Athens some years later; loathed by his fellow citizens, he died of starvation.[152]

At Sparta, meanwhile, Arginusae was seen as yet another calamity; morale was accordingly very low. The fleet, now at Chios, was run down, and those who had supported Callicratidas urged for peace with Athens, fearful that a continuation of hostilities would see the re-emergence of their opponent Lysander. Envoys were sent to Athens: on offer was the surrender of the Spartan fortress at Decelea in return for peace. Yet the Athenians turned it down: most of the people refused to consent, being completely deceived by Cleophon who prevented the conclusion of peace by coming into the assembly, drunk and wearing body armour, and protesting that he would not allow it unless the Lacedaemonians surrendered all the cities; Lysander, on cue, assumed command of the fleet for the rest of the war.[153]

The battle of Aegospotami (405 BCE) was a crushing defeat for the Athenians and the defining conflict for Athens and for Greece as a whole, effectively bringing a close to the Peloponnesian War.

The executed Athenian commanders were replaced by Conon, Adeimantus, and Philocles. On the Spartan side, Callicratidas had died in the battle of the Arginusae Islands and because it was not permitted to appoint the same navarch twice, Lysander was officially appointed as second in command to Aracus. It was, however, Lysander who really commanded the fleet.

Both sides spent time repairing their fleets. Lysander was able to rekindle his close relationship with the wealthy Persian prince Cyrus. He soon raised the money to begin rebuilding the Spartan fleet. Indeed, when Cyrus was recalled to Susa by his father Darius, he appointed Lysander as satrap of Asia Minor. With his fleet in good order, Lysander manoeuvred into the Hellespont. His aim was to regain control of some of the cities lost in recent years and to block the Athenian food supply from the Black Sea. Establishing a base at Abydos, Lampsacus was his first target which he took by storm.

The Athenians tailed Lysander into the Hellespont with 180 ships and took up position at Aegospotami, opposite Lampsacus. The next morning, the Athenians formed outside Lampsacus, but Lysander refused to emerge, and the Athenians returned to Aegospotami. Lysander dispatched some of his fastest ships to follow the Athenians and glean intelligence. This went on for the next three days: a cause of concern to Alcibiades who was observing events from his fortress overlooking the Hellespont. He tried to convince the Athenian generals to move up the coast to the more secure city of Sestos since they were currently on a harbourless, exposed beach with no ready source of supplies. He also claimed that several Thracian kings would provide him with an army; if the generals would offer him a share of the command, he would use this army to help the Athenians. The generals declined this offer and rejected his advice; Alcibiades went home.

Lysander made his move on day five. Our two sources have differing accounts of the start of the battle. Diodorus records that Philocles, the Athenian commander for the day, set sail with thirty triremes, and ordered the rest of his fleet to follow. Some deserters then divulged this split to Lysander who put to sea with his whole fleet, defeated Philocles and then attacked the rest of the unprepared Athenian fleet. At the same time, a Peloponnesian army landed on the European shore and captured the Athenian fleet.

In Xenophon, Lysander made the most of the Athenians' habit of leaving their ships to forage for food; Lysander crossed the Hellespont and attacked the disorganised Athenians. Conon and a mere nine ships escaped the disaster, but the remaining 170 were all captured along with some 3,000–4,000 Athenian sailors. Conon knew that he had lost the war and sailed to Cyprus into exile with Evagoras, a friendly ruler there.

Now the Athenians and their alliance fell to pieces: Byzantium and Chalcedon were the first of a number of Athenian-held cities to surrender to Lysander; in each case he allowed the garrisons to return to Athens. News of the defeat reached Athens on the state trireme 'Paralus'. With no fleet the Athenians realised that they were certain to be besieged by land and sea. The city was soon surrounded by two Peloponnesian armies and blockaded by Lysander's fleet, and the siege of Athens began.[154] For Athens, the war was over: she could not feed herself or communicate with her empire without control of the sea.

Lysander returned to Lampsacus with victory filling his sails. Using an earlier Athenian atrocity when the captured sailors of two ships were thrown overboard to their deaths as justification, Lysander and his allies slaughtered Philocles and 3,000 Athenian prisoners, although sparing other Greek captives. Lysander's fleet then headed slowly for Athens, capturing cities along the way. Only Samos put up any resistance: the government there, fiercely loyal to Athens, refused to give in; Lysander simply left a besieging force behind him.

Xenophon tells us how news of the defeat reached Athens:

> ... a wailing sound ran from Piraeus through the long walls to the city, one man passing on the news to another; and during that night no one slept, everyone was in mourning, not just for the dead, but rather more for themselves.[155]

The Athenians dreaded the retribution that the victory-drunk Spartans might exact on them and resolved to resist the siege—a hopeless cause. Athens was soon on the verge of starvation, and the city surrendered in March 404 BCE. The walls of the city were torn down and a pro-Spartan oligarchic government was established—the Thirty Tyrants' regime. Aegospotami marked the end of twenty-seven years of war, elevating Sparta to a position of unassailable dominance throughout the Greek world and establishing a political order that would endure more than thirty years.

How had Athens survived for so long after the earlier disaster at Syracuse? Firstly, they were assisted by the dilitariness of their enemies: Corinth and Syracuse were slow to get their fleets into the Aegean, and Sparta's other allies seemed in no rush to furnish ugently needed troops or ships. Some Ionian states who went over to Sparta expected protection, and many, disaffected accordingly, rejoined the Athenian side. The Persians dithered over the funds and ships they promised which played havoc with battle plans. Significantly, at the start of the war, the Athenians had prudently laid aside some money and 100 ships that were to be used only as a last resort, as indeed they were.

The world of ancient Greece was comprehensively transformed by the Peloponnesian War. Athens lost her place at the apogee of international influence and power and was reduced to subjection, while Sparta replaced Athens as the dominant power in Greece. The economic and social costs of the war were manifest right across Greece; poverty was rampant throughout the Peloponnese; huge swathes of countryside were laid waste, cities were totally wrecked; Athens itself was utterly devastated, never to regain its pre-war prosperity. Civil war was endemic throughout the complex and ever-changing network of *poleis*. The Peloponnesian War vividly marked the cataclysmic end to the fifth century BCE and the glory that was Greece in her golden age.

Conflict and Greek Women

If you believed Hector in the *Iliad* when he asserts that fighting battles was the exclusive preserve of men, you would have to accept that women played no part, directly or indirectly, in the serial warmongering that pervades real world ancient Greek history. Given the subdued profile of women generally in Greek society and their social, civic, and political unobtrusiveness that was thereby fostered, it may come as some surprise to learn that women were by no means totally excluded from military strategy-making, nor were they completely absent from combat situations; in sieges and street-fighting, women sometimes did their bit. Indeed, some women played exceptional and significant parts in the Greek war machine, starting with Homer, despite the haughty pronouncements of Hector and Telemachus. Throughout Greek history, a significant number of women had a hand in the causation, direction, or conduct of wars and battles. Deception, military intelligence, diplomacy, tactical excellence, courage, and ferocity are just a few of the martial qualities exhibited by the women in this chapter, which is adapted from my *Women at War in the Classical World*.[1]

The female of the species, of course, features prominently in the Greek and Roman pantheons and in mythical representations of war: we have Andromache, Athena and the Amazons, for example; she is present in epic poetry with Helen of Troy, Chriseis, or Briseis, and in drama in the shape of the vengeful or victimised women of the tragedies, or as the 'revolting' women in the comic *Lysistrata*. In the real world, she populates the strange foreign countries described with some incredulity by Herodotus, in particular Queen Tomyris, Artemisia, and Pheretima; she is present too as a poet warrior in Telesilla.

Behind the celebrities, we know, but often forget, that the everyday women in ancient Greece who married soldiers (and there must have been countless thousands of them down the years) were typical army wives, just getting on, quietly in the background, with providing the routine support that army wives have always provided in the extended absences of warrior husbands: holding the household (the *oikos*) together, running the farmstead, raising the children, and schooling the next generation of hoplites. This all too important domestic function apart, there were camp followers and the women of the ubiquitous baggage train: foraging for, selling and cooking rations, working the wool, making and mending military clothing, organising worship in the field, nursing casualties and burying the dead, and selling their bodies. On the home front and just behind the front line, never was there more making do and mending. All of this was essential, but usually unnoticed, support for the soldiers and sailors, but it was also indicative of a determined need among women to assist, subsist and survive in war-torn environments, or else to exploit the system and the situation, working the black markets and profiting from war, usually just to scrape the most basic of livings.

This chapter seeks to redress the balance between men and women in ancient Greek warfare and accords military women their rightful place in the annals of Greek military and social history. We shine a light on the role of mythical and fictional military women and deities in Homer, the tragedians and the comic playwrights; the bellicose Amazons are discussed as are belligerent women in Herodotus in contrast to the comparative reticence of Thucydides on matters female. The women of the obscure *Tractatus de Mulieribus* are revealed in the context of catalogues of the woman warrior, along with similar works by Plutarch and Polyaenus. We then follow the relatively prominent role of Spartan women in the military.

Greek goddesses play a significant role in the prosecution of war among mortals. Enyo, Athena, Hera, and Thetis all have major responsibilities for aspects of warfare. Victory (Nike) too, that pinnacle of fighting success, was a female goddess. However, despite the pre-eminence of female divinities, the father of the gods himself, Zeus, had some patronising advice for Aphrodite when she emerged injured from the battlefield wounded by Diomedes: war is not for you, my child: 'you stick to the marriage bed— Ares and Athena will look after military matters'.[2]

It is with Homer that we first come across the widely held axiom of the classical Greek and Roman worlds that war is man's work while wool-working is the preserve of women; the two lie at different poles of Greek societal and gender convention and, according to most Greeks, never should the two meet or be confused. The one defines men, the other women; war is a badge of maleness, wool an emblem of the good wife and homemaker. Hector and Telemachus, as noted, are unequivocal about the differentiation in Homer, and ever since then it echoed down through classical life and literature as a mantra for 'normal life' and the much-desired preservation of the *status quo*. At the same time, though, we can show that it has been undermined by a momentous gender role reversal in which women were seen to go off warring and, occasionally, men are left holding the bobbins and shuttles.

The world, as we know, is not always normal. Herodotus is staggered to report that Egyptians are all crazy: 'the women go to market and men stay at home and weave [the exact opposite to Greek practice]. Women even urinate standing up and men sitting down'. Aristophanes's Lysistrata attests that war is as much the responsibility of women as of men; she turns the conventional political landscape on its head when she dresses up the *proboulos* in women's clothes and teaches him the ways of wool while she and her comrades take over the running of the city, the complicated affairs of which include directing the Peloponnesian War, a conflict that can be disentangled just as a ball of 'womanly' wool can.[3] Elsewhere, an armoured Athena, female goddess, protects an embattled Athens while effeminate Cleisthenes has his shuttle.[4] Diodorus Siculus reports that the Amazon men of Libya stay home, weave, and look after the children while their women go off fighting wars. Pindar's Cyrene eschews the loom and prefers to slay wild beasts with her sword.[5] Euripides's Ague goes one better, getting self-fulfilment by killing animals with her bare hands.[6] The Bacchants too have deserted the loom for a life much more challenging. When he observes Artemisia's military excellence and belligerence, a bemused Xerxes reflects that his men are acting like women and she like a man. The warlike Amazons consign their men to a life of wool-working. Herodotus cites the Amazonian mission statement: 'We are armed with the bow and javelin and we ride horses. We don't know anything at all about women's work.'[7] Throughout Greek history, exceptional women are described as exhibiting *andreia*, with all its connotations of manliness and bravery.

Men, of course, were the protagonists in the Trojan war: Homer's *Iliad* is the denouement of the ten-year conflict with Achilles, Patroclus, Hector, Agamemnon, Ajax, Aeneas, and Deiphobus among the many, often squabbling, alpha male warriors. Yet there would not have been a Trojan war without women, both as the very *casus belli* itself and as characters who influenced the action and direction of the war. Helen, Queen of Sparta, must take responsibility for causing the war when she allowed herself to be abducted by Paris, while Briseis and Chryseis both played a role far more influential than their status as spoils of war would suggest. Hector's wife, later war widow, Andromache, tried to influence her husband's actions and strategy, while ever-patient, faithful army wife Penelope, in the *Odyssey*, endured virtual widowhood for twenty years as she waited, and waited, and waited, in the hope that Odysseus would come back home and dispel the repellent suitors circling around her shark-like, with an eye on her virtue. Achilles's mother, Thetis, was, a significant influence in her son's agonising decision—to fight or not to fight—in the war against Troy.

Women, though, have no active role on the battlefield here, with the notable exception of the Amazon Penthesilea. Homer's women do, nevertheless, have a vital function in narrating the tragedy that befalls Troy as we might expect, as war widow victims at funerals and in the mourning of dead heroes.[8] With the exception of Helen and of Homer himself, the destruction of Troy is always described from the perspective of Trojan women, which gives them an important role as exclusive narrators of the Trojan catastrophe. This is best illustrated when the women of Troy mob Hector at the Scaean Gate, desperate for news of their fathers, husbands, sons and brothers. Hector is evasive and prescribes prayer. Homer, however, comes straight to the point when he interjects into the action the doom-laden words: 'grief [*kedea*] awaits many'.[9] Hector's mother, Hecuba, takes control of the situation and advises Hector to sacrifice to Athena in order to enlist her protection of the Trojan wives and children from the marauding Diomedes. Despite their physical absence from the field of battle, Homer's female characters remain at the heart of the ten-year conflict.

Homer's *Iliad* tells us all about the final days of the ten-year long Trojan War. A number of the extant Greek tragedies and some of the non-extant works, incuding the earlier Theban Cycle, continue the story by revealing some of the terrible things that happened to the Trojan women captives and to the Greeks when they got home. Women, as in the *Iliad*, played a leading, and tragic, role in a number of these sequels, none of which, by definition, ended well. The fate and actions of women as a consequence of war is also explored in Aristophanic Greek comedy. The famous example is, of course, the *Lysistrata*, one of a number of plays based on fantasy situations in which the norms of Athenian society are absurdly contravened and contraverted.

The *Lysistrata* (the name translates as 'Army Disbander') was performed in 411 BCE and is the story of one woman's extraordinary but mad mission to end the Peloponnesian War—an ancient Athenian peace movement. Lysistrata persuades the women of Greece to withhold sex with their husbands and lovers until they negotiate a peace; however, all it achieves in the end is a battle between the sexes. Nevertheless, it does show how inept men can sometimes be, and the ability of women to intrude onto the traditional martial territory of men.

Greek men presumably believed that women had a value, and a unique role to play in their world beyond their obvious biological function, and that role included involvement in things military, either as goddesses or, in the mortal sphere, in a purely supportive and background capacity as wives, mothers, daughters, or concubines. However, this was acceptable only so long as any proactive or combative activities were safely cocooned in mythology or in dramatic fictions and did not impinge on their real world as real women. Herodotus, 'the father of history', was to change all that in the middle of the fifth century BCE.

One of Herodotus's aims when he wrote his landmark history was to illuminate the differences between the foreign and the Greek. The behaviour of 'barbarians' (foreigners) in 'barbarian' (foreign) countries and civilisations is one of the prominent features to emerge from Herodotus's ethnographical excursions around the Mediterranean. Unlike Thucydides, who virtually ignores women because they are apparently not relevant either to war or history, Herodotus mentions 375 women as individuals or in groups, seventy-six in an ethnographical context. Additionally, there are queens and regents, princesses, and royal mistresses, all wielding influence of some kind or another. Four of these foreign queens—Nyssia, Tomyris, Artemisia I, and Pheretime—exhibit impeccable political and strategic military skills that are as good as any man's, doubtless much to the indignation and anxiety of many a Greek man. Herodotus presumably believed that women, foreign women at least, had a valuable role to play in aspects of war and government and were, therefore, essential characters in his history. He is also anxious to show how their actions were in just reaction to wrongs inflicted on them by their men, how a breach by these men of the *nomos* (the law) was rightly avenged.

Women, as Herodotus may have been aware, had form in this area. Shammuramat was a wife of King Shamshi-Adad V and, on his death in 811 BCE, ruled the Neo-Assyrian Empire as its regent for five years until her son, Adad-nirari III, came of age. She was empress regnant of Assyria between 811 and 808 BCE; as one of the first known women to rule an empire, it is assumed that she wielded military power in the execution of that rule. The empire was extensive, extending from the Caucasus Mountains in the north to the Arabian Peninsula in the south, and western Iran in the east to Cyprus in the west. Shammuramat is often associated with Semiramis, the legendary wife of King Ninus, succeeding him to the throne of Assyria. The account of her life by Diodorus Siculus writing in the first century BCE, reveals her to be one of the first women to be used as a pawn in the political machinations of ruling men-folk and as a cause of conflict at the highest level.[10] Semiramis married Onnes, one of Ninus's generals, and fought alongside him at the capture of Bactria. Nevertheless, Ninus was so taken by Semiramis's bravery there that he compelled Onnes to 'willingly give her to him, offering in return for this favour, his own daughter Sonanê as wife'. Onnes was not interested, so Ninus 'threatened to put out his eyes unless he immediately complied with his commands'. Onnes was now terrified, 'fell into a kind of frenzy and madness', and hanged himself. Ninus then married the obviously influential Semiramis; she bore him a son called Ninyas.

What exactly was it that attracted both Onnes and Ninus to Semiramis? Diodorus describes her as 'endowed … with understanding, daring, and all the other qualities which contribute to distinction', qualities that she was able to apply impressively in a military context. When Semiramis arrived in Bactria and observed how the siege was going, she noted that all the attacks were being made on the plains and at vulnerable positions, but that no one ever assaulted the acropolis because of its strong position, and that its defenders had left their posts there to reinforce those who were under pressure on the walls below. Consequently, taking with her the soldiers trained in scaling rocky heights, and making her way with them up through a difficult ravine, she seized part of the acropolis and gave a signal to that effect to those who were besieging the wall down on the plain. The defenders of the city, terrified at the seizure of the acropolis, deserted the walls and gave up all hope of saving themselves.

Ninus conquered Asia but was fatally wounded by an arrow. Semiramis then masqueraded as her son and fooled her late husband's army into following her because they believed they were following Ninyas; she went on to reign as queen regnant for forty-two years, conquering much of Asia in that time. Her duping of the Assyrian army is one of the first examples we have of a woman apparently acting like a man to achieve masculine power and authority, as perfected later by many others, not least Jean d'Arc. Often, as we shall see, the illusion of masculinity was thrust upon women by incredulous men struggling to equate or reconcile what they believed to be exclusively man-like achievements with a woman. Roman Agrippina the Elder is a later example in the first century CE, described as exhibiting masculine qualities in her adroit marshalling of the rebellions legions of her husband, Germanicus, on a troublesome German frontier.

Semiramis was hungry for more: she took on the monumental task of founding the city of Babylon:

> And after securing the architects of all the [known] world and skilled artisans and making all the other necessary preparations, she gathered together from her whole kingdom two million men to complete the work.[11]

She then reinforced it with a high brick wall surrounding the city. She built several palaces in Persia, along the Euphrates and Tigris rivers including Ecbatana, and annexed Libya and Aethiopia to her empire. Somewhat bored with peace, Semiramis declared war on king Stabrobates of India, 'since she had great forces and had been at peace for some time she became eager to achieve some brilliant exploit in war'.[12] Well aware that she was at a strategic disadvantage due to the absence of elephants in her army, she inventively and ingeniously had her engineers create a herd of faux elephants to deceive the Indians into thinking she was deploying the real thing. Camels and river boats were also used to good effect.

She laughed off Stabrobates's slander when he called her a whore—another common theme when men call into question and judge a women's sexual behaviour in order to discredit them—and his threats to crucify her when he had defeated her. Semiramis's strategy worked, but she was wounded in the counterattack and her army retreated west of the Indus. Even in retreat, she remained resourceful, causing the slaughter of many Indians on an overcrowded pontoon bridge:

> She cut the fastenings which held the bridge together; ... the pontoon bridge, having been broken apart at many points and bearing great numbers of pursuing Indians, was brought down in chaos by the violence of the current and caused the death of many of the Indians.

Diodorus Siculus 2, 19, 9

One legend involved King Ara the Beautiful of Armenia after whom Semiramis allegedly lusted; she asked Ara to marry her, but he refused. Indignant at this regal snub, she assembled her armies and invaded Armenia; during the battle, she slew Ara. The tabloid reports got even worse when Pliny the Elder and Hyginus both record that Semiramis's sexual voracity strayed into bestiality when she had sex with a horse.[13] Semiramis also earned the reputation for being a witch—another frequent and effective way of disparaging a prominent and successful woman. Making the most of this, though, she responded by pretending to raise Ara's body from the dead. This ended the war.

In the eighth century BCE, an Arabian woman called Samsi reigned as queen. She bravely rebelled against Tiglath-Pileser III the king of Assyria, who became the first foreign ruler to subdue the Arabs when he attacked and defeated Samsi; he forced her surrender and imposed on her a tribute to enable her to remain in power as a puppet, which she did for the next twenty years. That tribute included gold, silver, male and female camels, and all types of spices. Her defeat, however, was significant: the Assyrians took from her numerous prisoners of war, 30,000 camels, and more than 20,000 oxen as booty. An inscription tells us that 9,400 of her soldiers were killed, while 5,000 bags of various lucrative spices, religious icons, and armaments and her estates were seized. When she fled to the desert, Tiglath-Pileser set fire to her remaining tents and she was said to have fled the battlefield like a 'wild she-ass of the desert'. Profound as this defeat was, it shows clearly the military power and wealth she formerly enjoyed and the prodigious size of the armed forces she commanded.

So the precedent for successfully belligerent women was clearly there for Herodotus to see; these descriptions would have informed his writing on ancient Greek women's role in war, and that of the Greeks' neighbours.

'Cruel' and 'unusually militaristic' are three apt words to describe Queen Tomyris of the Scythian Massagetae; at the same time, though, her actions against Cyrus can be seen as just desserts for his duplicity. Strabo, Polyaenus, Cassiodorus, and Jordanes, as well as Herodotus, all refer to her. She is notorious for slaying King Cyrus the Great (*c.* 576–530 BCE), the founder of the Achaemenid Empire, when he invaded her country. Herodotus shows his readers how Tomyris easily saw through the king's proposal of marriage as an ill-disguised desire to topple her and enslave the Massagetae; she wisely rejected him.

Tomyris showed more wisdom and foresight when Cyrus began building bridges in order to cross the frontier river dividing their territories; she warned him three times to end the aggression against her country.[14]

Cyrus then made the mistake of duping Tomyris's army, under the command of her son, Spargapises, into drinking copious amounts of wine while at battle readiness; Cyrus had slyly left a stash behind on the battlefield when his army withdrew. Scythians, however, were not used to drinking wine, being much more partial to hashish and fermented mare's milk; accordingly, they drank themselves stupid and, while under the influence, were victoriously subdued by Cyrus's Persians. Spargapises was captured; Tomyris warns that her patience is running out, and that she will give Cyrus his fill of blood if he does not release her son.[15] Yet when Spargapises had persuaded Cyrus to remove his bonds, he promptly committed suicide. A vengeful mother Tomyris challenged Cyrus to a second battle, promising him that fill of blood. Herodotus melodramatically describes it as the 'fiercest of all the battles waged between the barbarians'. Tomyris was victorious: Cyrus was killed; Tomyris cut off his head and crucified his corpse; she then shoved his head into a wineskin full of human blood.

To the ancient Greeks themselves, women and war simply did not mix. Herodotus's sensational telling of this escapade was designed not just to illuminate what he saw as the perverse and blood-thirsty behaviour of barbarian women compared with the civilised women of Greece, but to demonstrate just how far removed from Greek women they were. At the same time, though, he does expose Tomyris's good political and military sense, and exhibits some sympathy when he shows that, despite her victory, Tomyris has ultimately lost because she has lost her son. Herodotus's general description of the Massagetae, including their partiality for routine human sacrifice, and the prurient descriptions of the allegedly permissive sexual *mores* of barbarian women are manifestations of how the Greeks deployed psychological warfare of a kind by attacking the soft, vulnerable underbelly of their enemy by denigrating and slurring the sexual behaviour of their women—an insidious, prejudicial and demoralising tactic.

The story of Pheretima (d. 515 BCE), wife of the Greek Cyrenaean King Battus III and the last queen of the Battiad dynasty, provides another cautionary lesson for Herodotus's audience. When Arcesilaus, Battus's son, left Cyrene for Barca, Pheretima ruled the city as regent but Arcesilaus was murdered by exiled Cyrenaeans intent on revenge. Pheretima sped to Arysandes, the Persian governor of Egypt, seeking help in avenging the death of her son; Arysandes loaned her Egypt's army and navy, at the head of which she marched to Barca and demanded the surrender of those Barcaeans responsible for the murder of Arcesilaus; when the Barcaeans refused to own up, Pheretima laid siege to their city for nine months and finally took the city when Amasis, her Persian commander, tricked the Barcaeans. Pheretima, still crazed by vengeance, ordered the Barcaean wives' breasts to be cut off, and enslaved the rest of the Barcaeans to the Persians.

Such an atrocity was appalling enough, but for it to be committed by a woman, however strong her maternal love for a lost son, would have shocked many Greeks. Herodotus is at pains to show that such war crimes committed by a foreigner, and a woman foreigner at that, would not go unpunished. Pheretima returned to Egypt and gave the army and navy back to the governor. However, while there, she contracted a contagious parasitic disease, and died in late 515 BCE. Herodotus tells us that she was eaten alive by the worms spawned by her disease—punishment by the gods for her butchery of the women of Barca.[16]

The impressive military exploits of Artemisia I and her exemplary military service to Xerxes is described under the battle of Salamis.

Artemesia II of Caria was wife of King Mausolos (r. 387–353 BCE) with whom she ruled in consort. Herodotus described her as 'wondrous'. Decrees and laws were issued in joint names and honours were heaped on them, as an egalitarian regal couple. When Mausolos died, Artemisia ruled on her own for some years maintaining the reputation of the name Artemisia for prowess in battle.

Her expressions of grief for her husband are legendary: she is even reputed to have concocted and drunk a potion comprising her husband's bones and ashes. She organised prestigious poetry and oratory competitions to honour her late husband and completed the building of his mausoleum which became one of the Seven Wonders of the World, known as the Mausoleum of Halicarnassus. She embarrassed the people of Rhodes when she beat off an attack; the Rhodians found it hard to accept that they had been repelled by a barbarian, and a woman barbarian at that.[17]

According to Vitruvius, the conflict came about when the Rhodians tried to free themselves from the Carians after the death of Mausolos. When they sent a naval expedition to Halicarnassus, Artemisia was one step ahead; she stationed her troops and ships in a discreet harbour and positioned the town's inhabitants on the walls, whence they 'welcomed' the approaching Rhodian ships.[18] The Rhodian soldiers disembarked; Artemesia's ships attacked the Rhodian vessels now empty of troops and killed the crews. Artemisia then commandeered the Rhodian ships and sailed them back to Rhodes, crewed by Carians in disguise; here they were welcomed by the

Rhodians who thought that their navy was returning victorious. Atremisia's forces entered the town and executed the leading citizens.

Artemesia II also exemplifies how the pen can be mightier than the sword. In the words of Polyaenus:

Artemisia planted soldiers in ambush near Latmus [in modern western Turkey]; and herself, with a large train of women, eunuchs and musicians, celebrated a sacrifice at the grove of the Mother of the Gods, which was about seven stades distant from the city. When the inhabitants of Latmus came out to see the magnificent procession, the soldiers entered the city and took possession of it. Thus did Artemisia, by flutes and cymbals, possess herself of what she had unsuccessfully tried to obtain by arms.[19]

The poet Telesilla (fl. 510 BCE) was from Argos; she is just as famous for her military prowess and martial activities as she is for her poetry. Pausanias describes the brave military action of this soldier-poet at Argos.[20] After his invasion of Argive lands in 510 BCE, the battle of Sepeia saw Cleomenes, king of Sparta, defeat and wipe out the hoplites of Argos and massacre all the survivors. So, when Cleomenes attacked Argos, there were no male warriors left to defend it. Telesilla took the initiative when she posted on the city walls all the slaves and all the males normally exempt from military service because they were too young or too old. She collected weapons from sanctuaries and homes, armed the women, and drew them up in battle positions. The Spartans tried to terrify the Argive women with their battle cry but they remained unperturbed and fought bravely, standing their ground. The Spartans had realised that destroying the women of Argos would be a cheap victory, while defeat would mean a shameful and ignominious disaster, so they left the city.

Plutarch adds some fascinating detail relating to cross-dressing and bearded ladies.[21] He suggests that the battle took place on the first day of that month (the Fourth month or Hermaeus), 'on the anniversary of which they celebrate even to this day the "Festival of Impudence", at which they clothe the women in men's shirts and cloaks, and the men in women's robes and veils'.

Herodotus alludes to the Telesilla incident when he tells us about an oracle, told by a Pythian priestess, which predicted that female should conquer male:

But when the time shall come that the female conquers in battle, driving away the male, and wins great glory in Argos, then many wives of the Argives shall tear both cheeks in their mourning.[22]

Hydna of Scione, also known as Cyana, (fl. 480 BCE) brings to mind an early version of a Royal Marine commando. Hydna was an accomplished swimmer and diver and was responsible for the almost single-handed destruction of the Persian fleet.

According to Pausanias, Hydna and her father volunteered to help in the war with the Persians during a critical battle.[23] Hydna was schooled by her father, Scyllis of

Scione, an expert diver and an expert swimmer. When Xerxes's fleet was assailed by a violent storm off Mount Pelion, Hydna and Scyllis completed its destruction when they swam 10 miles in stormy waters to where the Persian navy was moored for the night. Knives in hand, they silently swam among the boats, cutting their moorings; rudderless in the wind and waves, the ships crashed together—some sank; most were badly damaged.

Herodotus is explicit in his telling of the decisive action taken by Athenian women against less patriotic fellow Athenians; the first instance is in response to the treason advocated by Lycidas when he was disposed, possibly by bribery, to accept a proposal made by the Persian Mardonius to defect to the Persians and renounce Greece. This would be in return for autonomy, land, and money for rebuilding wrecked temples. The Athenians were so angered by this preposterous suggestion that they surrounded Lycidas and stoned him to death. The women of the city then took it upon themselves to attack Lycidas's house and then stone his wife and children to death. Protection of the homeland was obviously the motivating factor; the incident demonstrates quite clearly how willing, and able, the patriotic women of Athens were to perpetrate terrible retribution in order to preserve their freedoms and honour in the face of a shameless enemy.[24]

Herodotus gives another instance of Athenian female bellicosity after the doomed expedition to Aegina when the Argives came to help the Aeginetans. Only one Athenian survived to return safely to Attica. When the wives of the Athenian troops learned this, they were outraged: they mobbed the man each demanding from him to know where her husband was; they then stabbed him to death with the brooches they wore on their tunics. The Athenian authorities were equally appalled and perplexed by this and could think of no other way to punish the women than change their dress to the Ionian style. Until the incident, Athenian women had worn Dorian dress, but this was now changed to a style that would obviate the need for brooch-pins.

Diodorus has a similar example of determined female fortitude, this time in the face of a siege imposed by the Carthaginian general Himilcon on the people of Gela in Sicily in 405 BCE. The plan was to evacuate the women and children to Syracuse because of the danger faced by the city and its inhabitants. The women, however, had other ideas and insisted they remain and endure the same fate as their menfolk. The valiant women remained in Gela and only went to Syracuse with the men when the city was surrendered. In the meantime, though, they performed a valuable role coordinating the activities of snatch parties preying on the Carthaginians.[25] They were just the sort of women a city needed when under seige; Diodorus continues:

> The Geloans defended themselves boldly; for the bits of the walls which fell during the day they rebuilt at night, with the women and children helping. Those women who were physically the strongest were armed and always in battle, while the rest of the Geloans stood by to attend to the defences and everything else with all eagerness.

Diodorus Siculus 13, 108, 2f

Another siege provides more evidence of women offering logistic support. Usually reticent when it comes to reporting women in war, Thucydides notes how in 429 BCE, women were life-savers at the seige of Plataea as executed by the Spartans. The Plataeans had prudently evacuated most of their non-combatant citizens to Athens ('their wives and children and oldest men and most of the noncombatants'), leaving a rearguard force of 400 Plataean and eighty Athenian troops, as well as 110 women 'to bake their bread for them': γυναῖκες δὲ δέκα καὶ ἑκατὸν σιτοποιοί. This tells us that female bakers, or cooks, were the norm in a garrison and in a city under siege even when all the other civilians had left. Moreover, this was not just a case of token staffing: there was one woman catering for every four soldiers and the women accounted for one in five of those left to resist the siege. Two years later, the Plataeans surrendered; the men were executed and the bread-making women enslaved—such is the importance of bread, and women.

In another rare piece of reportage on women, Thucydides tells us about the brave and resourceful womenfolk of Corcyra (modern Corfu), who made a perfect nuisance of themselves around 427 BCE hurling down roof tiles onto the heads of the besieging enemy. Greek men of the time would have it that such behaviour could not be more unseemly for a woman, for a Greek women at that. Yet it demonstrates again that, given the need and opportunity, women were quite able and prepared to fight valiantly for their city.[17] Slaves too joined in, further emphasising the absurdity of the situation and its distance from the social norm. Thucydides does not mince his words: to him it was simply and emphatically *para phusin* (unnatural). Be that as it may, the action of the women was intrumental in the Corcyran victory and Thucydides's blasé description, despite his reservations, suggests that this sort of thing was not exceptional.[26]

Support of a very different kind was provided by the prostitutes who went with the Athenians on the nine-month seige of Samos. There is no reason to believe that, like the breadmaking, this was not usual practice and women formed an integral part of logistic support in all its manifestations. Aptly, the prostitutes set up a temple to Aphrodite there.

Recent excavations have revealed that the city of Eretria attempted to protect their women and children from sieges by building a series of forts (fortified farmhouses essentially), which acted as emergency refuges outside the city. Besieged cities often fell eventually, so it was natural for the authorities to make what provision they could to protect non-combatants.

In 480 BCE, the women and children of Delphi were shipped to Achaia; the Athenians evacuated slaves and children, and presumably women, to the safety of Troezen, Aegina, and Salamis; in 431 BCE, the Plataeans and Athenians, up against Thebes, evacuated non-combatants to Athens. Brasadas moved women and children out to Olynthus fearing the reaction of Athens when Mende and Scione defected; the Agrigentes stayed one step ahead of the Carthaginians by moving women and children first to Gela, then Syracuse, and then to the Italian mainland. When Scione fell, the fighting men were executed and the remaining women and children were enslaved; the Athenians took Mende and declared it open for pillaging with no apparent slaughter; they also siezed Torone and reduced the women and children there to slavery. In a surprising reversal of practice, and a rare show of compassion, the defenders were sent to Athens and freed; things reverted to type, however, at Melos where the defenders were executed and the women and children enslaved. In 220 BCE, Lyttos in Crete was taken while its defenders were away on an expedition and its remaining population transported; the defenders returned only to find a ghost town. Worse happened at Abydos when Philip V of Macedon came calling; the defenders, fearing the worst, cut the throats of the women and children and then committed suicide themselves.

Where a surrender was negotiated, women naturally featured in the terms—there are about fifteen known instances of this in the fifth and fourth centuries BCE. Thucydides describes one such case at Potidaea in a case eerily familiar today, when safe passage was allowed for the defenders, women, children, and auxiliaries; the refugees could take one extra item of clothing (except for women who could take two) and a fixed amount of money for the journey.[27]

Cities helped other cities. An advantage of cities sending their vulnerable people to places of safety was the welcoming reception of those destinations, as in the case of the Troezenians when they took in the Athenians and the Athenians when they took in the Plataean women and children between 429 and 427 BCE. Individuals too showed generosity. Demosthenes records how Satyros, a comic actor, negotiated with Philip II to secure the release of the imprisoned daughters of Apollophanes of Pydna who were enslaved by the king at Olynthus; he compares this unfavourably with the Athenian ambassadors who sexually assaulted another female prisoner at Olynthus at a banquet.

Timessa, from Arkesine, also helped save a number of citizens; this is according to an inscription which is noteworthy because Timessa, unusually for a Greek woman, paid the ransom. Although it was not uncommon for wealthy citizens to pay ransoms on behalf of others, and about a hundred surviving decrees record public gratitude for such actions, Timessa is the only woman known to pay such a ransom.

Defensive work undertaken by women was not always carried out in a siege situation. In 417 BCE, the Argives began a massive construction project, building walls down to the sea in anticipation of a Spartan attack. The entire able-bodied citizenry was mobilised, including women and slaves.

Pausanias leaves us an account of Marpessa (or Choira, Sow), who was 'braver than the rest' in the defence of Tegea against the Spartans under King Charillus in the seventh century. The battle was inconclusive until Marpessa rallied the women of Tegea, who took up arms. Marpessa's contingent made all the difference and the Tegeans won the day, taking many prisoners including the prize catch that was the King of Sparta.[28] The jubilant women marked the occasion with a celebration in honour of Ares in which Marpessa's weaponry, rather than an effigy of Marpessa, was displayed; at the same time, the women denied the men any share of the meat from the sacrifices. These women were not just being mean to their men or greedy with their meat; they were reinforcing the role-reversal implicit in taking up arms (traditionally men's business) with a further reversal of roles when they sacrificed and ate sacrificial meat—an action that was, in this context, normally the exclusive preserve of men.

Plutarch describes the Phocian women who offered to commit suicide if their army was beaten by the Thessalians. While this may have been partly motivated by the very real fear of rape, it nevertheless also demonstrates extreme loyalty and bravery. Luckily, the Phocian army won the day.[29]

We have seen how Thucydides, somewhat grudgingly perhaps, describes an episode of targeted tile slinging. Thucydides's belligerent Corcyran women were not the only women to pick up and aggressively hurl a roof tile in anger. Four years before this episode, in 431 BCE, roof tiles were also the weapon of choice for the Plataeans when attacked by the Thebans. The Plataean women and slaves repaired to the roof tops and orchestrated a fusillade of tiles, setting the scene for an eventual rout of the attackers.[30] Indeed, Diodorus insists that it was the intervention of the women that tipped the balance in favour of the defenders. When the Thebans panicked, they left a number of their men behind who were taken prisoner.

Bombardment by tile, though, was no guarantee of military success for the women slingers: Polyaenus has the story of the female inhabitants of an unspecified Acarnanian town who made a rooftop assault on the Aitoleans attacking them. The defence failed and Acarnanian men and women died clinging together as one; significantly, the women gave up their resistance once their menfolk had perished or were captured.[31]

The biggest defeat in this situation, though, was suffered by the Selinuntians in 409 BCE at the hands of a 100,000-strong Carthaginian force, equipped with siege equipment, rampaging through Sicily. The whole town of Selinus was mobilised including elderly men, children and women, the latter distributing missiles and provisions. The wall was breached, and the subsequent hand-to-hand fighting involved not only the Selinuntian soldiers but the women too; according to Diodorus: 'many gathered to the aid of the defenders'. The Carthaginians retreated and messages were sent out from Selinus to Acragas, Gela and Syracuse requesting relief. The following day saw a repeat with the inhabitants fighting to the last roof tile when they effectively ran out of ammunition. The Carthaginians raised the town killing 16,000 citizens, capturing 5,000; only 2,600 escaped. A shocked Diodorus describes euphemistically how the women suffered 'terrible indignities, and some had to watch their daughters of marriageable age suffering treatment inappropriate for their years'. This may have included emulation of the old Assyrian atrocity of impalement where hands and heads were cut off, the hands tied around the necks of the victims, their heads stuck on swords and spears. That same year, as we have seen, Hannibal Mago took Himera: all the surviving soldiers were executed as a sacrifice to the memory of his grandfather Hamilcar and the women and children shared out among his troops. The city itself was totally destroyed, its buildings, including the temples, were razed to the ground.[32]

Diodorus is important because, first and foremost, he describes the atrocities endured by women and girls; a life of slavery awaited the women who survived 'under masters who spoke an unintelligible language and were nothing short of bestial'. He also clearly tells how women became embroiled in the close combat when the walls were breached, and emphasises how essential it was for women to participate in the conflict for the good of the city and its survival: in the chaos, 'the magnitude of the crisis was so great that it called for even the aid of their women'.

A report by Pausanias would suggest that roof-top tile-slinging by women defenders was typical behaviour and roof tiles unleashed by women were raining down on besiegers all the time.[33] Apparently, at the beginning of the Second Messenian War in the early seventh century BCE, a bad storm prevented the women of Eira from taking to the rooftops for a tile barrage on the attacking Spartans below.

Plutarch reports on the unusual, almost comic, death of Pyrrhus in 272 BCE after he was wounded by an Argive—not a hero of any kind, simply 'the son of a poor old woman' who was viewing the action in a teichoscopy:

> His mother, like the rest of the women, was at this moment watching the battle from the roof, and when she saw that her son was fighting with Pyrrhus she was distressed by the danger he was in, so, picking up a tile with both hands hurled it at Pyrrhus. It hit his head just below his helmet and crushed the vertebrae at the base of his neck, making his sight blurred and his hands drop the reins. Then he sank down from his horse ...

Plutarch continues to describe how the old mother's well-aimed tile was followed by a very messy decapitation of the dazed and injured Pyrrhus. Her missile has been called 'the most historically significant roof tile'.[34]

The *teichoskopeia* (teichoscopy) is an epic device in which observers on the city walls describe the battle scenes raging below them; since the people watching from the walls are non-combatants, they are usually women and eldery men. Apart from providing commentary on the action below, the teichoscopy also gives us an insight into the effects of battle on women or on a particular woman, especially in relation to combatants who may well be husband, brother, father, or son, or someone else close to them.

Probably the most famous, and certainly one of the earliest, teichoscopy is Helen's in Homer's *Iliad*. Helen is busy at her loom when she is approached in her bedchamber by Iris, disguised as her sister-in-law Laodice, the daughter of Priam. Helen is taken to the walls where Priam asks her to point out the Achaean heroes she sees on the Trojan plain where the Greek and Trojan armies are preparing for the duel between Menelaus and Paris, former and current husbands of Helen. Helen thus becomes a vital source of military intelligence for the Trojans. In a parade of heroes, she points out Agamemnon, Odysseus, Telamonian Ajax, and Idomeneus; she praises both the Greek and the Trojan armies, an indication perhaps of the paradoxical situation she finds herself in—she, a Greek woman, is now firmly ensconced in the Trojan camp. The stakes are high, not only because whoever wins the duel will win Helen, but more crucially, he will also ultimately win the war for either Greece or Troy. Helen watches Menelaus defeat Paris and then witnesses Aphrodite saving Paris, divine interference which serves to extend the war and results in many more casualties. What she sees of the duel turns Helen against Paris; she wishes him dead, praises the might of Menelaus, and challenges Paris to resume the duel, sure that he will be slain. Paris is unimpressed and can think only of bedding Helen while Menelaus desperately tries to find Paris in order to finish him off.

Hesiod's *Shield of Heracles* features a teichoscopy on the shield and is notable not just for the striking image of women wailing and tearing their cheeks—which must have been typical female behaviour on the walls—but also the fact that it was there on the shield in the first place, indicating that, for women, watching proceedings from the walls was itself typical behaviour in myth and in real life.

Plutarch gives us the pleasing story of the gutsy women of Chios who were appalled when their menfolk signed a treaty with the hostile and agressive Erythraeans. One of the injurious terms imposed on the Chians was that they were to surrender on oath all of their clothes, apart from one cloak and a tunic (*himation* and *chiton*). To extricate their men from such a humiliation the women, keen to protract hostilities, told them to explain to the Erythraeans that, in their dialect, cloak and tunic translated as shield and spear. The Chians thus retained their weapons and were able to make a safe escape.[35]

Around 379 BCE, the women of Sinope, a city on the Black Sea, were particularly inventive—when attacked by the Persian Datames, they dressed up in imitation armour (actually bronze pots and pans) to give the impression that the defending forces were more numerous than they really were. Aeneas Tacticus adds the footnote that the women were not permitted to throw anything because you can spot a woman a mile off by the way she throws. He also tells that Pisistratus had women board his Athenian ships to fool the Megarians into believing that they were up against a much stronger force.[36]

Women were an essential component of the army baggage train. Perhaps the most famous example of this is given by Xenophon in his *Anabasis*—the 'March of the 10,000' when in 401 BCE the baggage train supported by Greek mercenaries hired by Cyrus the Younger in his bid to take the Persian throne certainly included women.[37] After the battle of Cunaxa when the Persians reached the Black Sea, the baggage train was deemed too cumbersome (literally too much 'baggage') so they put everyone age forty or over, the sick, injured, children and women and actual baggage, onto boats while the younger people marched along the coast. However, we do know that some women remained with the troops: there was at least one slave dancer still in the company of a lucky Arcadian when the army reached Paphlagonia.[38] There were attempts to conceal women and boys, which were obviously successful because women provided life-saving encouragement to floundering soldiers during a perilous river crossing. They were also busied preparing food for the troops.

Baggage trains were, of course, valued highly by the troops, for many different reasons. They were so important that victorious soldiers were known to defect to the defeated army if the baggage train was captured by them and herded away behind enemy lines. This confirms that, particularly among mercenaries, when their wives, concubines, or mistresses were in those trains, the bond of affection between them was greater than loyalty to one army or another.

Catalogues and handbooks of one kind or another were common in the Greek world; 'types' of men and women feature prominently and include various war-related catalogues of armies in the *Iliad*; chthonic catalogues of women in the *Odyssey*; and Neanthes of Cyzicus's *About Illustrious Men* in the third century BCE. Charon of Carthage compiled two collections four books long listing illustrious men and women in short biographies and anecdotes. Photius (codex 161) tells us about the fourth-century-CE sophist Sopatros and his twelve books, one of which extracts brave exploits of women by Artemon of Magnesia and another describes 'women who achieved a distinguished name and great glory'. Theophrastus (frr 625-7) gives us a list of women who caused wars or destroyed houses. They all probably do show that cataloguing, including the cataloguing of warlike women, was good publishing business and many more were compiled than have survived.

There was also no shortage of advice on how to prosecute a war or win a battle. Of the extant works of military strategy and warfare in the earlier part of the first century BCE, there was the *Poliokretika* or *How to Survive under Siege* by Aeneas Tacticus (fl. fourth century BCE), 19–42 of the *Histories* on military matters, especially camps by Polybius (*c.* 200–*c.* 118 BCE), and author of the lost *Tactica*. These, along with Plutarch's, *De Mulierum Virtutibus* (*On the Bravery of Women*) and the anonymous, undatable *Tractatus de Mulieribus*, an obscure Greek work describing fourteen mainly valiant Greek and barbarian women, are of interest to us.

In Plutarch's *De Mulierum Virtutibus*, a section of his *Moralia*, there are fifteen ethnic groups of women from various parts of Greece, and twelve individuals.[39] Of the Trojan women, he emphasises the initiative they took in establishing a homeland for the Trojans in Italy:

> It suddenly occurred to the women that for a happy and successful people any sort of a settled habitation on land is better than all that wandering and voyaging, and that the Trojans must create a homeland, since they could not recover what they had lost. So, altogether they burned the ships.

Plutarch, *De Mulierum Virtutibus*, 1

Of the plucky Persian women, he tells how they lifted up their clothes and made heroes out of their erstwhile cowardly warriors:

> When Cyrus incited the Persians to revolt from king Astyages and the Medes he was defeated in battle. The Persians fled to the city, with the enemy not far from forcing their way in with them, so the women ran out to meet them, and, lifting up their tunics, said, 'Where are you rushing to so fast, you who are biggest cowards in the whole world? Surely you cannot, in your retreat, slink in here from out there.' The Persians, mortified at the sight and the words, chided themselves for being cowards, rallied and, engaging the enemy once more, routed them.

De Mulierum Virtutibus, 5

Celtic women exhibited marvellous skills of diplomacy, thus preventing internecine bloodshed:

> Before the Celts crossed over the Alps and settled in that part of Italy where they now live, a dire and persistent factional discord broke out among them which went on and on to the point of civil war. The women, however, put themselves between the armies, and, taking up the issues, arbitrated and decided them with such irreproachable fairness that a wonderful friendship of all towards all came about between both states and families. As a result of this the Celts continued to consult with the women regarding war and peace, and to decide through them any disputed matters with regard to their allies.

> *De Mulierum Virtutibus*, 6

They also inspired cross-dressing by brave and inventive Etruscan women:

> When the Etruscans took Lemnos and Imbros, they forcibly abducted Athenian women, to whom children were born. The Athenians expelled these children from the islands on the grounds that they were half- barbarian; nevertheless, the refugees put in at Taenarum and made themselves useful to the Spartans in the war with the Helots. For this they received citizenship and the right of intermarriage … the wives of the prisoners came to the jail, and after many prayers and entreaties, were permitted by the guards to go just close enough to greet and to speak to their husbands. When they had gone inside the women made their husbands quickly change their clothes, leaving theirs for their wives; then, putting on their wives' clothes they walked out with their faces covered.

> *De Mulierum Virtutibus*, 8

Plutarch's women are indeed well named by Plutarch. Their military talent extends to tactical excellence, clever deception, and other elements of psychological warfare—leading from the front, setting a good example, ruthlessness, compassion and modesty. We can identify the same laudable traits in the women described by Polyaenus.

Polyaenus (fl. mid second century CE), in his *Strategems*, covers much of the ground and characters we have met in Plutarch with the addition of more women, and some extra detail not offered by Plutarch. Five of Polyaenus's women feature in the *Tractatus de Muliebris*: Semiramis, Rhodogyne, Tomyris, Pheretime, and Artemisia but, interestingly, only Polyaenus's Rhodogyne and Artemisia bear any similarity to the account given in the *Tractatus*. Some of the entries are biographies while others describe a particular stratagem. Here are some of the women described by Polyaenus; they demonstrate a wide range of involvement by women in military affairs exhibiting bravery, self-sacrifice, patriotism, and diplomacy.

We have already met the resourceful Semiramis (*c.* 811–806 BCE), but this inscriptional information is of additional interest; it reads like an extract from her *curriculum vitae*—a complete military all-rounder:

> Semiramis received intelligence of the revolt of the Siraces while she was in her bath; and without waiting to have her sandals put on or her hair done, she got out immediately and took to the field. Her exploits are recorded on pillars, in these words:'Nature made me a woman, but I have raised myself to rival the greatest of men.… I have built walls which are impregnable; and with iron forced a way through inaccessible rocks. At great expense I have made roads in places which before not even the wild beasts could cross.

Strategemata 8, 26

Cheilonis also uses cross-dressing to affect the release of her husband:

> When Cheilonis, the daughter of Cleadas, and wife of Theopompus, learnt that her husband was taken as prisoner-of-war by the Arcadians, she went to Arcadia to visit him. The Arcadians, seeing the affection she had shown, allowed her to visit him in his cell; once there she changed clothes with him, and so he made his escape, while she remained in prison. Before long Theopompus had the chance to seize a priestess of Artemis while she was celebrating in a procession at Pheneus; the inhabitants of Tegea released Cheilonis in exchange for the priestess.

Strategemata 8, 34

Poycrete uses shrewd subterfuge to rid her county of the Milesians:

> The Milesians, with the help of the Erythraeans, made war on the Naxians; Diognetus, the the Milesian general, ravaged their country, and brought away considerable booty, including a number of women, among whom was Polycrete. Diognetus fell in love with Polycrete who lived with him not as a slave, but as his wife. In the Milesian camp a local festival was celebrated, at which the Milesians give themselves up to drinking and pleasure. Polycrete requested Diognetus' permission to send a small present of the sumptuous fare that was prepared to her brothers back home; so, she moulded up a piece of lead in a cake, and ordered the messenger to tell her brothers that it was intended only for their use. On the lead she inscribed a message to the effect that if they attacked the Milesian camp, they might surprise the enemy while they were drunk and sleeping. The Naxian generals accordingly attacked, and were victorious. Polycrete was highly honoured by her citizens for her service; and at her insistance they allowed Diognetus to continue his reign and keep his possessions.

Strategemata 8, 36; see also Plutarch, Moralia 254

Eryxo plans the successful assassination of the tyrant Laarchus (*Strategemata* 8, 41); Chrysame takes control and wins the day with some judicious use of magic (*Strategemata* 8, 43); and courageous Leaena renders herself speechless under torture:

> Aristogeiton had a mistress, whose name was Leaena. Hippias ordered her to be interrogated by torture, so as to determine what she knew of the conspiracy; after she had long bravely endured the various tortures that were visited on her, she cut out her tongue with her own hand, lest any more pain should extort from her any information.

Strategemata 8, 45

Proud and noble Axiothea prefers death to slavery:

> When Ptolemy, king of Egypt, sent a powerful force to dispossess Nicocles (fl. *c.* 374 BCE) of the kingdom of Cyprus, both Nicocles and his brothers, rather than submit to slavery, committed suicide. Axiothea the wife of Nicocles, wishing to emulate them ... Axiothea ... first stabbed herself, and then threw herself into the fire to save even her dead body from falling into the hands of the enemy.

Strategemata 8, 48

Mania was a woman warrior of the first order:

> Mania, the wife of Zenis prince of Dardanus, governed the kingdom after the death of her husband, with the assistance of Pharnabazus. She always went to battle drawn in a chariot; she gave out orders while in action, formed her lines, and rewarded every man who fought well, as she saw he deserved. And—what has scarcely happened to any general, except herself—she never suffered a defeat.

Strategemata 8, 52; see also: Xenophon, *Hellenica* 3, 1

[The Anonymous] *Women Intelligent & Brave in War* is a literal translation of this somewhat obscure catalogue of women. We do not know the author, when it was written, what genre it was intended to be in, and what the real title was. It sometimes goes under *Tractatus De Mulieribus Claris in Bello* but *Gunaikes en Polemikois Sunetai kai Andreia* may be nearer the mark, given that this what is in the manuscript. Of the featured fourteen women included, two are not warrior women at all and some (for example, Argeia and Lyde) do not exhibit any military qualities. The *Tractatus* remains a valuable adjunct to Plutarch, Polyaenus, and to the other primary sources of women war warriors.

The fourteen women are Semiramis; Zarinaea; Nitocris the Egyptian; Nitocris the Babylonian; Argeia; Dido; Atossa; Rhodogune of Parthia; Lyde; Pheretime; Thargelia; Tomyris; Artemisia I of Caria; and Onomaris.

Zarinaea, Nitocris of Egypt, Argeia, Theiosso (Dido), Atossa, Lyde, and Thargelia are of particular interest because they do not feature in Plutarch or Polyaenus, although we do, of course, know them from other sources; Onomaris is more interesting still as the *Tractatus* is the only surviving source for her. They are all described in short, pithy thumbnail sketches.

The *Tractatus* entry tells us how Zarinaea, when her husband and brother, Cydraeus, king of the Sacians, died she married Mermerus, ruler of Parthia. Zarinaea fought in a battle against the Persians and was wounded; she was pursued and caught by a Stryangaeus who spared her life. Mermerus later captured and killed him despite Zarinaea's plea that he be spared. An indignant Zarinaea then released some prisoners with whom she conspired to kill Mermerus; she then allied with the Persians. The author's source is Ctesias (*FGrH* 688 F7).

Nitocris was militarily adept and deceptive. She was, apparently, cleverer even than Semiramis, diverting the river running through her city in order to hamper the progress of any enemy incursions. She also built her tomb over the city gate to trick Darius who would expect to find treasures inside. All he got was an inscription berating him for his greed. Thargelia of Milesia married Antiochus, king of the Thessalians; when he died, she ruled Thessally for thirty years, repelling a Persian invasion through diplomacy.

Onomaris was a distinguished Galatian, a Gaulish-Celtic tribe. She showed great leadership and military prowess. When her country was beset by 'scarcity', she took control of events because no man was willing to lead the Galatians to a new, more rewarding, life elsewhere. In this respect, she is reminiscent of Artemisia I, who also came forward to take up power in the absence of any man. Onomaris pooled all the resources owned by her tribe, in order presumably to deter envy and superiority and to foster communal ownership and led her people over the Ister in a mass emigration; she then defeated the locals there and ruled the new land. These events probably took place in the fourth or third centuries BCE. Onomaris typifies the not unusual high social status of Celtic women, some of whom rose to prominence as leaders of men; Boudica and Cartimandua are famous examples. Four out of Plutarch's twenty-six women are Celts.

Ten of the fourteen *Tractatus* women are non-Greek, nine of the ten are from different countries, while the four Greeks are each from different *poleis*; they are all queens. The geographical diversity and regal status may suggest a deliberate decision to demonstrate the ubiquity of warrior women in the Mediterranean world and the relatively high number of queens who exerted independence and power. Most got to be where they were by dint of their being wives, mothers, or widows of reigning or former reigning kings; none of the widows show a need or desire to remarry. They are their own women, women powerful now in their own right; some go on to be more famous than their husbands, as in the case of Tomyris and Artemisia. They all hold on to their power tenaciously. Physical appearance is irrelevant to the author of the *Tractatus*. We know from other sources that some of the fourteen were beautiful, but our author focuses, by and large, on their military or political qualities. Guile and ingenuity are key weapons and stratagems in their world of war—part of the 'intelligence' alluded to in the work's title that some of our women have in spades; Semiramis, Artemisia, the two Nitocrises, Dido, and Atossa all use deception to good effect.

Women played an active and vital role in keeping the renowned war machine at Sparta well-oiled and efficient. Since Spartan men were preoccupied with military training, bonding with comrades in mess life, and constantly doing battle, it fell to women to run the farms and homesteads back home and keep the *polis* going in their absence. Working the wool was never as important a part of the Spartan woman's life as it was in the rest of Greece; she had many more important things with which to fill her day. No history written by a Spartan survives; we have, therefore, to rely on the prejudiced, xenophobic, and hostile writings of other Greeks for our picture of Sparta and Spartan society. Polemic and propaganda no doubt tinge what has come down to us.

Sparta was a military society.[40] The army and the wars it fought were everything to the Spartans. Lycurgus in the eighth century BCE summed it up nicely when he said that Sparta's walls were built of men, not bricks. Women of childbearing age were essential in keeping the war machine in good working order. Indeed, the zeal with which they applied themselves to this work for the state, this war-related industrial baby production, may in fact have diminished the Spartan woman's natural maternal instincts if the following encounter is true; it occurred when a mother is told of the death of her five sons in battle and she retorts to the messenger: "'don't tell me about that you fool; tell me whether Sparta has won!" And when he declared that it was victorious, "Then," she said, "I accept gladly also the death of my sons'".[41] Just as 'sensitive' was the wife and mother who told her son or husband departing for yet another war to come home carrying his shield, or, if not, carried on it.[42] The bereaved mothers of the fallen at the battle of Leuctra in 371 BCE are said to have had smiles beaming on their faces out of sheer pride.

Women's production of male children was just as important to the Spartan *polis* as a man fighting in the Spartan army. Women who died in childbirth and men who died in battle were honoured in equal measure—with the privilege of having their names inscribed on their gravestones. By the same token, producing a son who turned out to be a coward was a cause for great shame and sorrow. One traitor, Pausanias, met a terrible end when he took refuge in a sanctuary to Athena. His mother, Theano, instead of pleading for his life, picked up a brick and placed it in the doorway. Very soon, others followed her lead and completely bricked up the temple door. Pausanias eventually died a slow death from suffocation and starvation inside. Plutarch, in his *Lacaenarum Apophthegmata* (*Sayings of Spartan Women*), cites three Spartan mothers who killed their cowardly sons with their own hands.

As noted, Spartan men were preoccupied, obsessed even, with their military careers and, though usually marrying from their mid-twenties, did not see very much of domestic or family life before the age of thirty. Their wives, therefore, played a vital and active economic and domestic role in raising their children and managing the household. It was they who were wholly responsible for raising sons until they were aged seven when they left to join the junior army (*agoge*)—the start of their extensive and intensive training. It was, therefore, crucial that women of the citizen class be in tip-top condition physically and mentally to prepare them for quality conception and the very best in motherhood. Like women in the rest of Greece, the wife stayed at home but, unlike her sisters elsewhere she was educated in the arts and took training in athletics, dancing and chariot racing: a strong, fit and educated mother delivered strong babies for a strong army for a strong Sparta.

The military achievements and aspirations of Sparta and the Spartans held such a fascination to other Greeks that Plutarch compiled a book on the famous sayings of Spartan women, the *Lacaenarum Apophthegmata* in the *Moralia*; some of these refer to the roles played by women in the Spartan military world. Two are attributed to Gorgo (d. between between 518 and 508 BCE) the wife of Leonidas I: Gorgo was famed for her military and political judgement and wisdom. She was the daughter of a king of Sparta, the wife of another, and the mother of a third. When she was about eighteen (Herodotus says eight or nine), Gorgo precociously but astutely told her father, the vacillating King Cleomenes, to dismiss the tyrant Aristagoras of Miletus, who requested military aid for cash from Sparta for his rebellion against Persia. Gorgo also rose to the occasion when a mysterious blank wax tablet was sent to Sparta from the exiled king Demaratus, then residing at the Persian court, regarding a Persian attack on Greece:

> When it had arrived at Lacedemon, the Lacedemonians were not able to make head or tail of it until at last, as I am informed, Gorgo, the daughter of Cleomenes and wife of Leonidas, suggested a plan of which she had herself thought up, bidding them scrape the wax and they would find writing on the wood; and doing as she said they found the writing and read it, and after that they informed the other Greeks.[43]

Here are more excerpts from Plutarch's *Lacaenarum Apophthegmata*, all illustrating the bellicose mind-set of Spartan women. The following shows the high regard with which women held war heroes:

> When Brasidas, Argileonis' son, was killed [at the battle of Amphipolis in 422 BCE] some citizens of Amphipolis arrived at Sparta and visited her; they asked if Brasidas had met his death with honour and in a way worthy of Sparta. And when they proceeded to tell of his greatness, and declared that he was the best of all the Spartans, she said, 'My son was a good and honourable man, but Sparta has many a man even better than him'.[44]

To Spartan women, cowardice is anathema:

> When a messenger came from Crete bringing the news of the death of Acrotatus [son of Areus I, king of Sparta who fell at the battle of Megalopolis in 265 BCE], she said, 'When he met the enemy, was he not bound either to be killed by them or to

kill them? It is more pleasing to hear that he died in a manner worthy of myself, his country, and his ancestors than if he had lived forever a coward.[45]

Cowardice carries a heavy price:

> Damatria heard that her son had been a coward and unworthy of her, and when he arrived home, she murdered him. This is the epigram referring to her:
> Sinner against our laws, Damatrius, slain by his mother, was of the Spartan youth; she was of Sparta too.[46]

There is no hiding place or escape for cowards:

> Another, when her sons had run away from battle and come to her, said,'Where have you come now in your cowardly flight, vile sinners? Do you intend to slink in here where you came out of? And so saying she pulled up her dress and showed them where.
> One woman, seeing her son coming towards her, asked, 'How is our country?' And when he said, 'everyone's' dead,' she picked up a tile and, hurling it at him, killed him, saying, 'And so they sent you to bring the bad news to us!'[47]

Disability is no bar to potential bravery; no help for heroes here: 'Another, as she accompanied a lame son on his way to the field of battle, said,'At every step, my child, remember to be brave.'[48]

In the first half of the seventh century, King Polydorus of Sparta defeated the Argive army but then, when he attacked the city of Argos, he found himself up against the women of Argos, the only survivors there.

Spartan women rose to the occasion against the Messenians when the Spartan forces were busy fighting outside the city; a squadron of Messenians stationed itself menacingly outside the apparently defenceless city, so the women took up arms and repelled the attackers. When the Spartans returned, they believed their armoured women to be Messenians and would have attacked them had not their wives and daughters removed their armour to reveal who they really were. The Christian author Lactantius (*c.* 250–*c.* 325 CE) primly reports that the men and women soldiers lost no time in reacquainting themselves with each other; his suggestion is that they just had sex with the first woman they came across, regardless of whose wife she was: 'But the men, recognising their wives, and excited to passion by the sight, rushed to promiscuous intercourse, for there was no time to discriminate.'[49] The war monument at Messene bears the names of twenty-four fallen, ten of whom are women.

Timycha of Sparta (early fourth century BCE), and her husband Myllias of Croton, were part of a group of Pythagorean pilgrims who were attacked by Syracusan soldiers on their way to Metapontum, in defiance of the tyrant Dionysius the Elder. Beans were taboo to Pythagoreans so when they had the option of running through a field of beans to escape, they declined. Instead, they fought and died, with the exception of the pregnant Timycha and her husband, who were taken prisoner. Dionysius interrogated her about the taboo, but, mindful of her duty to preserve Pythagorean mysteries, she refused to answer. Instead, she bit off her tongue and spat it out at his feet in a supreme gesture of defiance, and to ensure her silence.

Yet it was not always unalloyed bravery. When the Theban army invaded Sparta after the battle of Leuctra in 371 BCE, the Spartan women were beside themselves, hysterical with fear—a reaction that was probably much more common than the bravery and defiance we have been hearing about. We know more about the valour shown by military-minded women because it was a relatively unusual phenomenon; the terror and extreme distress exhibited by a civilian population (non-combatant men, women, and children) on the approach of a hostile and foreign army must have been, and always has been, unbearable. In this case, the Spartan women had never seen an enemy before or experienced the atrocities and indignities which were no doubt rumoured to unfold. Even so, those populations which had been subdued before would have been similarly terrified. Xenophon describes the ineffably tense situation:

> Keeping the River Eurotas to their right they moved on, burning and plundering houses full of many valuable things ... the women could not even endure the sight of the smoke, since they had never seen an enemy before.[50]

Plutarch adds the detail. Agesilaüs was even more harassed by the commotion and shrieks and the running about throughout the city, where the elder men were enraged at the state of affairs, and the women could not keep quiet, but were totally beside themselves when they heard the shouts and saw the fires of the enemy. A boast Agesilaüs had often made, and was now regretting, was that 'no Spartan woman had ever seen the smoke of an enemy's fires'.[51]

Xenophon sums up the awful reality of the situation captured populations, men and women and slaves, found themselves in: 'It is a law established for all time among all men that when a city is taken in war, the people and property of the inhabitants belong to the captors.'[52]

For the ancient Greeks, rape came with the sanction of the gods. The Greek gods and heroes were rape role models. Zeus raped Leda in the form of a swan, and Europa in the guise of a bull. He raped Danae disguised as the rain. He raped Alkmen masquerading as her own husband. Zeus raped Ganymede. Antiope was raped by Zeus; Cassandra was raped by Ajax the Lesser; Chrysippus was raped by his tutor Laius; Persphone was raped by Hades; Medusa was raped by Poseidon; Philomela was raped by her brother-in-law; the daughters of Leucippus, Phoebe and Hilaeira, were abducted, raped, and later married to Castor and Pollux.

Homer rated a slave woman at four oxen and an iron tripod at twelve oxen; although it must be said in a glimpse of mitigation that both the enslaved Briseis and Chryseis are loved or admired by Achilles and Agamemnon.[53]

The Greeks did little, though, without the sanction of the gods; war and battle were no exceptions. Religion safeguarded the sacred nature of treaties; it demanded the security and inviolability of envoys and it upheld the sanctity of temples and anyone taking refuge in those temples. As we have seen, armies on the move were always accompanied by a flock of sheep fattened up for sacrifice: the rites of bloodletting (*sphagia*) prevailed at every critical juncture, whether it was before crossing a river, invading a border, striking camp, or even starting the battle. Often the sacrifices were preceded by a meal, washed down by generous amounts of wine—that meal could be the soldiers' last supper, the alcohol injected courage and unrestrained abandon, fuelling pillage and rape in victory when a city or town was mercilessly sacked, with men, women, and children raped and mutilated.

Moreover, the Greeks considered the rape of women acceptable behaviour within the 'rules' of warfare; vanquished women were just another item of war booty, later to be redeployed as wives, concubines, slaves, or recycled war trophies. The practice goes back at least to the *Iliad*, where Andromache speculates on what will happen to her when Troy loses the war.

Moreover, in Greece, women came under the definition of property. The rape of a woman was a property crime, committed against the man who owned the woman. If this was the case in everyday, normal civilian life, what chance did the vanquished woman have after a siege? In wars fought by the Greeks and way before that, particularly in the often repellent postcript to sieges, the systematic rape of women, men, and children on the losing side was, as with Xenophon, par for the course, with the odious assumption that it was an expectation, a duty even. It has been so, to a greater or lesser extent, ever since. This may account for the absence in Herodotus of descriptive episodes of rape; rape was simply quite normal battle or siege aftermath behaviour. His mention of the rape of Phocian woman by Persian troops in 480 BCE is a rare case. 'Barbarian' Xerxes impaled Sataspes for raping the daughter of Megabyzus, but probably because it was an infringement of Megabyzus's property rights; the same is probably true in his description of Paris's abduction of Helen where the offense is committed against Menelaus and not Helen who is merely his property. Herodotus points out that the higher the status of the victim then the heavier the penalty for committing rape; he compares the penalties for rape enshrined in the Gortyn Code that vary according to the standing of the victim and describes how sexual voracity corresponds with political lust and tyranny.

Generally speaking, the historians are silent on the issue of war rape. Other than the case of the Phocians referred to above there is nothing else that has survived. Whether this is due to the fact that it was standard practice and not worth the mention, or because of some shame or embarrassment on the part of the historian it is impossible to tell. However, it is difficult to believe that, in reality, rape was more often than not a terrible finale to the numerous sackings and defeats where women and children were taken into captivity and enslaved—given what we know about warfare before and after the Greeks. In 1919, in the wake of the First World War, Helen Law posed this question, showing, it seems, that nothing much had changed when it comes to the banalty of war rape:

> How far the silence of the historians is to be regarded as proof that other and perhaps worse atrocities were not committed. It is conceivable that other acts of violence were not recorded because they were regarded as unimportant or not unusual enough to be interesting, or were suppressed to shield the perpetrator of the deed.

Thucydides describes how the Thracians sacked Mycalessus and the women and children were put to the sword; but were the women raped beforehand?[54] The pupils in a boys' school there were certainly massacred. How often was rape committed during the euphemistic enslavement of women when women were enslaved in 427 BCE when the Spartans established that the Plataeans had never helped them against the Thebans and up to 200 Plataean men were slaughtered and the town was razed; when the women and children of Mytilene had a lucky escape when the Athenians rescinded a command that they be enslaved; when the women of Scione were enslaved and their men slain after the town revolted around 423 BCE; or when Cleon captured Torone and sold the women into slavery and sent the men away to Athens in 422 BC? Isocrates tells us that when the Melians refused to compromise when the Athenians refused their request to remain neutral Melos was besieged, the men were butchered, the town was destroyed and the women and children found themselves enslaved. Mass deportation of all inhabitants including wives and children occurred at Aegina in 431 BCE and Histiaea.

War, as Homer said, may be man's work, but it is, at same time, the curse of many a woman.

No Greek or Roman woman was ever conscripted into, press-ganged, volunteered, or signed up for a place in the ranks of a Greek army. There was simply no place for women in the army or the navy. However, our survey of women and conflict clearly shows that women played a significant role in many aspects of battle and war.

Endnotes

Introduction

1. Garlan, *War in the Ancient World*, p. 17

Chapter One

1. britishmuseum.org/explore/highlights/highlight_objects/me/t/the_standard_of_ur.aspx
   The Narmer Palette, or the Great Hierakonpolis Palette, features some of the earliest hieroglyphics. Robert Brier refers to the Narmer Palette as 'the first historical document in the world': *Daily Life of the Ancient Egyptians* p. 202. See also Spalinger, *War in Ancient Egypt.*
2. See Copper, *The Curse of Agade* p. 52; Klein, *The Royal Hymns of Shulgi*, p. 131; and Hamblin, *Warfare in the Ancient Near East.*
3. See Saggs, *Civilisation Before Greece and Rome*, p. 177ff.
4. *Exodus* 17, 14, 16. *1 Samuel*, 15, 3.
5. See Luckenbill, *Ancient Records of Assyria and Babylonia II*, p. 314.
6. *2 Kings* 8, 12; 15, 16.
7. *Zechariah* 14:2 and *Isaiah* 13:16; *Lamentations* 5, 11 (All King James Version).

Chapter Two

1. For example, Molloy, *Swords and Swordsmanship in the Aegean Bronze Age* (2010) and Konsolaki, *Cranial Trauma in Ancient Greece*
2. Bakas, *The Evidence of Military Traumas in the Minoan and Mycenaean Burials*
3. For example, Beckman, *Hittite Chronology*, p. 23: 'A terminus *ante quem* for the destruction of the Hittite empire has been recognised in an inscription carved at Medinet Habu in Egypt in the eighth year of Ramesses III (1175 BCE). This text narrates a contemporary great movement of peoples in the eastern Mediterranean, as a result of which 'the lands were removed and scattered to the fray. No land could stand before their arms, from Hatti, Kode, Carchemish, Arzawa, Alashiya on being cut off. [i.e.: cut down]'.

Chapter Three

1. Finley, *Ancient History*, p. 67. Thucydides 1, 15, 3–5.
2. See Bagnall, *The Peloponnesian War*; Grainger, *Hellenistic and Roman Naval Wars.*

3. See Low, *War, Death and Burial in Classical Sparta* in which she cautions against taking the overtly militaristic view of Sparta at face value. *Palatine Anthology* 7, 11, 2.
4. See Xenophon, *Constitution of the Lacedaemonians*, 3, 16.

Chapter Four

1. Dio Chrysostom: *The Eleventh Discourse Maintaining that Troy was not Captured*
2. Wood, 'Preface' of *In Search of the Trojan War* (2 ed.)
3. See Rutter, 'Troy VII and the Historicity of the Trojan War', Dartmouth College dartmouth. edu/~prehistory/aegean/?page_id=630#L27Top;
4. Latacz, *Evidence from Homer*.
5. Korfmann, *Was There a Trojan War?*
6. *The Times*, 20 August 2001.
7. Herodotus 6, 86
8. *Naturalis Historia* 6, 3, 10
9. Herodotus 4, 110–117
10. Strabo, *Geographia* 5, 50
11. Euripides, *Hercules Furens*, 408 *ff*; Apollonius Rhodius, *Argonautica*, 2, 777 *ff* and 966ff; Diodorus Siculus, *Bibliotheca Historica*, 4, 16; Ps.-Apollodorus, *Bibliotheca*, 2, 5, 9; Pausanias 5, 10, 9; Quintus Smyrnaeus, *Posthomerica*, 6, 240 *ff*; and Hyginus, *Fabulae*, 30
12. Plutarch, *Theseus*
13. Pliny, *Naturalis Historia* 34, 75
14. Diodorus Siculus 3, 54–56. See also Strabo, *Geography* 12, 8, 6 and Tzetzes on Lycophron, 243
15. Pausanias, 4.4.1–3
16. Pausanias, 4.5.8
17. Pausanias, 4.7.10
18. Pausanias, 4.6.6., 4.7.1
19. Pausanias, 4.7.3
20. Pausanias, 4.8.7; 4.8.1; and 4.8.4. For the apparent anachronism here relating to the deployment of the phalanx, see Snodgrass, *The Hoplite Reform and History*, 110–122
21. Smith, *Early History of Peloponnesus and Sparta to the end of the Messenian Wars, B.C. 668.* p. 10
22. Pausanias, 4.15.4
23. Pausanias, 4.15.7–16, 4
24. Pausanias, 4.17.2-9; Tyrtaeus *fragment* 5 in Edmonds, J. M., *Greek Elegy and Iambus*, Harvard. 'The Spartans themselves in their wars march in time to the poems of Tyrtaeus which they recite from memory ... after the Lacedaemonians prevailed over the Messenians because of the generalship of Tyrtaeus, they established the custom in their campaigns that, after dinner and the hymn of thanksgiving, each sing in turn the poems of Tyrtaeus; their military commander acts as judge and gives a prize of meat to the winner', Athenaeus, *Deipnosophistae* 14.630f, trans. Douglas E. Gerber, *Greek Elegiac Poetry*, Loeb (1999), pp. 33–44
25. Plutarch, *Septem sapientium convivium* 10, 153f. (*Moralia* 153f–154a).
26. Thucydides, *History of the Peloponnesian War* 1, 15, 3. See also Herodotus 5, 99; Plutarch, *Amatorius* 17 (*Moralia* 760e–761b)
27. For example, Tausend: *Der Lelantische Krieg—ein Mythos?*

Chapter Five

1. Pausanias, 2.24.8–9
2. The word *hoplon* is usually used in the plural (*hopla*) to denote all arms, with hoplites indicating a man at arms.

3. Herodotus 1, 82
4. Herodotus 6, 77–7. Cf Cicero, *De Officiis* 1, 10, 33; Plutarch, *Moralia* 245 c–e; Pausanias 2, 20, 8 and 3, 4, 1. See Hendriks, *The Battle of Sepeia*
5. Herodotus 1, 60; 1, 64; Aristotle, *The Athenian Constitution* 14; 15
6. Herodotus 7, 154
7. Herodotus 1, 166. Polynices and Eteocles, sons of Oedipus and descendants of Cadmus, fought over Thebes and killed each other. Hence a Cadmean victory means one where victor and vanquished suffer alike.
8. Herodotus 1, 167
9. Dionysius of Halicarnassus 7, 3–4
10. Dionysius, 7, 3–11; Diodorus Siculus, *Frag. lib.* 7. in the *Excerpt, de Virt. et Vit.*; Suda, *Aristodemos*
11. Diodorus 7, 5–6; Livy 2, 14, 5–9
12. Diodorus 12, 9–10; Strabo, 6, 1, 13

Chapter Six

1. Pliny, *Natural History* 5, 112; Herodotus 5, 28
2. Herodotus 5, 11, 5, 23
3. Herodotus 5, 30
4. Herodotus 5, 31; 5, 32
5. Herodotus 5, 33
6. Herodotus 5, 30
7. Herodotus 5, 34
8. Herodotus 5, 35
9. Herodotus 3, 46–47, 54–56
10. Herodotus 5, 96
11. Herodotus 5, 99
12. Herodotus 5, 116
13. Herodotus 5, 101–102
14. Herodotus 5, 103–104
15. Herodotus 5, 123–126
16. Herodotus 5, 104
17. Herodotus 5, 108–109; 113
18. Herodotus 5, 112–113
19. Herodotus 5, 118–119
20. Herodotus 5, 119–120
21. Herodotus 5, 121
22. Herodotus 5, 126–127
23. Herodotus 6, 9–10
24. Herodotus 6, 6–16
25. Herodotus 6, 19–20, 22, 25
26. Herodotus 6, 26
27. Herodotus 6, 28–30
28. Herodotus 6, 31–32
29. Herodotus 6, 94
30. Herodotus 6, 33
31. Herodotus 5, 105
32. Herodotus 6, 14; 5, 28; 6, 3
33. Herodotus 6, 42–43

Chapter Seven

1. Herodotus 6, 44
2. Herodotus, 6, 45
3. Lind. Chron. D 1–59 in Higbie (2003)
4. Herodotus 6, 97; 6, 99
5. Herodotus 6, 100-1
6. Herodotus 6, 95
7. Herodotus 6, 94; Cornelius Nepos, *Miltiades*, 4; Plutarch, *Moralia*, 305B; Pausanias 4, 22; Suda, *Hippias*; Plato, *Menexenus*, 240A; Lysias, *Funeral Oration*, 21; and Justinus 2, 9
8. Herodotus 6, 109
9. Cornelius Nepos, *Miltiades* 4
10. Herodotus 6, 117
11. Herodotus 6, 112
12. Herodotus 6, 105–6
13. Herodotus 5, 116
14. Herodotus 6, 114
15. Xenophon, *Cynegeticus* 6,13. Plutarch, *On the Malice of Herodotus* 26, 862a. Aristophanes, *The Knights*, gives the number of sacrificed goats at 1,000, while Aelian says 300.
16. Plutarch, *Theseus* 35
17. Pausanias 1, 32, 5; 1, 15, 3
18. Plutarch, *On the Glory of Athens* 347 CD
19. Lucian, *True History* 177
20. Herodotus 7, 21; 7, 25; 7, 7
21. Herodotus 7, 145; 161
22. Herodotus 7, 32
23. Herodotus 7, 62–80; 26; 37
24. Herodotus 7, 35
25. Herodotus 7, 55–56
26. De Souza (2003), p. 41; Holland (2006), p. 237
27. Herodotus 7, 97
28. Herodotus 7, 174
29. Herodotus 7, 173
30. Herodotus 7, 200; 7, 215
31. Herodotus, 8, 2; 8, 8; 7, 210
32. Ever since Ephialtes's betrayal, '*ephialtes*' has meant nightmare in Greek; Ephialtes is also used in Greek as a synonym for traitor, just like Quisling or Judas.
33. Herodotus 7, 223
34. Diodorus Siculus 11, 6
35. Herodotus 8, 7; 8, 13–14
36. Herodotus 8, 10
37. Herodotus 8, 11
38. Herodotus 8, 14
39. Herodotus, 8, 16–17
40. Herodotus 8, 19–21
41. Herodotus 8, 13
42. Plutarch, *Themistocles* 8, 2
43. Herodotus 8, 23
44. Herodotus 8, 22
45. Herodotus 8, 50; 8, 71
46. Herodotus 8, 70–95. See also Aeschylus, *Persae* 353–432; Diodorus Siculus 11, 16–19; Plutarch, *op. cit.*, 12–15

47. Herodotus 8, 75
48. Herodotus 8, 44–48
49. See Chrystal, *Women at War in the Ancient World* from which this is taken.
50. Herodotus 7, 99, 3
51. Pallene is the ancient name of the westernmost of the three headlands of Chalcidice in the Aegean Sea. Its modern name is Kassandra Peninsula.
52. Herodotus 8, 88. Polyaenus, *Strategems* 8, 53, 4
53. Herodotus 8, 93
54. Polyaenus, *op. cit.*
55. Herodotus 7, 99; 8, 68; 8, 88; 8, 93
56. Aristophanes, *Lysistrata*, 675
57. Diodorus Siculus 11, 16–19
58. Herodotus 8, 97
59. Herodotus 9, 7–9; 9, 11
60. Herodotus 9, 13
61. Herodotus 9, 28–29; 9, 15
62. Herodotus 9, 25; 9, 33; 9, 39–41
63. Herodotus 9, 49
64. Herodotus 9, 51–52
65. Herodotus 9, 90–104; Diodorus 11, 34–36
66. Herodotus 9, 114
67. Herodotus 9, 115–118
68. Herodotus 9, 118–121
69. Thucydides 1, 94
70. Thucydides 1, 95

Chapter Eight

1. Thucydides 1, 96; 1, 99
2. Plutarch, *Aristides* 26
3. Herodotus 7, 107; Plutarch, *Cimon* 7
4. Thucydides 1, 100; 1, 101
5. Polyaenus, *Strategemata* 8, 67
6. Thucydides 1, 101
7. Plutarch, *Cimon* 12; Thucydides 1, 101
8. Plutarch, *Cimon* 13
9. Simonides 45; translated by J. H. Merivale
10. From the end of the seventh century BCE, Sparta was the most powerful city-state in the Peloponnese and could count the powerful *poleis* Sparta acquired (two powerful allies, Corinth and Elis) among its allies. Sparta aggressively added more allies through diplomacy and military intervention. The Peloponnesian League came about when Sparta defeated Tegea and offered them a permanent defensive alliance. Many other states in the central and northern Peloponnese joined the league, which eventually embraced all Peloponnesian states with the exception of Argos and Achaea.
11. Thucydides 1, 104
12. Thucydides's numbers; Ctesias (*Persica* 36) says that the Athenians sent forty ships, whereas Diodorus (11, 74) says 200, with Thucydides.
13. Herodotus 3, 12
14. Thucydides 1, 110; 1, 109
15. Thucydides 1, 109; Diodorus 11, 74–75
16. Diodorus 11, 77
17. Thucydides 1, 110

18. Thucydides 1, 112
19. Plutarch, Cimon 19; Thucydides 112
20. Diodorus 12, 1
21. Herodotus 7, 165; Diodorus 11, 20
22. Diodorus 20–22; Herodotus 7, 165–7
23. See Lee, *The Fight for Ancient Sicily*

Chapter Nine

1. A modern term to describe the cities subject to Sparta and bound by unequal treaties to 'have the same friends and enemies as the Spartans, and to follow the Spartans wheresoever they may lead'; such as Xenephon, *Hellenica* 2, 2, 20; 4; 6; 2. See Lendon, *Thucydides and the 'Constitution' of the Peloponnesian League*.
2. Thucydides 2, 9
3. Herodotus 9, 35; Pausanias 3, 11
4. Thucydides 1, 105; Diodorus 11, 78
5. Thucydides 1, 105–106; Diodorus 11, 79
6. Thucydides 1, 107–108; Diodorus 11, 80; 11, 83
7. Thucydides 1, 108; 1, 111; Diodorus 11, 88
8. *Oxford Classical Dictionary, ad loc.* See also Woodhead: *The Institution of the Hellenotamiae*
9. Thucydides 1, 113; Diodorus 12, 6
10. Thucydides 1, 139, 2; Plutarch *Pericles* 30, 2
11. Thucydides 1, 139; 1, 67, 4.
12. Aristophanes, *Acharnians* 530-7; Diodorus 12, 39, 4–5; trans. C. H. Oldfather.
13. Thucydides 1, 115–116; Plutarch, *op. cit.*, 25
14. Thucydides 1, 116; Diodorus 12, 27–28; Plutarch, *op. cit.*, 26
15. Thucydides 1, 29; Diodorus 12, 30–31
16. Thucydides 1, 48
17. Thucydides 1, 49; Diodorus 12, 33
18. Thucydides 1, 56
19. Thucydides 1, 56–63; Diodorus 12, 34
20. Plutarch, *Alcibiades* 7
21. Xenophon, *Memorabilia* 4, 4, 1; 1, 6, 9
22. Plato, *Laches* 181b
23. Plato, *Symposium* 219e–221b
24. Xenophon *Apology*, 1, 18
25. Thucydides 5, 25, 1. Lysias provides the first use of the term, at Harpocration under *Archidameios polemos* in a lost speech.
26. Thucydides 1, 67–68
27. Thucydides 2, 12
28. Thucydides 2, 14
29. Thucydides 2, 16
30. Thucydides 2, 18; *Constitution of Athens*, 2
31. Thucydides 1, 73–75
32. Strabo, *Geographia*, 13, 600
33. Thucydides 1, 22, 1
34. Thucydides 8, 11, 3; Strabo 9, 396. See Hornblower (1995). *The Fourth-Century and Hellenistic Reception of Thucydides* p. 6
35. Thucydides 2, 48; 2, 56
36. Glanders is a zoonotic infectious disease primarily found in equines but can be contracted by other animals, such as dogs, cats, and goats. Humans can catch it through close contact with these animals.

37. Plutarch, *Pericles* 35
38. Thucydides 2, 79
39. Thucydides 2, 80–82
40. Thucydides 2, 83–84
41. Thucydides 2, 85–86
42. Thucydides 2, 86; 90–92
43. Thucydides 3, 3–4
44. Thucydides 3, 5–6
45. Thucydides 3, 15
46. Thucydides 3, 19
47. Thucydides 3, 25
48. Thucydides 3, 27–28
49. Thucydides 3, 35–36; trans. Benjamin Jowett., 1881
50. Thucydides 3, 50–51
51. Thucydides, 3, 71, 1
52. Thucydides 3, 81, 4
53. Thucydides 3, 91
54. Thucydides 3, 97–98
55. Thucydides 3, 90
56. Thucydides 3, 103
57. Thucydides 3, 107–108
58. Thucydides 3, 109
59. Thucydides 3, 110; 112
60. Thucydides 3, 111
61. Thucydides 3, 114
62. Thucydides 4, 25
63. Thucydides 4, 25, 7–9
64. Thucydides 4, 25, 10–11
65. Thucydides 4, 3–23
66. Thucydides 4, 26–40
67. Thucydides 4, 42–44
68. Thicydides 4, 53–54
69. Thucydides 7, 44
70. Thucydides 4, 90–96
71. Plato, *Symposium*, 220d–221c
72. Thucydides 4, 100
73. Thucydides 4, 122; 130–131
74. Thucydides 4, 134
75. Thucydides 4, 104
76. Thucydides 4, 105
77. Thucydides 5, 26, 5
78. See Agelarakis, 'Physical anthropological report on the cremated human remains of an individual retrieved from the Amphipolis agora', 72–73
79. Thucydides 1, 117
80. Thucydides 4, 104–105
81. Thucydides, 5, 18, 1–19; 5, 18 2, 23, 1–24, 1. There are two texts: the real treaty that ended the war, and a document in which Sparta and Athens concluded a defensive alliance. Translation by Rex Warner. Plutarch *Nicias* 9, 7
82. Thucydides 5, 17, 2, Plutarch, *op. cit.*, 10, 2
83. Thucydides 5, 18
84. See Legon, *The Peace of Nicias* (1969)
85. Legon, *op. cit.*, p. 323

86. *Oxford Classical Dictionary, ad loc.* p. 1041
87. Thucydides 5, 65
88. Diodorus 12, 79, 6
89. Thucydides 5, 64–74
90. Herodotus 8, 48; Thucydides 5, 84
91. Thucydides 3, 91
92. Thucydide 6, 8
93. Combat radius or radius of action in naval terms can be defined as 'the maximum distance a ship can travel away from its base along a given course with normal load and return without refueling, allowing for all safety and operating factors'. *Dictionary of Military and Associated Terms*, US Department of Defense, 2005.
94. Thucydides 5, 116
95. Xenophon, *Hellenica*, 2,2, 9: Plutarch, *Lysander*, 14, 3
96. Thucydides 5, 84–116
97. Xenophon, *op. cit.*, 2, 2, 3
98. Isocrates, *Panegyricus* 100; *idem, Panathenaicus* 62–63
99. The entry is Λιμὸς Μηλιαῖος (Fames Meliæa)
100. Thucydides 3, 86
101. Thucydides 4, 1–9; 4, 65
102. Thucydides 5, 4. Diodorus 12, 54
103. Thucydides 5, 4; 6, 6; 6, 8; 6, 46
104. Thucydides 6, 8; 6, 9; 6, 10–14
105. Thucydides 6, 16–18
106. Thucydides 6, 20–26
107. George Grote (1794–1871): 'The Mutilation of the Herma' from his *History of Greece*.
108. Thucydides 6, 49
109. Thucydides 6, 42–43
110. Thucydides 6, 67–71; Plutarch, *Nicias* 16
111. Herodotus 9, 73
112. Thucydides 6, 97; Plutarch, *op. cit.*, 17
113. *Mothax* (μόθαξ) means 'stepbrother'; in this context *mothakes* were either offspring of Spartiate fathers and helot mothers or children of poor Spartiates. They were allowed to fight in the army along with *perioeci*.
114. Thucydides 6, 98
115. Thucydides 6, 101
116. Thucydides 7, 5–6
117. Thucydides 7, 22–24
118. Thucydides 7, 34, 1
119. Thucydides 7, 37–41
120. Thucydides 7, 43–44
121. Thucydides 7, 52–53
122. Thucydides 7, 59–71; Plutarch, *op. cit.*, 25
123. Plutarch, *op. cit.*, 30
124. Thucydides 6, 93, 104; Plutarch, *op. cit.*, 19, 21, 27, 28; *idem, Lysander*, 16, 17; Diodorus 12, 7, 8, 28–32; Polyaenus 1, 39, 42
125. Thucydides 8, 10; 20, 1
126. Thucydides 8, 24
127. Thucydides 8, 25
128. Thucydides 8, 41–2
129. Thucydides 8, 55
130. Thucydides 8, 61
131. Thucydides 8, 62

132. Thucydides 8, 95
133. Thucydides 8, 14–18
134. Thucydides 8, 80
135. Thucydides 8, 99
136. Thucydides 8, 101–103
137. Thucydides 8. 104–106; Diodorus 13, 39–40
138. Thucydides 8, 107
139. Diodorus 13, 45–46; Xenophon, *Hellenica* 1, 1, 4–8; Plutarch, *Alcibiades* 27
140. Diodorus 13, 49; Xenophon, *op. cit.*, 1, 1, 11–18; Plutarch, *op. cit.*, 28
141. Diodorus 13, 64; Xenophon, *op. cit.*, 1, 2, 7–10
142. Diodorus 13, 59, 4–60
143. Diodorus 13, 61–62
144. Diodorus 13, 66; Xenophon, *op. cit.*, 1, 3, 4–7; Plutarch, *op. cit.*, 30
145. Plutarch, *op. cit.*, 31
146. Diodorus 13, 69; Xenophon *op. cit.*, 1, 4, 22
147. Hellenica, Oxyrhncia 4; Diodorus 13, 71; Xenophon, *op. cit.*, 1, 5, 11–14; Plutarch, *op. cit.*, 35 4–6; *idem, Lysander* 5, 1–2
148. Xenophon, *op. cit.*, 1, 5, 20
149. Diodorus 13, 77–79; Xenophon, *op. cit.*, 1, 6, 15–18
150. Diodorus 13, 97–99; Xenophon, *op. cit.*, 1, 6, 26–34
151. Xenophon, *op. cit.*, 1, 7, 15
152. Xenophon, *op. cit.*, 1, 7, 35
153. Aristotle, *Constitution of the Athenians* 34
154. Diodorus 13, 105–106; Xenophon, *op. cit.*, 2, 1, 18–28; Plutarch, *Lysander* 9, 4–11
155. Xenophon, *op. cit.*, 2, 2, 3

Chapter Ten

1. Much of this is adapted from the chapters on ancient Greek women in my *Women at War in the Ancient World*.
2. Homer, *Iliad* 5, 330–430
3. Aristophanes, *Lysistrata* 567ff
4. Diodorus Siculus *Library of History* 3, 53
5. Pindar, *Pythian Ode* 9, 19–22
6. Euripides, *Bacchae* 1,236
7. Herodotus 4, 114, 3
8. For example, *Iliad* 24, 723–746; 748–760; 761–776
9. Homer, *Iliad* 6, 241
10. Diodorus Siculus, 2, 4ff. See also Polyaenus, *Strategems* 8, 26
11. Diodorus 2, 7, 2
12. Diodorus 10, 16
13. Pliny the Elder, *Natural History* 8, 155; Hyginus, *Fabulae* 243, 8
14. Herodotus 1, 206, 1
15. Herodotus 1, 212, 3
16. Herodotus 4, 205ff. Pheretima lives on in the name of the worm that infested her: *pheretima* is a genus of earthworm found in New Guinea and other parts of Southeast Asia; the worms are still used as a medicine in China and carry biological agents efficacious in the treatment of epilepsy. The *Pheretima aspergillum* worm contains hypoxanthine, a herb used as an antipyretic, sedative, and anticonvulsant. It lowers blood pressure and contains a platelet-activating factor.
17. Demosthenes 15, 23
18. Vitruvius *De Architectura* 2, 8, 15

19. Polyaenus, 8, 53, 4

20. Pausanias, *A Description of Greece* 8, 48, 4–5

21. Plutarch, *Virtutes Mulierum* 4

22. Herodotus 6, 76

23. Pausanias 10, 19, 1

24. Herodotus 9, 5, 1–2; 5, 84, 1

25. Diodorus Siculus 13, 108, 2f

26. Thucydides, *History of the Peloponnesian War* 3, 74, 2; 2, 78f; 3, 68

27. Thucydides 2, 70, 3

28. Pausanias 8, 48, 4–5

29. Plutarch, *Moralia* 244 b–d

30. Thucydides 2, 4; Aeneas Tactitus 2, 6; Diodorus 12, 41

31. Polyaenus 8, 69

32. Diodorus 13, 55–57f; Xenophon, *Hellenica* 1, 1, 37

33. Pausanias 4, 21, 6

34. Plutarch, *Pyrrhus* 34, 1–4; Pausanias 1, 13, 8; Polyaenus 8, 68. By William Barry, *Roof Tiles and Urban Violence*, p. 55

35. Plutarch, *Virtutes Mulierum* 3

36. Cornelius Nepos, *On Great Generals* 14; Aeneas Tactitus 40, 4–5; 4, 8–11

37. Xenophon, *Anabasis* 5, 3, 3; 6, 1,11–13; 4, 1, 10–15; 3, 2, 25; 4, 8, 27; 5, 4, 33; 4, 3, 18–19

38. *Inscriptiones Graecae* 3, 69

39. Plutarch, *Moralia* 242E ff

40. See though Low, *War, Death and Burial in Classical Sparta*, in which she cautions against taking the overtly militaristic view of Sparta at face value.

41. Plutarch, *Lacaenarum Apophthegmata* 6, 7

42. *Op. cit.*, 6, 16

43. *Op. cit.*, 3, 1; Cf Herodotus, 4, 51; 7, 239

44. Plutarch, *op. cit.*, 2, 1

45. *Op. cit.*, 4, 2. Cf similar sentiments spoken by a Spartan woman, quoted by Teles in Stobaeus, *Florilegium*, 108, 83

46. *Op. cit.*, 5, 1; cf *Palatine Anthology* 7, 433

47. *Op. cit.*, 6, 4

48. *Op. cit.*, 6, 13; *cf* Plutarch *Moralia*, 331 b; Stobaeus, *Florilegium* 7, 29; Cicero, *De Oratore*, 2, 61

49. Plutarch, *Moralia* 231c. Lactantius, *Divine Institutes* 1, 20, 29–32

50. Xenophon, *Hellenica* 6, 5, 28

51. Plutarch, *Agesilaüs* 31, 4–5

52. Homer, *Iliad* 23, 703–705

53. Xenophon, *Cyrus* 7, 5, 73

54. Thucydides 7, 29

55. Thucydides 3, 68; 3, 50; 4, 122; 5, 3

56. Isocrates 4; 12; 3, 27; 1, 114

Bibliography

Adcock, F. E., 'The Archidamian War, B.C. 431–421', in *Cambridge Ancient History, Vol. 5* (Cambridge, 1992); *The Greek and Macedonian Art of War* (Berkeley CA, 1957)

Adie, K., *Corsets to Camouflage: Women and War* (London, 2003)

Adkins, A. W. H., 'The Arete of Nikias: Thucydides 7.86', *Greek, Roman and Byzantine Studies* 16, 379ff (1975).

Afflerbach, H. (ed.), *How Fighting Ends: A History of Surrender* (Oxford, 2012)

Agelarakis, A., 'Physical anthropological report on the cremated human remains of an individual retrieved from the Amphipolis agora', in *Excavating Classical Amphipolis by Ch. Koukouli-Chrysantkai*, BAR International Series 1031, 72–73 (2002)

Allen, S. H., *Finding the Walls of Troy: Frank Calvert and Heinrich Schliemann at Hisarlik* (Berkeley, 1999)

Andrewes, A., 'The Mytilene Debate: Thucydides 3.36–49', *Phoenix* 16, 64–85 (1962); Thucydides on the Causes of the War, *Classical Quarterly* 53 (1959)

Andrews, J. A., 'Cleon's Hidden Appeals: Thucydides 3.37–40', *Classical Quarterly* 50, 45–62 (2000)

Angel J. L., 'Skeletal Material from Attica', *Hesperia* 14 (1945)

Anglim, S., *Fighting Techniques of the Ancient World 3000 BCE–AD 500* (London, 2002)

Ash, R., 'Epic Encounters? Ancient Historical Battle Narratives and the Epic Tradition' in Levine, *Clio and the Poets: Augustan Poetry and the Traditions of Ancient Historiography* (Leiden, 2002), 253–73

Askin, K. D., *War Crimes Against Women: Prosecution in International War Crimes Tribunal* (Amsterdam, 1997)

Åstrom, P., 'The Cuirass Tomb and Other Finds at Dendra Part I: The Chamber Tombs', *Studies in Mediterranean Archaeology iv* (Göteborg, 1977)

Austin, N. J. E., 'Ammianus on Warfare', *Latomus* 165 (1979)

Badian, E., *From Plataea to Potidaea: Studies in the History and Historiography of the Pentecontaetia* (Baltimore MD, 1993)

Badian, E., 'The Peace of Callias', *Journal of Hellenic Studies* 107, 1–39 (1987)

Bagnall, N., *The Peloponnesian War: Athens, Sparta, and the Struggle for Greece* (New York, 2006)

Bakas, S., *The Evidence of Military Traumas in the Minoan and Mycenaean Burials* koryvantesstudies.org/studies-in-english-language/page211-2/ (2016)

Bakogianni, A. (ed.), *War as Spectacle: Ancient and Modern Perspectives on the Display of Armed Conflict* (London, 2016)

Baldwin, B., 'Cleon's Strategy at Amphipolis', *Acta Classica* 11 (1968)

Balot, R., 'The Freedom to Rule: Athenian Imperialism and Democratic Masculinity', in Tabachnick, D. E. (ed.), *Enduring Empire: Ancient Lessons for Global Politics* (London, 2009), 54–68

Barber, E. W., *Women's Work: The First 20,000 Years—Women, Cloth and Society in Early Times* (New York, 1994)

Barker, P. F., *From the Scamander to Syracuse, Studies in Ancient Logistics.* Diss, University of South Africa (November 2005)

Bar-Kochva, B., *The Seleucid Army* (Cambridge, 1976)

Barkworth, P. R., 'The Organisation of Xerxes' Army', *Iranica Antiqua* 27: 149 –167 (1993, retrieved 3 July 2017)

Beard, M. R., *Women as a Force in History: A Study in Tradition and Realities* (New York, 1946)

Beckman, G. M., *Writings from the Ancient World: The Ahhiyawa Texts* (Atlanta: Society of Biblical Literature, 2012)

Beckman, G. M. 'Hittite Chronology', *Akkadica* 120 (2000)

Blok, J. *The Early Amazons* (Leide, 1994)

Boardman, J. (ed.) *The Cambridge Ancient History. Volume IV: Persia, Greece and the Western Mediterranean c. 525 to 479 B.C.* (2nd ed.) (Cambridge, 1988)

Boardman, J., *The Greeks Overseas* (Harmondsworth, 1964)

Boot, M., *Invisible Armies: An Epic History of Guerilla Warfare from Ancient Times to the Present* (London, 2014)

Borm, H. (ed.), *Civil War in Ancient Greece and Rome: Contexts of Disintegration and Reintegration,* (Stuttgart, 2015)

Bosworth, A. B., 'The Humanitarian Aspect of the Melian Dialogue', *Journal of Hellenic Studies* 113 (1993), 30–44

Boudet, J., *The Ancient Art of Warfare* (London, 1966)

Bradeen, D. W., 'The Lelantine War and Pheidon of Argos', *Transactions of the American Philological Association* 78, (1947), 223–241

Bradford, E., *Thermopylae: The Battle for the West.* (Boston MA, 2004)

Bradley, G. (ed.), *Greek and Roman Colonization: Origins, Ideologies and Interactions* (Swansea, 2005)

Bragg, M. 'The Trojan War', BBC Radio 4 *In Our Time*, 31.05.2012, www.bBCE.co.uk/programmes/b01j6srl

Branigan, K., 'The Nature of Warfare in the Southern Aegean During the Third Millennium B.C.', in Laffineur, R. (ed.), *Polemos: Le Contexte Guerrier en Egee a L'Age du Bronze. Actes de la 7e Rencontre egeenne internationale* (Universite de Liège, 1999), pp. 87–94

Braund, S. (ed.), *Ancient Anger: Perspectives from Homer to Galen* (Cambridge, 2003)

Brosius, M., *Women in Ancient Persia: 559–331 BCE* (Oxford, 1998)

Brown, J., *Homeric Sites Around Troy* (Canberra, 2017)

Brouwers, J., *Henchmen of Ares: Warriors and Warfare in Early Greece* (Rotterdam, 2013)

Brownmiller, S., *Against Our Will: Men, Women and Rape* (Harmondsworth, 1975)

Bruce, I., 'The Corcyrean Civil War of 427 BCE', *Phoenix* 25 (1975)

Bryce, T., *The Kingdom of the Hittites* (Oxford, 2005)

Buck, R. J., *A History of Boeotia* (Edmonton, 1987)

Burns, A. R., 'The so-called 'Trade-Leagues' in Early Greek History and the Lelantine War', *Journal of Hellenic Studies* 49 (1929), 14–37

Bunt, P., 'Spartan Policy and Strategy in the Archidamian War', *Phoenix* 19 (1965)

Burgess, J. S., *The Tradition of the Trojan War in Homer and the Epic Cycle* (Baltimore MD, 2004)

Burn, A. R., 'Persia and the Greeks' in Gershevitch, I. (ed.), *The Cambridge History of Iran, Volume 2: The Median and Achaemenid Periods* (Cambridge, 1985)

Campbell, B., 'Teach Yourself How to be a General', *JRS* 77, (1987) 13–29; *Greek & Roman Military Writers* (London, 2004); (ed.) *Oxford Handbook of Warfare in the Classical World* (Oxford, 2013)

Campbell, D. B., *Greek and Roman Siege Machinery 399 BCE–AD 363* (Oxford, 2003); *Ancient Siege Warfare: Persians, Greeks, Carthaginians* (Oxford, 2005); *Besieged: Siege Warfare Ancient World* (Oxford, 2006)

Carey, B. T., *Warfare in the Ancient World* (London, 2005)

Cartledge, P., 'Spartan Wives: Liberation or Licence?' *CQ* 31 (1981) 84–105; *Thermopylae: The Battle That Changed the World.* (New York, 2006); *Surrender in Ancient Greece* in Afflerbach, *How Fighting Ends* (2012) 15–28

Casson, L., *Ships and Seamanship in the Ancient World* (Princeton, 1971)

Castleden, R., *The Mycenaeans* (London, 2005); *The Attack on Troy* (Barnsley, 2006)

Caston, V. (ed.), *Our Ancient Wars: Rethinking War through the Classics* (Michigan, 2016)

Cawkwell, G., *The Greek Wars: The Failure of Persia* (Oxford, 2005); *The Greco-Persian Wars* (Oxford, 2006)

Cerchiai, L., *The Greek Cities of Magna Graecia and Sicily* (New York, 2004)

Chadwick, J., *The Mycenaean World.* (Cambridge, 1976)

Chakravarti, P., *The Art of War in Ancient India* (2003 repr.)

Champion, J., *The Tyrants of Syracuse: 480–367 BCE v. 1: War in Ancient Sicily* (Barnsley, 2010); *The Tyrants of Syracuse: 367–211 BCE v. II: War in Ancient Sicily* (Barnsley, 2012)

Chapman, A., *The Female Principle in Plutarch's* Moralia (Dublin, 2007)

Chaniotis, A. (ed.), *Army and Power in the Ancient World* (Stuttgart, 2002)

Chavalas, M. V. *Women in the Ancient Near East (London,* 2013)

Chrystal, P., A Powerful Body of Women, *Minerva*, January–February 2014, 10–13; *Wars & Battles of the Roman Republic* (Stroud, 2015); *Roman Women: The Women Who Influenced Roman History* (Stroud, 2015); *Roman Military Disasters* (Barnsley, 2016); *Women in Ancient Greece* (Stroud, 2016); *Ancient Greece in 100 Facts* (Stroud, 2017); *Women in Ancient Greece: Seclusion, Exclusion, or Illusion?* (Stroud, 2017); *When in Rome: A Social History of Rome* (Stroud, 2017); *Women at War in the Ancient World* (Barnsley, 2017); *Roman Record Keeping & Communications* (Stroud, 2018); *Roman Republic into Roman Empire: the 1st Century BCE Civil Wars in Ancient Rome* (Barnsley, 2018)

Clayton, E. C., *Female Warrior* (London, 1879)

Cline, E. H., *1177 B.C.: The Year Civilization Collapsed.* (Princeton NJ, 2014); (ed.), *The Oxford Handbook of the Bronze Age Aegean* (Oxford, 2012)

Cloutier, G., *Andromache: Denial and Despair. The First-Year Papers* (Trinity College Digital Repository, Hartford, CT, 2013) www.digitalrepository.trincoll.edu/fypapers/37

Clutton-Brock, J., *Horse Power: A History of the Horse and the Donkey in Human Societies* (Harvard, 1992)

Cochrane, C. N., *Thucydides and the Science of History,* (Oxford, 1929)

Connolly, P., *Greece and Rome at War* (London, 2006)

Connor, W. R. *Thucydides* (Princeton NJ, 1984); *The New Politicians of Fifth-Century Athens* (New York, 1992)

Conwell, D. H., *Connecting a City to the Sea: The History of the Athenian Long Walls* (Leiden, 2008)

Cook, B. A. (ed.), *Women and War: A Historical Encyclopedia from Antiquity to the Present 2 Vols.* (Oxford, 2006)

Cooper, H. M. (ed.), *Arms and the Woman: War, Gender, and Literary Representation* (Chapel Hill NC, 1989)

Crawford, H., *Sumer and Sumerians* (Cambridge, 2004)

Crawford, M. H., 'War and Finance', *Journal of Roman Studies* 54, (1964) 29–32

Crowley, J. *The Psychology of the Athenian Hoplite: The Culture of Combat in Classical Athens* (Cambridge, 2012)

Curto, S., *The Military Art of the Ancient Egyptians* (Milan, 1971)

D'Amato R., *The Sea Peoples of the Mediterranean Bronze Age 1450–1100 BCE.* (London, 2015)

Dandamaev, M. A., *A Political History of the Achaemenid Empire* (trans. W. J. Vogelsang) (Leiden, 1989)

Davis, P. K., *100 Decisive Battles from Ancient Times to the Present: The World's Major Battles and How They Shaped History* (Oxford, 1999); *Besieged: 100 Great Sieges from Jericho to Sarajevo* (Oxford, 2001)

Dawson, D., *The Origins of Western Warfare: Militarism and Morality in the Ancient World* (Boulder, CO, 1997)

Deacy, S. (ed.), *Rape in Antiquity* (London, 1997)

Delbrück, H., *Warfare in Antiquity: History of the Art of War, Volume 1* (Lincoln, NE, 1920)

De Souza, P.

De Souza, P. *Piracy in the Greco-Roman World* (Cambridge, 1999); *The Greeks at War: From Athens to Alexander* (Oxford, 2004); 'Battle B Naval Battles and Sieges' in Sabin, *The Cambridge History of Greek and Roman Warfare Vol 1* (2007) 434–460; (ed.) *War and Peace in Ancient and Medieval History* (Cambridge, 2011)

De Ste. Croix, G. E. M., *The Origins of the Peloponnesian War* (London, 1972)

Dewald, C., *The Cambridge Companion to Herodotus* (Cambridge, 2006)

Dickinson, O., *The Origins of Mycenaean Civilization* (Götenberg, 1977); 'Invasion, Migration and the Shaft Graves', *Bulletin of the Institute of Classical Studies* 43 (1999), 97–107; 'Was there really a Trojan War?' in Gallou, C., *Dioskouroi* (Oxford, 2008), 189–97

Doenges, N. A., 'The Campaign and Battle of Marathon', *Historia* (1998), 1–17

Doerries, B., *The Theatre of War: What Ancient Greek Tragedies Can Teach Us Today* (London, 2015)

Donlan, W., 'Archilochus, Strabo and the Lelantine War', *Transactions of the American Philological Association* 101 (1970), 131–142

Dothan, T. K., *The Philistines and Their Material Culture.* (Jerusalem, 1982); *People of the Sea: The Search for the Philistines.* (New York, 1992)

Dougherty, C., 'Sowing the Seeds of Violence: Rape, Women and the Land' in Wyke, *Parchments of Gender* (1988), 267–84

Dowden, K., 'The Amazons: Development and Function', *RhM* 140 (1997), 97–128

Drews, R., *The End of the Bronze Age: Changes in Warfare and the Catastrophe Ca. 1200 B.C.* (Princeton NJ, 1993)

Druett, J., *She Captains: Heroines and Hellions of the Sea* (New York, 2005)

Du Bois, P., *Centaurs and Amazons: Women and the Pre-History of the Great Chain of Being* (Ann Arbor TX, 1982)

Ducat, J., 'Les Hilotes', *Hellenic Correspondence Bulletin*, suppl. XX (Athens, 1990)

Dull, C. J., 'Thucydides 1. 113 and the Leadership of Orchomenus', *Classical Philology* 72 (1977), 305–314

Evans, J. A. S., 'Herodotus and the Ionian Revolt', *Historia: Zeitschrift fur Alte Geschichte* 25 (1976), 31–32

Everson, T., *Warfare in Ancient Greece* (Stroud, 2007)

Fagan, G. G. (ed.), *New Perspectives on Ancient Warfare* (Leiden, 2010)

Fehling, D., *Herodotus and His 'Sources': Citation, Invention, and Narrative Art* (trans J.G. Howie) (London, 1989)

Ferrill, A., *The Origins of War: From the Stone Age to Alexander the Great* (Boulder CO, 1997)

Fields, N. (2004) *Mycenaean Citadels c. 1350–1200 BCE (3rd ed.)* (Oxford, 2004); *Bronze Age War Chariots* (Oxford, 2006); *Syracuse 415–13 BCE: Destruction of the Athenian Imperial Fleet* (Oxford, 2008)

Fink, D. L., *The Battle of Marathon in Scholarship: Research, Theories and Controversies Since 1850* (New York, 2014)

Finley, M. I., 'Introduction'. *Thucydides—History of the Peloponnesian War* (trans Rex Warner), (Harmondsworth, 1972); *The World of Odysseus* (London, 1978)

Forde, S., *The Ambition to Rule: Alcibiades and the Politics of Imperialism in Thucydides* (Ithaca NY, 1989)

Fornara, C., 'The Aftermath of the Mytilenian Revolt', *Historia: Zeitschrift für Alte Geschichte* (2010), 129–142

Fowler, R., 'How the *Lysistrata* Works', *EMC* 15 (1996), 245–59

French, A., 'The Tribute of the Allies', *Historia* 21 (1972)

Gabba, E., 'True History and False History in Classical Antiquity', *JRS* 61 (1981), 50–62

Gabriel, R. A., *A History of Military Medicine Vol 1: From Ancient Times to the Middle Ages* (New York, 1992); *The Great Armies of Antiquity* (London, 1992); *The Great Battles of Antiquity: A Strategic and Tactical Guide to Great Battles That Shaped the Development of War* (London, 1994)

Gaca, K. L., 'Girls, Women, and the Significance of Sexual Violence in Ancient Warfare' in Heineman, E. D., *Sexual Violence in Conflict Zones: From the Ancient World to the Era of Human Rights* (Philadelphia, 2011), 73–88; 'Ancient Warfare and the Ravaging Martial Rape of Girls and Women: Evidence from Homeric Epic and Greek Drama' in Masterson, M., *Sex in Antiquity: Exploring Gender and Sexuality in the Ancient World* (New York, 2015)

Gardiner, R. (ed.), *Age of the Galley: Mediterranean Oared Vessels since pre-Classical Times* (London, 2004)

Garlan, Y., *War in the Ancient World* (London, 1975)

Garland, R., *Athens Burning: The Persian Invasion of Greece and the Evacuation of Attica* (Baltimore MD, 2017)

Garlick, B. (ed.), *Stereotypes of Women in Power* (New York, 1992)

Garouphalias, P., *Pyrrhus: King of Epirus* (London, 1979)

Georges, P. B., 'Persian Ionia Under Darius: The Revolt Reconsidered', *Historia* 49 (2000), 1–39

Gera, D. L., *Warrior Women: The Anonymous Tractatus De Mulieribus* (Leiden, 1997)

Gerolymatos, A., *Espionage and Treason: A Study of the Proxenia in Political and Military Intelligence Gathering in Classical Greece* (Leiden, 1986)

Gill, C. (ed.), *Lies and Fiction in the Ancient World* (Liverpool, 1993)

Gillis, E., 'The Revolt at Mytilene', *American Journal of Philology* 92 (1971), 38–47

Gomme, A. W., 'The Athenian Hoplite Force in 431 BCE', *Classical Quarterly* 21 (1927); *An Historical Commentary on Thucydides Volume 1* (Oxford, 1945); 'Thucydides and Cleon, The Second Battle of Amphipolis', *Hellenika* 13 (1954); *An Historical Commentary on Thucydides Volume 2. Books II–III 2nd edition* (Oxford, 2016)

Graf, F., Women, War and Warlike Divinities, *ZPE* 55 (1984), 245–54

Grant, M. *Greek and Roman Historians: Information and Misinformation* (1995); *Cleopatra* (New York, 1992)

Grant de Pauw, L., *Battle Cries and Lullabies: Women in War from Prehistory to the Present* (Norman OK, 2000)

Green, P., *The Greco-Persian Wars.* (Berkeley, 1996); *Greek History 480-431 B.C., the Alternative Version* (Ann Arbor, 2006)

Grundy, G., *The Great Persian War and its Preliminaries; A Study of the Evidence, Literary and Topographical* (London, 1901)

Hackett, J., *Warfare in the Ancient World* (London, 1989)

Hall, H. R., 'The Peoples of the Sea. A Chapter of the History of Egyptology', *Recueil d'études égyptologiques dédiées à la mémoire de Jean-François Champollion* (1992), 297–329

Hamblin, J. W., *Warfare in the Ancient Near East to 1600 BCE* (New York, 2006)

Hamel, D., *The Battle of Arginusae: Victory at Sea and Its Tragic Aftermath in the Final Years of the Peloponnesian War* (Baltimore MD, 2015)

Hammond, N. G. L., 'The Campaign and Battle of Cynoscephalae in 197 BCE', *Journal of Hellenic Studies* 108 (1988), 60–82; 'The Construction of Xerxes' Bridge over the Hellespont', *Journal of Hellenic Studies* (1996), 88–107

Hansen, M. H., 'The Battle Exhortation in Ancient Historiography: Fact or Fiction?', *Historia* 42 (1993), 161–80

Hanson, V. D., 'The Status of Ancient Military History', *Journal of Military History* 63 (1999), 399–414; *The Wars of the Ancient Greeks* (London, 1999); *The Western Way of War: Infantry Battle in Ancient Greece 2nd ed* (Oxford, 2000); *Why the West Has Won: Carnage and Culture from Salamis to Vietnam* (Oxford, 2001); *A War Like No Other: How the Athenians and the Spartans Fought the Peloponnesian War* (New York, 2005); (ed.) *Hoplites: The Classical Greek Battle Experience* (London, 1991)

Hardwick, L., 'Ancient-Amazon Heroes: Outsiders or Women?', *G&R* 37 (1990), 14–36

Hasel, M. G., *Domination and Resistance: Egyptian Military Activity in the Southern Levant, ca. 1300–1185 B.C.* (Leiden, 1998)

Harris, R. 'Independent Women in Ancient Mesopotamia' in Lesko, B. S., *Women's Earliest Records*, 145-56, (Atlanta GA, 1989)

Harris, W. V., 'The Rage of Women' in Braund, *Ancient Anger* (2003), 121–43

Harrison, T., 'Herodotus and the Ancient Greek Idea of Rape' in Deacy, *Rape in Antiquity* (1997), 185–208

Harvey, D., 'Women in Thucydides', *Arethusa* 18 (1985), 67–90

Hassall, M., 'Rome and the Eastern Provinces at the End of the 2nd Century BCE', *Journal of Roman Studies* 64 (1974), 195–220

Hatke, G., *Aksum and Nubia: Warfare, Commerce, and Political Fictions in Ancient Northeast Africa* (New York, 2013)

Hawkes, C. (ed.), *Greeks, Celts and Romans, Studies in Venture and Resistance* (London, 1973)

Heath, E. G., *Archery: A Military History* (London, 1980)

Henderson, B., 'The Campaign of the Metaurus', *The English Historical Review* (1898)

Hendriks I. H. M., 'The Battle of Sepeia', *Mnemosyne* 33 (1980), 340–346

Herwig, H. (ed.), *Cassell's World History of Warfare* (London, 2002)

Herzog, C., *Battles of the Bible* (London, 1978)

Higbie, C., *The Lindian Chronicle and the Greek Creation of their Past* (Oxford, 2003)

Hignett, C., *Xerxes' Invasion of Greece* (Oxford, 1963)

Hindley, C., Eros and Military Command in Xenophon, *CQ* 44 (1994), 347–66

Hodkinson, S. (ed.), *Sparta and War* (Swansea, 2006)

Hogg, O. F., *Clubs to Cannon: Warfare and Weapons Before the Introduction of Gunpowder* (London, 1968)

Holland, T., *Persian Fire: The First World Empire and the Battle for the West* (London, 2006)

Holmes, R., *Acts of War: The Behaviour of Men in Battle* (London, 2004)

Holscher, T., 'Images of War in Greece and Rome', *Journal of Roman Studies* 93 (2003), 1–17

Hood, E., *The Greek Victory at Marathon*, Clio (Australian Capital Territory, 1995)

Hood, S., '"Last Palace" and "Reoccupation" at Knossos', *Kadmos* 4 (1965), 16–44; *The Home of the Heroes: The Aegean Before the Greeks* (London, 1974)

Hopwood, K., *Organised Crime in the Ancient World* (Swansea, 1999)

Hornblower, S., *The Greek World 479-323 BCE* (London, 1983); *Thucydides* (London, 1987)

Howard, D. (2011) *Bronze Age Military Equipment* (Barnsley); *A Commentary on Thucydides. 2 vols.* (Oxford, 1991–1996); 'The Fourth-Century and Hellenistic Reception of Thucydides', *The Journal of Hellenic Studies* 115 (1995), 47–68; 'War and the Development of Ancient Historiography' in Sabin, *The Cambridge History of Greek and Roman Warfare* (2005); (ed.) *The Oxford Classical Dictionary* 3/e (Oxford, 2003)

Hunt, P. (1998) *Slaves, Warfare, and Ideology in the Greek Historians* (Cambridge, 1998); The Slaves and Generals of Arginusae, *American Journal of Philology* 122 (2001), 359–80

Hunter, L. W., *Aieneiou Poliorketike* (Oxford, 1927)

Hutchinson, G., *Attrition: Aspects of Command in the Peloponnesian War* (Stroud, 2006)

Jackson-Laufer, G. M., *Women Rulers throughout the Ages: An Illustrated Guide* (New York, 1999)

James, S. L., *Companion to Women in the Ancient World* (Chichester, 2012)

Jameson, M., *Sacrifice Before Battle*, in Hanson, V. (ed.) *Hoplites* (1991), p. 220

Jarymowycz, R., *Cavalry: From Hoof to Track* (London, 2009)

Jenkins, T. E., 'Epistolary Warfare' in *Intercepted Letters: Epistolarity and Narrative in Greek and Roman Literature* (2006), pp. 51–59

Jestice, P. G., *Greek Women and War in Antiquity* in Cook, *Women and War* (2006), pp. 256–8.

Jones D. E., *Women Warriors: A History* (Washington DC, 1997)

Jones, M. J., *Roman Fort Defences to AD 117* (Oxford, 1975)

Kagan, D. (1969) *The Outbreak of the Peloponnesian War* (Ithaca, NY, 1969); *The Archidamian War* (Ithaca, NY, 1974); *The Peace of Nicias and the Sicilian Expedition* (Ithaca, NY, 1981); *The Fall of the Athenian Empire* (Ithaca, NY, 1987); *The Peloponnesian War* (New York, NY, 2003); *Men of Bronze: Hoplite Warfare in Ancient Greece* (Princeton, NJ, 2013)

Kallet, L., *Money and the Corrosion of Power in Thucydides: The Sicilian Expedition and its Aftermath* (Berkeley, 2001)

Kallet-Marx, L., 'Thucydides 2.45.2 and the Status of War Widows in Periclean Athens' in Rosen, R. M. (ed.), *Nomodeiktes: Greek Studies in Honor of Martin Ostwald* (1993) 133–143

Keaveney, A., The Attack on Naxos: A'Forgotten Cause' of the Ionian Revolt. *Classical Quarterly* 38 (1988), 76–81

Keegan, J., *A History of Warfare* (London, 1993)

Keeley, L. H., *War Before Civilisation: The Myth of the Peaceful Savage* (Oxford, 1996)

Kelder, J. M., 'Greece During the Late Bronze Age', *Journal of the Ancient Near East Society: Ex Oriente Lux*. 39 (2005), 131–179; *The Kingdom of Mycenae: A Great Kingdom in the Late Bronze Age Aegean*. www.academia.edu. (Bethesda, MD: CDL Press, 2010). Retrieved 10 August 2017; 'The Egyptian Interest in Mycenaean Greece', *Jaarbericht 'Ex Oriente Lux' (JEOL*, 2010), 125–140

Kelly, R. C. The Evolution of Lethal Intergroup Violence, *PNAS* 102(43) (2005), 15294–15298 10.1073/pnas.0505955102

Kelly, T. Did the Argives defeat the Spartans at Hysiai in 669 BCE? *American Journal of Philology* 91 (1970), 31–42

Kennell, N. M., *The Gymnasium of Virtue: Education and Culture in Ancient Sparta* (Chapel Hill, NC, 1995)

Kern, P. B., *Ancient Siege Warfare* (London, 1999)

Killebrew, A. E., 'The Philistines and Other 'Sea Peoples' in Text and Archaeology', *Society of Biblical Literature Archaeology and Biblical Studies*, 15 (2013)

King, C., 'The Homeric Corslet', *American Journal of Archaeology* 74 (1970), 294–96

King, I., 'Thinkers at War: Socrates', *Military History Monthly* 15 Jan. 2014

Kirkpatrick, S., 'Skeletal Evidence for Militarism in Mycenaean Athens', *Hesperia Supplements, Vol. 43, New Directions in the Skeletal Biology of Greece* (2009)

Klein, J. *The Royal Hymns of Shulgi, King of Ur* (Philadelphia PA, 1981)

Knight, D. W., 'Thucydides and the War Strategy of Pericles', *Mnemosyne* 23 (1970), 150–160

Konsolaki, E., 'Cranial Trauma in Ancient Greece: From Homer to Classical Authors', *Journal of Cranio-Maxillo-Facial Surgery* (2010)

Korfmann, M., 'Was There a Trojan War?' *Archaeology* 57 (2004)

Kraft, J. C., 'The Pass at Thermopylae, Greece', *Journal of Field Archaeology* 14 (1987), 181–98

Krentz, P., *The Thirty at Athens* (Ithaca, NY, 1982)

Krzszkowska, O., 'So Where's the Loot?' The Spoils of War and the Archaeological Record', in Laffineur, R. (ed.), *Polemos: Le Contexte Guerrier en Egee a L'Age du Bronze. Actes de la 7e Rencontre egeenne internationale* (Universite de Liège, 1998), pp. 489–498

Lacey, J., *The First Clash: The Miraculous Greek Victory at Marathon and Its Impact on Western Civilization* (Presidio Press; Reprint edition, 2011)

Lambert, S. D., 'A Thucydidean Scholium on the "Lelantine War"', *Journal of Hellenic Studies* 102 (1982), 216–220

Lang, M., 'Herodotus and the Ionian Revolt', *Historia* 17 (1968), 24–36

Laqueur, W., *Guerrilla Warfare: A Historical & Critical Study* (London, 1977)

Lardeen, J. A. O., 'The Constitution of the Peloponnesian League', *CP* 28 (1933), 259

Sparta and the Ionian Revolt: A Study of Spartan Foreign Policy and the Genesis of the Peloponnesian League, *Classical Philology* 27 (1932), 140; 'Orchomenus and the Formation of the Boeotian Confederacy in 447 B.C.', *Classical Philology* 55 (1960), 9–18

Latacz, J., 'Evidence from Homer', *Archaeology* 57 (2004); *Troy and Homer: Towards a Solution of an Old Mystery* (Oxford, 2003)

Lazenby, J. F., *The Defence of Greece 490–479 B.C.* (Warminster, 1993); *The Spartan Army* (Barnsley, 2011)

Lee, J. W. I., 'The Fight for Ancient Sicily', *Archaeology Archive* 64 (2011)

Lee, J., 'For There Were Many *hetairae* in the Army: Women in Xenophon's Anabasis', *Anc. W.* 35 (2004), 45–65

Lee, W. E., *Warfare and Culture in World History* (New York, 2011)

Legon, R. P., 'The Peace of Nicias', *Journal of Peace Research* (Special Issue on Peace Research in History) (1969), 323–334

Legon, R. P., Megara and Mytilene. *Phoenix* 22 (1968), 200–225

Leitao, D. D., *Sexuality in Greek and Roman Military Contexts* in Hubbard, *Companion* (2014), 230–243

Lendering, J., 'Sybota (433 BCE)', *Ancient Warfare* 2.3 (2008)

Lendon, J. E., 'Thucydides and the "Constitution" of the Peloponnesian League', *Greek, Roman and Byzantine Studies* 35 (1994), 159–177; 'The Rhetoric of Combat: Greek Military Theory and Roman Culture in Julius Caesar's Battle Descriptions', *Cl. Ant* 18 (1999), 273–329; *Soldiers and Ghosts: A History of Battles in Classical Antiquity* (New Haven CT, 2005)

Leteiner, D., 'The Failure of the Ionian Revolt', *Historia* (1982), 129–60

Libourel, J. M., 'The Athenian Disaster in Egypt', *American Journal of Philology* 92 (1971), 605–615

Liebeschuetz, W., 'Thucydides and the Sicilian Expedition', *Historia* 17 (1968), 289–306

Lightman, M., *A to Z of Ancient Greek and Roman Women* (New York, 2008)

Llewellyn-Jones, L., 'Sexy Athena: The Dress and Erotic Representation of a Virgin War Goddess', in Deacy, S. (ed.), *Athena in the Classical World* (Leiden, 2001), 233–57

Lloyd, A. B., *Marathon: The Crucial Battle That Created Western Democracy* (London, 2004); (ed.) *Battle in Antiquity* (Swansea, 1996)

Lorimer, H. L., 'The Hoplite Phalanx', *ABSA* 42 (1947), 122ff

Low, P., 'War, Death and Burial in Classical Sparta', *Omnibus* 65 (2013), 8–10

Luce, T. J., *The Greek Historians* (London, 1997)

Luckenbill, D. D., *Ancient Records of Assyria and Babylonia II* (Chicago, 1926)

Luginbill, R., *Thucydides In War and National Character* (Boulder, CO, 1999)

Luraghi, N., *The Ancient Messenians: Constructions of Ethnicity and Memory* (Cambridge, 2008)

Lynn, J. A., *Battle: A History of Combat from Ancient Greece to Modern America* (Boulder, CO, 2003)

Majno, G., *The Healing Hand: Man and Wound in the Ancient World* (Cambridge, MA, 1975)

Man, J., *Amazons: The Real Warrior Women of the Ancient World* (London, 2017)

Manville, P. B., 'Aristagoras and Histiaios: The Leadership Struggle in the Ionian Revolt', *Classical Quarterly* 27 (1977), 80–91

Marincola, J., *Greek and Roman Historiography* (Oxford, 2011)

Marozzi, J., *The Way of Herodotus: Travels with the Man Who Invented History* (Boston, MA, 2008)

Marsden, E. W., *Greek and Roman Artillery* (Oxford, 1969–71)

Martin, S., 'Private Lives and Public Personae' (1997) www.dl.ket.org/latin2/mores/women/womenful.htm

Matthews, R., *The Battle of Thermopylae: A Campaign in Context.* (Stroud, 2006)

Matthews, V. H. (ed.), *Gender and Law in the Hebrew Bible and the Ancient Near East* (London, 2004)

Mayor, A., *Greek Fire, Poison Arrows and Scorpion Bombs: Biological Warfare in the Ancient World* (London, 2009)

McDonald, J., 'Athens and the Hiera Orgas', Dillon, M. (ed.), *Religion in the Ancient World: New Approaches and Themes* (Amsterdam, 1996), 321-323

McGregor, M. F., *The Athenians and Their Empire* (UBCE Press, 1995)

Meiggs, R., *The Athenian Empire* (Oxford, 1972)

Meiggs, R. and Lewis, D., *A Selection of Greek Historical Inscriptions to the End of the Fifth Century B.C.* (Oxford, 1971)

Meiggs, R., 'The Chronology of the Peloponnesian War', *Proceedings of the American Philosophical Society* 115 (1971)

Meijer, F., *A History of Seafaring in the Classical World* (London, 1986)

Meritt, B. D., 'Scione, Mende and Torone', *American Journal of Archaeology* 27 (1923), 447–60

Midlarsky, M., *The Killing Trap: Genocide in the Twentieth Century* (Cambridge, 2005)

Mikalson, J. D., *Herodotus and Religion in the Persian Wars* (Chapel Hill, NC, 2012)

Molloy, B., 'Swords and Swordsmanship in the Aegean Bronze Age', *American Journal of Archaeology* 114 (2010), 'Martial Minoans. War as social process. Practice and Event in Bronze Age Crete', *Annual of the British School of Athens* 107 (2012)

Momigliano, A., *The Classical Foundations of Modern Historiography*, Sather Classical Lectures, 54 (Berkeley, CA, 1990)

Monoson, S. S., *Combat Trauma and the Ancient Greeks* (New York, 2014)

Montagu, J. D., *Battles of the Greek and Roman Worlds* (London, 2000); *Greek and Roman Warfare: Battles, Tactics and Trickery* (London, 2006)

Morkot, R. G., *Historical Dictionary of Ancient Egyptian Warfare* (Washington DC, 2003); *The A to Z of Ancient Egyptian Warfare* (Washington DC, 2010)

Morris, I. M., 'To Make a New Thermopylae: Hellenism, Greek Liberation, and the Battle of Thermopylae', *Greece & Rome* 47 (2000), 211–230

Morrison, J. S., *Greek and Roman Oared Warships* (Oxford, 1996)

Murray, O., *The Greek City* (Oxford, 1990); *Early Greece* (London, 1993)

Murray, W., *Hybrid Warfare: Fighting Complex Opponents from the Ancient World to the Present* (Cambridge, 2012)

Mylonas, G. E., *Mycenae and the Mycenaean Age* (Princeton, NJ, 1966)

Nakhai, B. A., *The World of Women in the Ancient and Classical Near East* (Newcastle 2008)

Nevin, S., *Military Leaders and Sacred Space in Classical Greek Warfare: Temples, Sanctuaries and Conflict in Antiquity* (London, 2016)

Newark, T., *Women Warlords: An Illustrated History of Female Warriors* (London, 1989)

Nilsson, M. P., 'The Introduction of Hoplite Tactics in Rome', *Journal of Roman Studies* 19 (1929), 1–11

Northwood, S., *Early Roman Armies* (London, 1995)

Nossov, K. S., *Ancient and Medieval Siege Weapons: A Fully Illustrated Guide to Siege Weapons and Tactics* (London, 2006)

Ober, J., 'Fortress Attica: Defense of the Athenian Land Frontier, 404-322 BCE', *Mnemosyne*, supplement 84, p. 108

Ogden, D., 'Homosexuality and Warfare in Ancient Greece', *Battle in Antiquity* (Swansea, 2009)

Olsen, B., *Women in Mycenaean Greece. The Linear B Tablets from Pylos and Knossos* (New York, 2014)

Omitowoju, R., *Rape and the Politics of Consent in Classical Athens* (Cambridge, 2002)

Ormerod, H. A., *Piracy in the Ancient World* (Liverpool, 1924)

Osborne, R., 'Polybius on Rome v. Greece', *Omnibus* 55 (2008), 26–27

Palaima, T., 'Mycenaean Militarism from a Textual Perspective', *Polemos: Warfare in the Aegean Bronze Age* (*Aegaeum*) 19 (1999), 367–378. Retrieved 10 July 2017

Parker, V., The Dates of the Messenian Wars, *Chiron* 21 (1999), 25–47

Payne-Gallwey, R., *The Projectile Throwing Engines of the Ancients* (London, 1907)

Peel, M. (ed.), *Rape as a Method of Torture* (London, 2004)

Pembroke, S., '*Locres et Tarente, le Rôle des Femmes dans la Fondation de Deux Colonies Grecques*', *Annales ESC* 25 (1970), 1,240–1,270

Pennington, R. (ed.), *Amazons to Fighter Pilots: A Biographical Dictionary of Military Women* (London, 2003)

Phang, S. (ed.), *Conflict in Ancient Greece and Rome: The Definitive Political, Social, and Military Encyclopedia* [3 volumes]; ABCE-CLIO Kindle Edition (2016)

Platias, A. G., *Thucydides on Strategy* (London, 2006)

Podoksik, E., Justice, Power, and Athenian Imperialism: An Ideological Moment in Thucydides' History, *History of Political Thought* 26 (2005), 21–42

Pollock, S., *Ancient Mesopotamia: The Eden that Never Was* (Cambridge, 1999)

Pomeroy, S. B., *Women's History and Ancient History* (1991), 197–217; *Women in Hellenistic Egypt* (New York, 2002); *Spartan Women* (Oxford, 2002)

Popham. M. R., The Last Days of the Palace at Knossos, *Studies in Mediterranean Archaeology* 5 (1964); 'The Destruction of the Palace at Knossos and its Pottery', *Antiquity* 40 (1966), 24-28

Postgate, N., *Early Mesopotamia: Society and Economy at the Dawn of History* (London, 1994)

Powell, A., *Athens and Sparta: Constructing Greek Political and Social History from 478 BCE*, (London, 1988); (ed.), *Hindsight in Greek and Roman History* (Swansea, 2013)

Powers, D. (ed.), *Irregular Warfare in the Ancient World* (Chicago, 2013)

Pritchett, W. K., *The Greek State at War* (Berkeley, 1971–1991)

Pryor, J. H., *Geography, Technology, and War: Studies in the Maritime History of the Mediterranean, 649-1571* (Cambridge, 1988)

Quinn, T., 'Thucydides and the Unpopularity of the Athenian Empire', *Historia* 13 (1964)

Qviller, B., 'Reconstructing the Spartan Partheniai: Many Guesses and a Few Facts', *SO* 71 (1996), 34–41

Raaflaub, K. A., Homer, the Trojan War and History. *Classical World* 91 (1998), 386–403; *Searching for Peace in the Greek World* in *War and Peace in the Ancient World*, 1–33 (Chichester, 2007); (ed.) *War and Society in the Ancient and Medieval Worlds* (Harvard, MA, 1999); (ed.) *War and Peace in the Ancient World* (Chichester, 2007)

Rankov, B., *Exploratio: Military and Political Intelligence in the Roman World* (London, 1995)

Rauh, N. K., *Merchants, Sailors and Pirates in the Ancient World* (Stroud, 2003)

Ray, F. E., *Land Battles in 5th Century BCE Greece: A History and Analysis of 173 Engagements* (2011); *Greek and Macedonian Land Battles of the 4th Century BCE: A History and Analysis of 187 Engagements* (New York, 2012)

Ray, J., 'Hatshepsut: The Female Pharaoh', *History Today* 44 (1994), 23-9

Redfield, J., 'The Women of Sparta', *CJ* 73 (1977), 146–161

Rees, O., *Socrates: The Warrior Philosopher*, www.academia.edu/12147327/Socrates_The_Warrior_Philosopher

Regan, G., *Backfire: A History of Friendly Fire from Ancient Warfare to the 21st Century* (London, 2002)

Rehak, P., 'The Mycenaean "Warrior Goddess" Revisited', in Laffineur, R. (ed.), *Polemos: Le Contexte Guerrier en Egee a L'Age du Bronze. Actes de la 7e Rencontre egeenne internationale* (Universite de Liège, 1998), pp. 227–240

Rhodes, P. J., *The Athenian Empire* (Oxford, 1985)

Rihll, T., 'Ancient Military Technology', *Omnibus* 62 (2011), 28–30

Roberts, A. (ed.), *Great Commanders of the Ancient World* (London, 2008)

Roberts, J. T., *The Plague of War: Athens, Sparta, and the Struggle for Ancient Greece* (New York)

Robinson, V. (ed.), *Morals in Wartime* (New York, 1943)

Rodgers, W., *Greek and Roman Naval Warfare* (Annapolis, 1937)

Roisman, R., *The Classical Art of Command: Eight Greek Generals Who Shaped the History of Warfare* (New York, 2017)

Romilly, J. de, *Thucydides and Athenian Imperialism* (Oxford, 1963)

Rusch, S. M., *Sparta at War: Strategy, Tactics and Campaigns* (London, 2011)

Russell, F. S., *Information Gathering in Classical Greece* (Ann Arbor, TX, 1999)

Rutter, J. B., 'Troy VII and the Historicity of the Trojan War' (2004), www.dartmouth.edu/~prehistory/aegean/?page_id=630#L27Top

Ryder, T. T. B., *Koine Eirene: General Peace and Local Independence in Ancient Greece* (Hull, 1965)

Sabin, P., *Lost Battles: Reconstructing the Great Clashes of the Ancient World* (2008); (ed.) *The Cambridge History of Greek and Roman Warfare Vol 1* (Cambridge, 2007); (ed.) (2007) *The Cambridge History of Greek and Roman Warfare Vol 2* (Cambridge, 2007)

Sacks, K. S., 'Herodotus and the Dating of the Battle of Thermopylae', *Classical Quarterly* 26 (1976), 232–248

Sage, M. M., *Warfare in Ancient Greece: A Sourcebook* (London, 1996)

Saggs, H. W. F., *Civilisation Before Greece and Rome* (London, 1989)

Salazar, C. F., *The Treatment of Wounds in Graeco-Roman Antiquity* (Leiden, 2000)

Salmonson, J. A., *The Encyclopedia of Amazons* (London, 1991)

Samons, L. J., *The Peloponnesian War. What's Wrong with Democracy?* (Los Angeles, CA, 2004)

Sancisi-Weerdenburg, H., 'Exit Atossa: Images of Women in Greek Historiography in Persia' in Cameron, A., *Images of Women in Antiquity*, 20–33 (London, 1993)

Santosuosso, A., *Soldiers, Citizens, and The Symbols of War: From Classical Greece To Republican Rome, 500–167 B.C* (Boulder, CO, 1997).

Sapounakis, J., 'Injuries to the head and neck in Homer's Iliad', *British Journal of Oral and Maxillofacial Surgery 45* (2007)

Schaps, D., 'The Women of Greece in Wartime', *Classical Philology* 77 (1982), 193–213

Schofield, L., *The Mycenaeans* (Los Angeles, CA, 2006)

Schulman, A. R., 'The Battle Scenes of the Middle Kingdom', *Jnl of the Society for the Study of Egyptian Antiquities* 12 (1982), 165–82; 'Military Organisation in Pharaonic Egypt in Sasson', *Civilisations of the Ancient Near East Vol 1*, 289–301 (New York, 1995)

Scott, J. A., 'Thoughts on the Reliability of Classical Writers, with Especial Reference to the Size of the Army of Xerxes', *The Classical Journal* 10 (1915)

Sealey, R., *A History of the Greek City-states, c. 700–338 B.C.* (Berkeley, CA, 1976)

Seevers, B., *Warfare in the Old Testament: The Organization, Weapons, and Tactics of Ancient Near Eastern Armies* (Grand Rapids, MI, 2013)

Sekunda, N., *The Spartan Army (560–330 BCE)* (London, 1998)

Shapiro, H. A., 'Amazons, Thracians and Scythians', *GRBS* 24 (1982), 105–114

Shaw, I., *Egyptian Warfare and Weapons* (Oxford, 1991)

Shay, J. M. D., *Achilles in Vietnam: Combat Trauma and the Undoing of Character* (New York, 1995); *Odysseus in America: Combat Trauma and the Trials of Homecoming* (New York, 2003)

Sheldon, R. M., *Ambush: Surprise Attack in Ancient Greek Warfare* (London, 2001)

Shepherd, W., *Plataea 479 BCE: The Most Glorious Victory Ever Seen* (Oxford, 2012); *Pylos and Sphacteria 425 BCE: Sparta's Island of Disaster* (Oxford, 2013)

Sherratt, S., 'The Trojan War: History or Bricolage?', *Bulletin of the Institute of Classical Studies* 53 (2010), 1–18

Shutt, R. H. J., 'Polybius; A Sketch', *Greece & Rome* 22, 50–57

Sidebottom, H., *Ancient Warfare: A Very Short Introduction* (Oxford, 2004)

Sidnell, P., *Warhorse: Cavalry in Ancient Warfare* (London, 2006)

Siefert, R., 'Rape in Wars: Analytical Approaches', *Minerva: Quarterly Report on Women and the Military* 11 (1991), 17–22

Siegfried, E., *Analytical Study of Battle Strategies Used at Marathon (490 BCE)* (US Army War College, Carlisle Barracks, PA, 2010)

Smith, W., 'Early History of Peloponnesus and Sparta to the End of the Messenian Wars, B.C. 668' in *A Smaller History of Ancient Greece* (chapter IV, pg 10) (2010), retrieved 27 June 2017, from www.ellopos.net/elpenor/greek-texts/ancient-greece/history-of-ancient-greece-4-668.asp?pg=10

Snodgrass, A. D., 'The Hoplite Reform and History', *Journal of Hellenic Studies* 85 (1965), 110–122

Snodgrass, M., 'The Linear B Arms and Armour Tablets—Again', *Kadmos* 4 (1965), 97–98

Sobol, D., *The Amazons of Greek Mythology* (Cranbury, NJ, 1973)

Spalinger, A. J., *War in Ancient Egypt* (Chichester, 2005)

Spaulding, O. A., The Ancient Military Writers, *Classical Journal* 28 (1933), 657–669

Stadter, P. A., 'The Motives for Athens' Alliance with Corcyra (Thuc. 1.44)', *GRBS* 24 (1983), 131–136

Stanford University, *Mortal Women of the Trojan War—Briseis (Hippodameia)*, web.stanford. edu/~plomio/briseis.html

Starr, C. G., *The Influence of Sea Power on Ancient History* (Oxford, 1989)

Strassler, R. B. (ed.), *The Landmark Thucydides: A Comprehensive Guide to the Peloponnesian War* (New York, 1996)

Strauss, B. S., *The Anatomy of Error: Ancient Military Disasters and their Lessons for Modern Strategists* (New York, 1990); *The Battle of Salamis: The Naval Encounter That Saved Greece—and Western Civilization.* (New York, 2004); *The Trojan War: A New History* (New York, 2006)

Stronk, J. P., *Ctesias' Persian History: Introduction, Text and Translation* (Dusseldorf, 2010)

Talbert, R., 'The Role of the Helots in the Class Struggle at Sparta', *Historia* 38 (1989), 22–40

Tartaron, T. F., *Maritime Networks in the Mycenaean World* (Cambridge, 2013)

Tausend, K., '*Der Lelantische Krieg—ein Mythos?*', *Klio* 69 (1987), 499–514,

Taylor, C. C. W., 'The Role of Women' in Kamtekar, *Plato's Republic in Virtue and Happiness* (2012)

Taylor, M. J., *Antiochus The Great* (Barnsley, 2013)

Thapliyal, U. P., *Warfare in Ancient India* (New Delhi, 2010)

Tipps, G. K., 'The Battle of Ecnomus', *Historia* 34 (1985), 432–465

Tritle, L. A., *From Melos to My Lai: A Study in Violence, Culture and Social Survival* (London, 2002); *A New History of the Peloponnesian War* (Chichester, 2010)

Turner, J., *Pallas armata, Military Essayes of the Ancient Grecian, Roman, and Modern Art of War* 1670–1 (New York, rept. 2011)

Turney-High, H., *Primitive War: Its Practice and Concepts* (Columbia, SC, 1949)

Tyldesley, J., *Hatchepsut: The Female Pharaoh* (New York, 1996)

Tyrrell, W. B., *Amazons: A Study in Athenian Myth-Making* (Baltimore, 1984)

Van Creveld, M., *Men, Women and War: Do Women Belong on the Front Line?* (London, 2001)

Van Der Veer, J. A. G., 'The Battle of Marathon: A Topographical Survey', *Mnemosyne* 35 (1982), 290–321

Van Wees, H., 'Heroes, Knights and Nutters: Warrior Mentality in Homer' in Lloyd (ed.) *Battle in Antiquity* 1–86 (Swansea, 1997)

Vikman, E., 'Ancient Origins: Sexual Violence in Warfare, Part I', *Anthropology & Medicine* 12 (1) (2005), 21–31

Walcot, P., 'Herodotus on Rape', *Arethusa* 11 (1978), 137–147; 'On Widows and their Reputation in Antiquity', *SO* 66 (1991), 5–26

Wallinga, H. T., 'The Ionian Revolt', *Mnemosyne*, 37 (1984), 401–437

Warner, R., *Athens at War* (London, 1970)

Warry, J., *Warfare in the Classical World* (London, 1980)

Wasinski, V. M., *Women, War and Rape: The Hidden Casualties of Conflict*, Diss. (University of Leeds, 2004)

Wasserman, F., 'Martin. Post-Periclean Democracy in Action: The Mytilenean Debate (Thuc. III 37-48)', *Transactions and Proceedings of the American Philological Association* 87 (1956), 27–41

West, A. B., 'The Chronology of the Years 432 and 431 BCE', *Classical Philology* 10 (1915), 34–53; 'Notes on Certain Athenian Generals of the Year 424–3 B.C.', *American Journal of Philology* 45 (1924), 141-160

West, M. L., 'Academic spat over Troy project', *The Times*, 20 August 2001

Westlake, H. D., 'The Naval Battle at Pylos and Its Consequences', *Classical Quarterly* 24 (1974), 211–226; *Individuals in Thucydides* (Cambridge, 2010)

Wet de, B. X., 'This So-Called Defensive Policy of Pericle', *Acta Classica* 12 (1969), 103–119

Wheeler, E. L., *Stratagem and the Vocabulary of Military Trickery* (Leiden, 1998)

Wheelwright, J., *Amazons and Military Maids* (London, 1989)

Whitehead, D., *Aineias Tacticus: How to Survive Under Siege* 2/e (Bristol, 2002)

Wicker, K. O., Mulierum Virtutes in H.D. Betz, *Plutarch's Ethical Writings and Early Christian Literature*, 106–34 (Leiden, 1978)

Wiedemann, T. E. J., 'Thucydides, Women and the Limits of Rational Analysis' in McAuslan, I., *Women in Antiquity* (Oxford, 1996), 83–90

Wilde, L. W., *A Brief History of the Amazons: Women Warriors in Myth and History* (London, 2016)

Wilkes, J. J., *The Illyrians* (Chichester, 1992)

Wiseman, T. P., 'Lying Historians: Seven Types of Mendacity', in Gill, *Lies and Fiction in the Ancient World* (1983)

Wood, M., *In Search of the Trojan War*, (London, 1985)

Woodhead, A. G., 'The Institution of the Hellenotamiae', *Journal of Hellenic Studies* 79 (1959), 149–152; *The Greeks in the West* (1962)

Woodruff, P., *Thucydides on Justice, Power and Human Nature.* (Indianapolis, IN, 1993)

Woods, M., *Ancient Warfare: From Clubs to Catapults* (Minneapolis, 2001)

Woolley, C. L., *Ur of the Chaldees*, rev. Ed. (Ithaca, NY, 1982)

Yadin, Y., *The Art of Warfare in Biblical Lands* (Jerusalem, 1963)

Ziegler, K., 'Tomyris', *RE* vi, A2 (1937), 1702–4

Ziolkowski, J., *Thucydides and the Tradition of Funeral Speeches at Athens* (New York, 1981)

Index